THE MEDAL FACTORY

KENNY PRYDE has been a cycling journalist since 1987, he edited *Winning: Cycle Racing illustrated* and *The Fabulous World of Cycling*, was a staff writer at *Cycling Weekly*; and editor-at-large of *Cycle Sport*. He has written for the *Guardian*, *Ride*, *VeloNews*, the *Herald*, *Scotsman* and *Irish Independent*.

THE MEDAL FACTORY

BRITISH CYCLING AND THE COST OF GOLD

KENNY PRYDE

PURSUIT

This paperback edition published in 2022

First published in Great Britain in 2020 by
PURSUIT BOOKS
an imprint of Profile Books Ltd
29 Cloth Fair
London EC1A 7JQ

www.profilebooks.com

1 3 5 7 9 10 8 6 4 2

Typeset in Quadraat by MacGuru Ltd
Printed and bound in Great Britain by
CPI Group (UK) Ltd, Croydon CR0 4YY

A CIP catalogue record for this book is available from the
British Library.

ISBN 978 1 78125 986 3
eISBN 978 1 78283 416 8

Special thanks to the women who've indulged
me for decades, Sandra and Katie

CONTENTS

INTRODUCTION

Viewed from the comfortable distance of 2019, it takes effort to recall that there was a period during which British Cycling and Team Sky were both widely acclaimed as unqualified successes. Certainly, inside cycling there were critics of both organisations, but fans, the wider public, sports federations and even captains of industry were all loudly impressed by what they had witnessed from 2004 to 2012.

Within British Cycling and Team Sky, among its riders, coaches and managers, British cycling was widely perceived as cutting edge on every front, in training and talent identification, from nutrition and sports psychology to technology. When you tallied up the international successes of these outfits on track and road, how could you fail to be impressed?

From being a derided sporting irrelevance ('men with shaved legs in skintight Bermuda shorts playing on kids' toys!') to knighthoods and cereal box endorsements, cycling moved to centre stage in British sporting culture, thanks to unstoppable success garnered via a collection of articulate and funny riders who became household names. In a ten-year period

British men and women were victorious in almost everything that was worth winning on road and track, from yellow and rainbow jerseys to medals at World, Commonwealth and European level; British cycling and its riders dazzled.

At the 2000 Sydney Olympics, we started to see riders in Team GB skinsuits winning medals; powerhouse Jason QueALEY in the kilo surprising everyone; 20-year-old Bradley Wiggins part of a medal-winning team pursuit quartet; the joyous confirmation of the track results in Athens four years later; Nicole Cooke's celebratory roar in a soaking Beijing road race in 2008; and, of course, the multiple glories of 2012 in France and London. And yet, in spite of all this, by 2016 British cycling ended up staring into the abyss, racked by self-doubt, excoriated in the media and criticised in Parliament. The metamorphosis of British cycling from centre of sporting excellence to den of iniquity is even more dramatic when you take a step back to take in the unprecedented turnaround that the management regime had set in motion in the previous two decades.

Was ever a sport so fulsomely praised before being brought to its knees as rapidly as British cycling? Gleefully celebrated in the national media as a medal factory then pilloried as a den of cheating sexist bullies in the space of a few weeks, British cycling and riders were subjected to a forensic public interrogation. Having worked its way to the top of world cycling after almost twenty years of struggle, British cycling's coaches, riders and reputation were all but destroyed in a six-month horrow show of grotesque headlines and allegations. How did it happen, to come so far and fall so fast?

This book tells the story of the people who transformed the sport of cycling in Britain, detailing how they built a winning culture, uncovering the histories that shaped the most successful British Olympic sports team in history. In doing so, those characters turned an underfunded niche sport into a mainstream pastime. Cycling travelled so far from its origins, scaled the highest heights at Olympic Games, World championships and Tours de France, yet ended up plumbing grim depths. The story of British Cycling's Medal Factory and its denizens is a remarkable one.

When accusations of sexism and bullying erupted in spring 2016, questions were asked in the Houses of Parliament, yet this wasn't the first time that British Cycling had been held up to scrutiny. Back in 1995, members of Parliament demanded changes after the chaos inside cycling's governing body came to light. Those parliamentary interventions led to revolutionary changes, and it is there that this story begins, with the arrival of the characters who would build the Lottery-funded Medal Factory.

This book reveals the happy coincidences, the happenstance, the hard work and alliances that helped revitalise and reshape the culture inside British Cycling, forging a squad, coaches and management that enjoyed staggering success over three full Olympic cycles.

The background of the key characters – Peter Keen, Dave Brailsford, Shane Sutton – as well as the myriad supporting players is uncovered, detailing how Olympic and World Championship successes were achieved and at what cost. The departure of the first performance director and Medal Factory architect Keen, the rise of Brailsford, the arrival of Team Sky, the frictions and rivalries that emerged are all exposed, as British Cycling and its riders continue their extraordinary rise.

This is an examination of British Cycling – and British cyclists – the tale of the people who helped fundamentally transform the sport and how they were brought down to earth. It's a tale of breathtaking vision, unswerving drive and inescapable hubris. From Peter Keen to Dave Brailsford, from Bradley

Wiggins to Chris Froome via Shane Sutton and many others, this is the story of the people who built British Cycling's Medal Factory and Team Sky.

1

THE ANNUS HORRIBILIS

'Where did it all go wrong? Well, where do you start?'

If the birth of the golden age of British cycling can be pinpointed to 29 July 1992 in Barcelona – to Lotus and Chris Boardman, a pursuit medal, gold – then the event that triggered its destruction also has a date. It was 2 March 2016. With the nation watching in expectation of another round of championship cycling medals and Union Jacks, British Cycling's world was instead about to crumble in front of their eyes.

That fateful day during the World track championships was when Great Britain women's sprinter Jess Varnish was interviewed by BBC television's Jill Douglas. Having finished fifth in the women's team sprint and thus failed to qualify for the upcoming Rio Olympics, Varnish explained that her preparation for those London World Championships had been little short of a disaster. In the context of such conventionally bland TV encounters, it was a veritable bombshell.

Offering a sympathetic question to the disappointed

non-qualifier, Douglas, in an 'arm-around-the-shoulder' tone, suggested, 'It must be bittersweet to have come so close?'

'Completely bitter,' countered Varnish, who was flanked by her sprint partner, Katy Marchant. 'We've been playing catch-up for two years after decisions that had been made above us.' Marchant added, 'People above us have made the complications for us and put us where we are now.'

Marchant had flashed across the line just eight hundredths of a second off fourth place and Olympic qualification. But, as a consequence of this and previous results, Team Great Britain would *not* be one of the twelve women's pairings taking part in the team sprint event that August in the Velódromo Municipal do Rio.

Varnish's disappointing result – normally little more than a footnote in a results archive – would go on to generate massive headlines, soul-searching and government inquiries. Varnish effectively fired the starting pistol on events that would see the reputations of riders, management, coaches and British Cycling irretrievably damaged over the following months. That seemingly minor outburst from a frustrated rider would result in British Cycling and its Olympic track squads coming close to unravelling in a tortured eighteen-month period.

Following Varnish's televised declarations in the Lee Valley track centre, the print media inside the velodrome followed up and amplified her criticisms of British Cycling coaches. Varnish elaborated to the *Daily Telegraph*'s cycling correspondent, Tom Cary:

> There's been no real plan. We have not been out there racing against the world. There have been other people that aren't even on the squad now trying to qualify the 'A-team' a place at the Olympics ... it's great they've been given an opportunity to go to a major championship, but

they're not there yet. It should not be their job. We put our lives on the line for this. I'm a 25-year-old athlete now, I've been around for a long time and you think 'should I keep putting my life in these people's hands?' It's my life, I only live once, is it going to be worth it? How many more times can I keep putting my life on hold, making these choices for my career, if it's not going to pay off, through no fault of my own?

Varnish's complaints were widely reported online on specialist sites and social media buzzed with indignation and support.

A couple of weeks later, on 20 April, news broke that British Cycling head of performance Shane Sutton had told Varnish in Manchester Velodrome that she would no longer be part of British Cycling's Olympic Podium programme. So not only would there be no Olympic track suit for Varnish that summer, there would be no £26,000 per annum tax-free grant any more either. Varnish, a professional bike rider supported by UK Sport and British Cycling for six years, no longer had a job or an income.

Many were quick to conclude that, following Varnish's public criticisms of British Cycling, she had obviously been the victim of a punishment sacking for speaking out so publicly against the regime. Sutton demurred, insisting that her performances at World Championships and previous World Cup track meetings simply hadn't been good enough, and presented his case in forthright style. 'The evidence doesn't lie. There were ten events which counted towards [Olympic] qualification. Jess participated in eight, Katy in seven. [Varnish] had a golden opportunity to qualify. But then because she didn't, she looked to blame everyone else,' retorted Sutton, never one to gild the lily.

Given that Varnish had been on various funded British

Cycling squads since the age of 16, it was certainly true that she had had a good run. 'She's been with us a long, long time. She qualified 17th for the Sprint in London [2016 World Championships], so her chances of medalling in Rio were very slim if not none. And she hasn't gone as quick as she went three years ago. There is no point in carrying on and wasting UK Sport's money.' Even the famously plain-speaking Sutton would struggle to get more blunt than that. 'It wasn't that we "got rid" of Jess. It was just that [her contract] was up for renewal and we didn't renew it.' Her younger team sprint partner, Katy Marchant, who had also been highly critical, kept her place and her job, and went on to Rio, where she would win a bronze medal in the individual sprint.

The coaching team had come to the conclusion that if Varnish wasn't fast enough for Rio, it was highly unlikely Varnish would improve by the time of the Tokyo Olympics in 2020.

In fact, it had been Varnish's coach, Iain Dyer, who had informed Sutton in post-World Championships debrief sessions that Varnish wasn't making progress, and Sutton, in the end, had agreed that she should be taken off the programme. In a sense, Varnish's fate had been sealed by Dyer, not that this detail gained any traction at the time, because Sutton had broken the news.

Just two days after her deselection became public knowledge, a back-page lead story on Varnish appeared in the *Daily Mail* highlighting accusations of sexism and bullying that would, in the end, cost Sutton his job. Varnish, reckoning that there was no chance of a comeback, had opted to go out swinging, with a bang rather than a whimper. The *Daily Mail* pushed her story with the headline, 'Sensational claims against British Cycling chief from axed star Jess Varnish "I was told to go and have a baby ... and my bum was too big."' The headline was accompanied by a half-page photo of Varnish in a Team GB skinsuit from years earlier. Social media feeds blazed with conspiracy theories and outrage, while the story was widely shared.

Just four days after Varnish's tales of misogyny and bullying hit the newsstands, GB Paralympic cyclist Darren Kenny told the *Daily Mail* that Sutton had often disparaged Paralympians training in Manchester Velodrome by calling them 'gimps' and 'wobblies'. Sutton, who had immediately been suspended by British Cycling following Varnish's initial accusations pending an investigation, resigned that same day, 26 April 2016.

In between the first Varnish story and Kenny's Paracycling 'wobblies', former women's world road champion and 2008 Beijing Olympics road race gold medallist Nicole Cooke added her voice to the chorus of high-profile critics, in a piece she wrote for the *Guardian* on 25 April, with the headline 'Welcome to the world of elite cycling where sexism is by design'. In the thousand-word article, she said that 'I have my own personal experiences of Shane and sympathise with Jess. She was in the position so many have found themselves: speak out and your dreams will be destroyed and years of hard work wasted.'

Just behind Cooke, another former British World and Olympic champion came forward to recount her experiences. Victoria Pendleton, winner, among other things, of Olympic gold medals in Beijing and London as well as being six-time world sprint champion, had worked closely with Sutton from Beijing 2008 until she retired from the track following her final race at the London Games in 2012.

After leaving British Cycling, Pendleton had written a tough autobiography entitled *Between the Lines*, in which she criticised British Cycling's regime, saying that even in her sprinting pomp in Beijing senior coaches 'Jan Van Eijden and Iain Dyer were barely talking to me. Shane was prickly and Dave [Brailsford] seemed invisible … I felt increasingly isolated amid such cynicism and dissent' – a typical passage from a soul-baring volume. When Varnish went public, Pendleton became a vocal critic of her former coach and the regime around him. 'I would not be able to live with myself if I sat back and let people try to discredit [Varnish's] character. Not when I wholeheartedly believe her. My experiences [at British Cycling] were very similar,' she told the *Telegraph*'s Tom Cary. Varnish was gone, but by now so was Sutton.

So, a little over three months out from the opening ceremony of the 2016 Rio Olympic Games, British Cycling had lost its head of performance, and coaches' nerves were fraying under a tide of negative news stories and comment pieces. What impact would Sutton's departure and the manner in which it happened have on the morale of the British cycling team and the wider organisation? Funding administrator UK Sport had awarded British Cycling £29 million since the London Olympics to prepare for Rio, and that investment was coming under scrutiny, leaving the organisation and its staff reeling.

Then, for good measure, a week prior to the women's Olympic road race, the media revealed that Britain's reigning world road race champion Lizzie Armitstead (now Deignan) had been charged with an anti-doping violation following three infractions in a year. Armitstead had allegedly missed one out of competition test in August 2015, then was guilty of a paperwork error in October and missed another test in June 2016. The 27-year-old risked a two year ban but her appeal to the Court of Arbitration for Sport was successful, meaning she could compete in Rio. Armitstead rode under a cloud and, yet again, British riders were in the news for the worst reasons.

It wasn't all bad news for British Cycling in 2016, however. That July, Team Sky's Chris Froome won his third Tour de France before going on to claim a bronze medal in the Rio Olympics road time trial, while in the Rio velodrome his former teammate and sparring partner Bradley Wiggins claimed his fifth Olympic gold medal and helped set a new World and Olympic record in the team pursuit to boot.

British riders returned from Rio laden with medals – just as they had four years earlier in London and four years before that, in Beijing. In spite of Sutton's departure and the ongoing media fallout, the medal haul from Rio was astonishingly good, with twelve medals in total, six of which were gold. For a brief period there was a hiatus in the bad news summer, as the performances at the Tour and the Rio Games helped efface the Varnish-inspired inquiry and Armitstead's missed tests. British riders won a combined total of thirty-three medals at the Rio Olympics and Paralympics.

Was the beleaguered British Cycling finally out of the woods? Far from it, because hidden somewhere in the shadowy undergrowth, Fancy Bears were stirring. Fancy Bears? How could such a quirky-sounding outfit of anonymous internet hackers be the harbingers of more bad news for British Cycling?

Barely had the team stepped off the specially decorated British Airways plane from Rio when, on 15 September, the Fancy Bears hackers revealed the results of their server-busting digging. They had broken into athletes' confidential medical records in the World Anti-Doping Agency (WADA) database and uploaded files on its site. The documents contained details of twenty-five Western athletes' applications and use of Therapeutic Use Exemption (TUE) certificates; it was the Bears' attempt to prove that Russia (which had been excluded from the Rio Games over State-organised doping allegations) had been victimised by biased sporting authorities. In short, they believed that Russian athletes had been unfair victims of politically motivated suspensions.

The TUE certification system was WADA's attempt to control athletes' use and abuse of medicines that could also have performance-enhancing properties. Included in its list were medicines used to treat asthma, pollen allergies, tendinitis, bronchial infections and colds. WADA had been established in 1999, but it struggled to frame medical guidelines that pleased all parties. It was a much-debated area of sports medicine that was clearly open to abuse by unscrupulous athletes as well as team and federation doctors, in all manner of sports.

The Fancy Bears' conflation of the TUE-regulated use of 'medicines' with the State-sanctioned administering and covering up of erythropoietin (EPO) and anabolic steroid use was risible, but some of the mud slung stuck. If nothing else, the hacked information provoked a long-overdue debate around the increasing medicalisation of all sport.

Corticosteroids, taken via pill, infusion or injection, have an anti-inflammatory effect, and have long been used to treat tendinitis in cyclists, although they also are used to treat severe pollen allergies and asthma. Additionally, they stimulate the body to metabolise fat, 'leaning out' patients, and, in some subjects, provide a sense of euphoria. The timing and use of large doses of corticosteroids like Triamcinolone had long been used as a performance enhancer and, in the 1960s and 1970s, 'cortico' was a key doping product until it was superseded by much more effective and sophisticated performance-enhancing methods. It was still being abused throughout the 1990s.

Among the high-profile British names revealed to have applied for TUEs at various times were both Froome and Wiggins. Froome had been granted a TUE to enable him to use the corticosteroid Prednisolone on two occasions, for five 40 mg doses on both occasions, firstly prior to the 2013 Critérium du Dauphiné and secondly in April 2014, permitting him to take seven doses of 40 mg prior to the Tour de Romandie. Wiggins had applied for and been granted permission for injections of 40 mg of Triamcinolone on three occasions – on 29 June 2011, prior to the start of the Tour de France, and a year later, on 26 June 2012, for the same dose of Triamcinolone. Wiggins' final Fancy Bears hack revealed a TUE was granted on 2 April 2013, prior to his ill-fated attempt to win the general classification of the Giro d'Italia, and again it was for Triamcinolone.

For context, Wiggins was one of respectively fifty-five, forty-six and thirty-one riders who were granted TUEs by the Union Cycliste Internationale (UCI) medical commission during those three seasons – other riders and substances whose identities remain unknown, subject to considerations of medical confidentiality.

Of the two substances used by Froome and Wiggins under TUE authorisation, Triamcinolone was the more potent and considered the most questionable treatment by allergy experts. 'That sort of dose to treat an allergy is almost unheard of,' said one World Tour team manager who had spoken to his medical staff; 'it's the sort of product and dose that you might give someone if they couldn't get out of bed, who had suffered a really bad allergic reaction.'

In Froome's case, the Prednisolone he took was to combat exercise-induced asthma, and nobody who had seen Froome racked by a rib-cracking cough on a mountain summit finish could doubt he had a real problem. The issue here was more one of the proportionality and timing of the dose rather than the potency of the product, concerning though that was.

The rapidity with which Froome's TUE certificate was awarded also caused eyebrows to be raised, given there were reports that the TUE committee of three experts asked to consider that the application had been bypassed by UCI Medical Commission head Dr Mario Zorzoli, who granted Team Sky doctor Alan Farrell's request. In fact, Zorzoli would later privately admit that he only tended to consult the three other experts on the panel if he thought the substance, timing and rider were 'at it' and, in this case, he had thought nothing of it and effectively rubber-stamped the request. Zorzoli, beset on all sides by reams of evidence of sophisticated industrial-scale doping in the sport in recent years, was just relieved that if riders were going to use corticosteroids, at least they were now letting him know beforehand. In comparison to the years of post-dated doctors' scripts and justifications for riders caught red-handed, at least they were *pre*-dating their misdemeanours.

After the Fancy Bears data hacks, there would be new lines of inquiry and indelicate questions for British Cycling and its riders to face about their medical histories. As far as WADA, the UCI and UK Anti-Doping regulations were concerned, Wiggins, Froome and Team Sky had followed the appropriate rules, but the Fancy Bears hack revealed how close the 'we race clean' ethos espoused by Team Sky flirted with the black arts of cortisone doping that had been practised in cycling for over forty years. Speaking to Sky News at the launch of the new team in January 2010, when Wiggins said, 'We'll do everything we can to be as good as we can in July,' who could have guessed what that might include?

These cycling stories all played out during a febrile summer, when various British sporting organisations were making news for the worst reasons. An elite GB Canoeing coach was under investigation for sexual impropriety with athletes, as was a coach from the UK Sport-funded Archery GB. Around the same time, the GB Bobsleigh team was being investigated for racism, its funding administered directly by UK Sport rather than its national federation. And, speaking of racism, the English women's national football team manager was accused of the same, and lost his job.

Almost as high profile as the issues faced by British Cycling, distance runner and national hero Mo Farah's relationship with his coach Alberto Salazar came under fierce media scrutiny. Consequently, the ethics and precise nature of the medical support offered to British athletes and bike riders was under scrutiny as never before. The revelations of TUE use and the ethical questions raised were troubling – but the rules had not been broken; there was at least that for Team Sky supporters to cling to. However, quite remarkably in this annus horribilis for British Cycling, there was still worse to come.

Someone nursing a grudge – or with little sense of what would ultimately be unleashed – contacted the Daily Mail journalist and serial British Cycling tormentor Matt Lawton and suggested to him that he should ask questions and find out what was in a Jiffy bag that had been delivered to Wiggins and Team Sky at the French Critérium du Dauphiné stage race back in June 2011. The date was – not coincidentally – around the time the Fancy Bears hack had revealed Wiggins had been granted limited permission to use Triamcinolone, that corticosteroid with its myriad of medical uses and several useful performance-enhancing side effects.

Lawton's scoop – another Daily Mail back-page lead story exclusive – broke on 6 October 2016 with the unambiguous headline 'Wiggins drug probe'. On subsequent days, the story got increasingly convoluted and drew in more characters whose connections and work experience careened between British Cycling and Team Sky. If Varnish's story had been a relatively localised affair – women's racing inside British Cycling – the Jiffy bag imbroglio explicitly tied British Cycling to Team Sky, as medical staff, records, storage and transportation crossed unhindered and apparently unrecorded between the two entities.

Lawton's story revealed that a Jiffy bag had been hand-delivered to Team Sky by Simon Cope, then the GB women's road team manager. It appeared that Cope had collected the package from Manchester Velodrome, flown to Geneva, hired a car and driven to La Toussuire in the French Alps to deliver the package and its mystery contents. What sort of small package would have merited such expensive and bespoke transportation? In light of the Fancy Bears hacking story and the focus on Wiggins' use of cortisone, the insinuation was clear, even if the details were utterly opaque.

Thus, on top of Varnish's accusations of bullying, Pendleton and Cooke's retro-criticism and Armitstead's missed dope tests, in addition to the use of Triamcinolone and Prednisolone revealed by the Fancy Bears hack, there was now also a mysterious Jiffy bag, whose contents were unknown and whose transportation was decidedly expensive. The clear implication in the *Daily Mail* story was that there was some kind of doping going on or, at the very least, WADA anti-doping regulations were being bent to the point of snapping.

The Jiffy bag story was even more of a reputational disaster than the revelation of the TUE-approved use of Triamcinolone – at least in that there was a clear paper trail that led back to a hacked WADA database. The Jiffy bag was a veritable Schrödinger's cat of a story. What *was* in that bag? Was it nothing big or a big story? Never, in the history of sport, has a small padded bag been at the centre of a story that came close to the utter ruination of a major sports federation, a Tour de France winner and two sporting knights of the realm.

And, throughout those turbulent months, other stories of malfeasance inside British Cycling's Manchester headquarters emerged – whispers of nepotism, the sale of British Cycling clothing and equipment by staff, missing or shoddy medical records, stolen laptops and the inexplicable delivery of tubes of banned testosterone gel to the Manchester headquarters in 2011 – that all added to the paranoid atmosphere swirling around the velodrome complex that housed British Cycling. The fact that the recently removed head of performance, Shane

Sutton, could be linked to all these stories from 2011 to 2016 didn't help clarify anything, but rather gave material to those keen to paint a bigger, darker picture.

Between the Varnish declarations on 2 March and the *Daily Mail* story that launched 'Jiffy bag-gate' there were 218 days that laid waste to the reputation of a sporting institution that had taken twenty-four years to build. Almost a quarter of a century of coaching, innovation, world records, Olympic medals and four Tours de France had all been smeared, performances tarnished by allegations that were as serious as they were unexpected.

Such had been the torrent of bad news throughout 2016 – principally for cycling and athletics – that the select committee of the Department of Digital, Culture, Media and Sport (DCMS) decided an inquiry was required. On 28 October the chairman of the DCMS committee, Conservative MP Damian Collins, invited a number of figures involved to appear before them to explain themselves in a series of televised interviews.

With newspapers, television and online outlets turning up new angles and interviews, the sense that British Cycling was under attack was palpable. With the announcement of the parliamentary DCMS inquiry, by the end of 2016, there were no fewer than three high-profile inquiries going on into British Cycling and Team Sky. First out of the blocks was the Varnish-inspired Phelps independent review instigated by British Cycling and UK Sport back in March, examining allegations of bullying and sexism. Then came the UK Anti-Doping authority, which announced on 7 October it would get to the bottom of the mysterious Jiffy bag and its contents, followed by Collins' DCMS select committee inquiry into 'Combatting doping in sport', opening up another front.

If the Phelps and UK Anti-Doping investigations were carried out in private, the Collins' DCMS committee's grilling was screened live and extensively reported on a daily basis. It made for grisly viewing in which various figures were quizzed and found wanting by a collection of politicians intent, at the very least, on talking tough to people who mostly appeared underprepared.

On 19 December 2016 the former head of performance at British Cycling and current team principal at Team Sky, Sir Dave Brailsford, duly appeared in front of Collins' committee to answer questions about the Jiffy bag delivered by Simon Cope to Team Sky in June 2011 on the last day of the Critérium du Dauphiné which Wiggins had just won. It made for uneasy viewing, revealing as it did the intertwined relationship that existed between British Cycling and Team Sky.

In transporting the mysterious Jiffy bag, Cope, an employee of British Cycling, a federation bankrolled by the government via National Lottery funding and UK Sport, was essentially working for Team Sky, a professional World Tour team, which raised hackles among those who felt that Team Sky was wealthy enough not to poach staff. The explanation was that Cope's time – as well as that of any other employee, mechanic or masseur of British Cycling who was temporarily seconded to work for Sky – was charged to Team Sky, who then paid British Cycling.

Brailsford was in a quandary, caught on the hop, but he remained loyal to his former rider and medical staff. His initial explanation reported in the newspapers – that Cope had flown to France to see GB rider Emma Pooley – was nonsense, given that Pooley was racing in Spain at the time. From that point on, Brailsford was on the back foot, revealing, at best, that he didn't know what had been going on or, at worst, that he was covering something up. Not so much win-win, as a complete lose-lose scenario.

'Dave Brailsford doesn't like being laughed at,' noted one

former professional road rider, commenting on Brailsford's character. It turned out to be an accurate assessment, and a useful optic through which to view the Fancy Bears hack and the resulting fallout. Unfortunately for Brailsford, few were convinced by his answers in front of the DCMS committee, or those of Cope or Shane Sutton, while the doctor involved, Richard Freeman, didn't appear at the hearings, citing ill-health for his absence. Freeman also revealed that the laptop his medical records for the team would have been kept on had been stolen while on holiday in Greece, and that he wasn't very good at keeping records anyway. In the 'flying by the seat of our pants' and 'learning on the job' chaos of a new team and new processes and procedures, perhaps Freeman's defence was credible – though few critics were prepared to give him the benefit of the doubt. However, in the absence of any paper trail or solid evidence, people's position on the story depended on their like – or otherwise – of the team and the characters involved. (Ironically, it emerged in late 2018 that Freeman's laptop had indeed been stolen in Greece, and that UK Anti-Doping had had paper evidence of this fact all along.)

Dressed immaculately to face his parliamentary inquisitors, Brailsford insisted that Cope had transported Fluimucil, a decongestant medicine, and that was all there was to it. Brailsford's Fluimucil explanation was widely disbelieved, but, since there were no medical records to be found anywhere, that appeared to be the end of it. It was claimed that the team doctor at the Dauphiné – Dr Freeman – would surely have been able to source this at a local French pharmacy rather than contacting British Cycling physiotherapist Phil Burt, getting him to pop it in a Jiffy bag at Manchester Velodrome, and subsequently getting Cope to deliver said package via aeroplane and car.

Brailsford, trying to protect his reputation as well as that of Team Sky – not forgetting his legacy at British Cycling – was ill-prepared for the media onslaught that rained down upon him. That Sutton was peripherally involved in the 2011 tale of the mystery package as well as the 2016 sexism and bullying storyline – also under his watch while Brailsford was at British Cycling – simply coated another layer of grimy suspicion to Brailsford's hitherto gleaming public reputation.

The pressure on Brailsford was immense. The combination of the Russian hack exposé of the TUEs used by Wiggins and Froome as well as Brailsford's initially contradictory statements attempting to explain the 2011 Dauphiné mystery package merely added to the discomfort. For Team Sky supporters it was clear that certain sectors of the media were out for Brailsford's head and had decided how this story was going to end – and it wasn't going to be a happy one for Brailsford.

Not that he knew it at the time – nor could anyone – but the traumas of 2016 were little more than a foretaste of what would unfurl in September 2017, when Chris Froome would return an 'adverse analytical finding' for the asthma drug Salbutamol on his way to winning the Tour of Spain. The leak of this information – which should have remained private until Froome and the relevant authorities had decided whether or not there was a doping case to answer – would precipitate months of confusion and rancour.

And throughout 2016, one man, more than most, could watch the various threads of these intertwined stories unravel, revealing ugly details and crashing reputations. One man, in fact, who had had more to do with the birth of that modern British Cycling organisation that had been pilloried and questioned so relentlessly that summer.

Peter Keen, by then director of sport policy at Loughborough University, was the man who had 'invented' so much at British Cycling, an academic turned British Cycling head of performance, the policy-writing visionary who had detailed the 'World Class Performance Plan', who had first hired Dave Brailsford at British Cycling, who had signed up junior pursuiter Bradley Wiggins, the coach who had guided Chris Boardman to Olympic gold and a Tour de France yellow jersey and overseen the massive leap forward in British cycling in the 1990s. Following events from a safe distance, Keen was bemused and saddened at what he witnessed.

True, Keen was no longer party to the minutiae and backstories of the participants in this sporting soap opera, but he had watched the parliamentary select committee interrogate Brailsford, Sutton and Simon Cope with a sense of disappointment. He clarified:

> It was disappointing in the sense that I watched Shane being questioned and it was obvious he was completely unsuited to the job he had been asked to do. He was so unprepared and out of his depth, it was clear this was just not his area and it amazed me that he had been promoted and put in that position in the first place; it wasn't where his strengths lay. But I have to say that I was shocked by the questioning, because it revealed how little that the select committee members knew or understood about the demands of high-performance sport and what it entailed.

Keen was not alone in his disappointment. There were several other characters who had been instrumental in the development of British cycling – and British Cycling, the organisation – in the previous twenty years who watched their sporting legacy be dismantled piece by piece with a combination of anger, frustration and sadness. Men like former British Cycling Federation (BCF) president and coach Jim Hendry, national coach Doug Dailey and Brian Cookson, president between 1997 and 2013. There were many others of course, too many to mention, but without Hendry, Dailey and Keen there would be no Brailsford, no Team Sky, and Britain would probably still be waiting for its first Tour de France winner.

How could a sporting federation that had risen so high have been brought so low, with such breathtaking speed? British Cycling had taken twenty years to build and about nine months to ruin. The foundations on which modern British cycling were built had been laid by these people together with the coaches, sports scientists, talent team coaches, technical staff, mechanics, nutritionists and the strength and conditioning teams, along with their programmes, logistics and technical staff. In 2016 British Cycling was a world power and the former Cinderella federation and its few part-time staff now had a membership that had grown from 11,000 in the early 1990s to over 130,000.

All of that now in ruins – now, in DCMS chair Collins' infamous phrase, 'no longer fit for purpose'.

In fact, the interrogation of British Cycling by members of the House of Commons was not a new phenomenon. Some of those with long memories and years served in the trenches of sports administration – Hendry, Cookson and Dailey among them – had already been there and done that. In 1995, when British Cycling was still wandering the sporting wilderness, underloved and underfunded, questions had been asked about the management and running of the sport by a federation that relied on a government body for its funding back then too.

That earlier furore had, in fact, been the catalyst for seismic changes that revolutionised the sport in the UK. Was a period of self-immolation actually required in order to stimulate new growth? Perhaps the traumas of Jess Varnish, TUEs, Jiffy bags and the three separate inquiries would be beneficial in the end? After all, it had worked before ...

2

CHEEKY YOUNG UPSTARTS

'Those who cannot remember the past are condemned to repeat it.'
George Santayana

In many lines of inquiry explored in 2016 there was a sense of déjà vu about what was uncovered at British Cycling. Many observers had heard these questions before, though the profile of the sport and the intervening years of success had altered the landscape. The sums of money involved in 2016 made the old BCF finances from twenty years previously look like chump change. However, no matter how much had progressed, the profound sense of crisis inside the organisation was the same.

Back in 21 November 1996, Labour MP Jon Trickett stood up in the House of Commons and said that the then British Cycling Federation wasn't up to the required standard. 'There has been much debate in cycling circles about ... the way in which the sport has been managed by the BCF. The BCF board stands guilty of, at best, a lack of vision and a timorous failure to realise the full potential of this beautiful and undeveloped sport, despite the fact that it receives £500,000 a year of public money.'

Trickett was well-informed and eloquent, expressing concern that the Sports Council, the principal funder of the BCF, had carried out an audit of the federation and found it grievously wanting. There were 'concerns' about the financial position of the federation and the recently opened Manchester Velodrome, the annual accounts, and 'inadequate financial accountability and control' of the organisation. Finally, the cherry on the cake, the Sports Council audit revealed 'actual, potential or perceived conflicts of interest involving some board members', as well as internal conflict in the Board.

In mitigation, the Sports Council, the government-funded body that disbursed £47 million a year to UK sports bodies in the pre-National Lottery era, hadn't actually produced its own annual report for three years, so when it came to keeping tabs on wayward sporting federations, it wasn't leading by example. Two months after Trickett made his remarks, the Sports Council was replaced by UK Sport, a new body set up to distribute National Lottery funds to sports governing bodies.

In tone, Trickett's remarks about a dysfunctional federation letting down its membership and government together with boardroom conflicts of interest were an uncanny foreshadowing of themes that would be repeated twenty years later by the Department for Digital, Culture, Media and Sport. The difference being that in the intervening two decades British cycling had scaled the dizziest heights of the sport, and that in 1996 Trickett spoke to an almost empty House of Commons to near universal media disinterest in that pre-internet media age.

If the concerns about misuse of public funds and inept leadership were broadly similar, the contrasts in other respects were astonishing. In 1996, Parliament asked why British cycling was so useless. In 2016, Parliament was asking how, precisely, the global successes of British cyclists had been achieved – two cost-benefit analyses from opposite ends of the sporting continuum. No one in 1996 was talking about cycling's 'duty of care' or the human and ethical price of a 'winning at all costs' mentality.

Ironically, the questions and problems raised by Trickett would help instigate a total overhaul of cycling's governing body, transforming the underperforming and underfunded BCF into British Cycling. The multiple successes of British Cycling, renamed in 1997 after the incorporation of BMX, cyclo-cross and mountain biking into a single governing body, would eventually raise very different questions about whether those costs – financial and psychological – were worth it.

In fact, Trickett's late November statement and the Sports Council audit had already been overtaken by events in Manchester. At the 1996 BCF annual general meeting on 2 November, the under-fire Board had been completely removed and replaced by an eleven-member executive committee that had been elected from the floor by club delegates at the conference. It was at that tumultuous meeting that Brian Cookson and Peter King – two key players in shaping the future of what would become British Cycling – came to the fore.

Neither King nor Cookson had attended that 1996 AGM with any revolutionary intent. According to Cookson, his election to the post of interim chairman at British Cycling had been on the basis that he 'had been the most mouthy and asked a lot of questions at the meeting'. This was, broadly, the same attitude by which Surrey accountant and Redhill CC club member Peter King became the chief executive, essentially because at that fraught meeting King had asked the then head of finance questions that he couldn't answer. In 1996, being bolshie, committed, engaged in the grass roots of the sport and agitating for change were key qualifications for high office.

Cookson, a 36-year-old who had been a race organiser and cycling official for decades, was eventually elected president of the – then – BCF in November 1997, and only relinquished that post when he moved up to cycle sport's top job, as president of the UCI, the governing body of world cycling, in September 2013.

However, in the first instance Cookson and the other ten members of the new emergency BCF board had to make sure that the Manchester Velodrome – the headquarters of British Cycling since autumn 1994 – stayed open. In light of how important the velodrome would become, as a centre of excellence and totemic location for so many Olympic medal-winning riders, it is shocking to discover how close the facility came to oblivion. The velodrome was a mismanaged object of ridicule, given little consideration by a BCF Board unable to see its transformational potential.

Twenty-four years later, Brian Cookson is blunt. 'We really were days from handing back the velodrome keys to Manchester City Council because there was an outstanding utility bill and if it had been closed, I doubt very much if it would ever have opened as a velodrome again; it would have been flats or a retail park, putting on car boot sales or something.'

This massive reversal of fortune was averted when a combination of the Sports Council and Manchester City Council came up with the money to pay the outstanding £130,000 bill. Without this, the headquarters of British Cycling, Team Sky, the location of the 2002 Commonwealth Games and three-time world track championships venue (1996, 2000, 2008) would have been clogged with trestle tables selling artisan chutney or hosting antiques fairs.

The velodrome had a twisted backstory. For a sporting body that was bereft of both international results and finances, late in 1992, there had been good news. That was the year that plans were announced for a brand-new world-class velodrome in Manchester, which would be Britain's first-ever permanent covered track. The cost – around £9.5 million – would be shared between central government and the Foundation for Sport and the Arts. The impetus for the project had been generated by Manchester's bid for the 2000 Olympic Games, and the project was signed off in the afterglow of Chris Boardman's 1992 Olympic triumph, British cycling's fleeting moment of gold medal glory and tabloid celebration.

Any city bidding for summer Olympic Games needs to be able to show the visiting International Olympic Committee executives big, shiny venues and, compared to an athletics stadium or an Olympic swimming centre, a velodrome was actually the least expensive option to construct. Manchester's losing Olympic legacy would become British Cycling's incalculable gain.

This was a crucial piece of infrastructure for a number of reasons, some more obvious than others. Work started in early 1993 and in September 1994 there was a world-class velodrome in Stuart Street, which was a shot in the arm, both for track racing and the prestige for a national federation. British cycling now had a velodrome headquarters it could be proud of, a building that suggested better times ahead, one that could serve as a national focus.

Astonishingly, however, not everyone was quick to grasp the potential of the velodrome as a headquarters, which, on its opening, the BCF was due to manage and run, rather than simply rent, as it does now. In fact, in spite of the years of planning and building, the BCF hierarchy hadn't given much thought to the practicalities of managing a state-of-the-art facility. Who, precisely, was going to run it?

As with so many jobs of that era, in tasks that overlapped performance and practicality, the job ended up in the lap of

Doug Dailey. The Merseysider had taken on the role of full-time paid national coach in 1986, imagining a future of hands-on coaching and squad preparation. What the former international roadman and Olympian actually found was a mountain of paperwork, zero budget, a GB team car that cost £1 ('we bought it from an UK pro team') and an underperforming, bloated squad of road and track riders, men and women.

Dailey got stuck in, doing the best he could with his team of volunteer coaches and part-time managers, whose sequestered estate cars and personal holiday allowances actually enabled foreign sorties to take place. There was no job that Dailey did not carry out at some point in his twenty-six-year career at British Cycling, from soigneur to airport taxi driver, from coach to baggage handler, finally bowing out at the end of 2012 after a stint as logistics chief.

Barely weeks before it was due to open, the then BCF president, Ian Emmerson, had approached Dailey and explained that since Dailey had previously been manager of Kirby Sports Centre, he'd be the best man for the job. Dailey hadn't even seen or been near the site during its construction; he hadn't had the time:

> As soon as we got back from the 1994 Commonwealth Games in Canada, he said I needed to get straight over there. When I got to the velodrome, it wasn't open to the public and I ended up deciding where the plugs were going and which way doors would open. Paul Hardy from the Racing Commission was in there too and we had Paul's wife on reception and his daughter in catering. I was like a supervisor, setting up badminton courts, mopping out changing rooms and arranging folding seats. And that was the basis on which it opened.

A measure of the shambolic nature of the organisation and its handling of the velodrome is further revealed when you learn that only months before it opened, BCF management had signed a new lease on its previous offices in Kettering. The fact that then BCF chief executive Jim Hendry lived in Kettering may not have been unconnected with this decision.

Amazingly, there were no serious plans to move the head-quarters to Manchester, even though there were plentiful offices, meeting rooms, storage and workshops in the brand-new building. And a velodrome. The BCF had a state-of-the-art cycling centre but no plans to move into it and, in spite of the obvious benefits, lobbying of the Board was still required to convince them to move. With more than two years' 'warning' that there was a velodrome about to open, the fact that there was no proper plan speaks volumes for the management vision of the BCF at the time. It's no surprise that questions were asked in Parliament.

It was in the flurry of communications and meetings between the BCF, Manchester City Council and the Sports Council that a spotlight was shone into the workings of the cycling federation that would have repercussions about its fitness to govern and run not just the velodrome, but the sport itself. Enter Jon Trickett MP and his troublesome questions.

Sprinter Chris Hoy – a future Olympic multi-medallist – was one of the many riders 'saved' and inspired by the new building. Hoy had been a promising junior who had drifted away from the sport for life as a student at Edinburgh University, but the new building drew him back. 'I was in the thick of what you might call "fresher life" when I got a letter from Doug Dailey,' recalls Hoy now, 'inviting me down to Manchester for squad sessions. It was just what I needed at that time, but if the velodrome hadn't opened, if there hadn't been that invitation to squad training, then that might have been the end of me.'

Hoy, of course, went on to win six Olympic gold medals, eleven World Championship golds as well as a pair of Commonwealth Games golds. In total, there's a box in Chris Hoy's wardrobe with thirty-seven Olympic, World, European and Commonwealth medals of assorted colours in it, all trained for in Manchester.

The year 1997, with its visionary new Board and velodrome rescue, might be seen as the point at which the seeds planted by Boardman and his coach Peter Keen at the Barcelona Games five years previously actually bore fruit. The regime and culture that subsequently developed in Manchester from those first signs of new life would last twenty years, until Jess Varnish and others spoke out.

If Boardman's Barcelona individual pursuit gold back in 1992 had turned out to be a false dawn, then four years later, at the Atlanta Olympics, there had been a more profound gloom, as male and female British track riders failed to make a medal ride-off in any discipline – a modern performance nadir.

In the four years after his Barcelona success, however, Boardman and coach Keen had taken their approach to training into the European professional peloton, and Boardman, riding for the GAN and Crédit Agricole teams, had enjoyed a healthy level of success, including setting a new hour record in Bordeaux Velodrome in 1993, winning the 1994 Tour de France prologue, and claiming a bronze medal in the time trial at the Atlanta Games. Boardman and Keen's high-profile triumphs added credibility to the training methods espoused by Keen and executed by Boardman. People were now paying closer attention, and it was no longer easy for an entrenched old guard to disregard Keen's methods, his 'scientific training stuff'.

Keen's approach to cycling – a focus on the physiological demands of specific events, detailed training sessions based on the power demands of climbing or time trialling, an analysis of the benefits of aerodynamics in time trials – was supported by Dailey, Hendry and Cookson. However, if innovative training and technologies had been crucial in producing Boardman's results, it would be hard to replicate that approach more widely, given the stunted BCF finances. Additionally, as far as Parliament and the membership of the BCF were concerned, there was also the small matter of the Board's gross mismanagement.

More broadly, Boardman's old gold had had significant repercussions, bringing together three characters – Boardman, Dailey and Keen – who would all be instrumental in guiding the all-conquering British Cycling juggernaut between 2008 and 2012. These three men – for whom cycling had been their work and their lives, racing and training on shoestring budgets, raised in the traditions of the British club cycling scene – would have a major impact in shaping the culture of the new organisation.

In the autumn of 1997, with a new Board that would virtually erase the previous regime, British Cycling was ready to move forward. New president Cookson and chief executive King were in place, Dailey was national coach and they – and their supporters – were left to pick up the pieces. What faced them was no small task; they had to try to reshape the sport, making it a credible organisation that would, in due course, attract National Lottery funding. However, slowly some semblance of order and relative calm returned to the backroom of British cycling.

The Manchester Velodrome, a genuinely world-class facility, was clearly a massive boost to the sport. In addition to being a prestigious world venue and a headquarters in the heartland of British cycling, the new National Cycling Centre would house the national squads and coaches in the one place. Coaches would meet and discuss ideas, while regional coach education was centralised and those newly inspired trainers could then return to the regions and try to apply these new strategies, spreading the word.

If those changes in British cycling's ideas and attitudes would take time to become embedded, then the immediate impact of the Manchester Velodrome was to invigorate track racing in a densely populated catchment area that had long been a stronghold of cycling talent, attracting curious riders to try the various disciplines. Track racing, once the domain of relatively few committed riders, was now a more attractive proposition: for the first time in British cycling history, track racing didn't depend on the vagaries of the weather.

For all that, the velodrome, Trickett's awkward parliamentary questions and the new Board and president represented a chance – and a need – for a fresh start for the BCF, which was still hopelessly short of funds. There was a new headquarters, there were new coaches and ideas, new technologies and applied sports science methods gaining traction in the country, but there was still precious little money to fund or implement any of the initiatives. Throughout the 1990s, British Cycling had had to make do with a budget comprised of a Sports Council grant of around £500,000, supplemented by annual membership fees of roughly £20 from its dwindling 9,000 members, declining in face of the easy appeal of mountain biking. There was no national squad sponsorship – not even from a bike brand, let alone blue-chip corporations like Sky or HSBC – and race levies and club affiliation fees weren't going to pay for many newfangled power-measuring SRM cranks costing £1,200 a pair.

Help, however, was at hand, in the shape of a Conservative government. Just over a year after the Barcelona Games, in 1993, Prime Minister John Major's Tories passed the National Lottery Act, and in November 1994 the first Lotto tickets – those paper triumphs of hope over experience – were issued. It had been decided that just under one third of the National Lottery revenues would go to a variety of government-designated 'good causes', one of which would be sport, with funds administered by a new quango, UK Sport, formed in July 1994. Almost overnight UK Sport found itself with financial resources the like of which the old Sports Council could never have conceived of.

The sums generated by the National Lottery and given to those various good causes (the arts, heritage sites, elite and grass-roots sport) were said by the Lottery to have topped £37 billion by 2017.

In 1997, however, British Cycling was still waiting for a portion of this largesse, and it wasn't in a healthy administrative position to claim its slice of that financial pie either. On road and track, for both men and women riders, it was business as usual, business as it had been for the past decade in British cycling, casting around for freakish talent and wondering how far the tiny budget could be stretched.

As the squads soldiered on, stronger rumours of Lottery funding started to filter out of Whitehall, and Dailey, involved in cycling and British Olympic sports politics for so long, got wind of this development. 'I recall meeting someone at the velodrome in 1995 who was drawing up the draft guidelines and briefing materials for Olympic sports about the funding. So there were a couple of years when we had the velodrome in Manchester, but without the funding to go with it.' There was light at the end of the tunnel, with talented riders, innovative coaching, a coherent, reformed organisation, proper funding and new blood – King, Cookson – allied to coaching and sports science talent (Keen, coaching coordinator Tony Yorke, sports scientists Louis Passfield and Simon Jones) that was primed and enthusiastic.

Keen would emerge as the most influential of these, in

many different areas – from training and nutrition to visionary thinking – and for those unaware of his long history with the sport, it's worth going back to the first meeting of the people who would be so tightly wrapped in the development of British Cycling – and cycling in Britain more generally. He first came to the attention of the then BCF back in 1986, when, as a young sports scientist, he was working on developing software and a test protocol for the groundbreaking Kingcycle ergometer. The national coach at the time, Jim Hendry, had heard about Keen, then working in Bishop Otter College in Chichester, through the coaching grapevine, and secured funding for him to develop the Kingcycle.

The Kingcycle was essentially a glorified turbo trainer that could be used to measure a rider's power output in watts, their heart rate, as well as enabling a VO_2 maximum figure and all manner of gas and blood analysis as the rider rode their own bike, strapped to the Kingcycle, staring at a monitor, their work rate controlled by an Amstrad 8256 computer, sweating and suffering. It was a portable, accurate piece of equipment, and the 'Kingcycle test' quickly became well-known on the UK cycling scene. As early as 1987, the phrase 'watts per kilogram' was already known and understood by many coaches and riders.

In January 1987 Keen met the 18-year-old Chris Boardman for the first time, when national coach Dailey had driven down a car full of track squad guinea pigs to be tested on an early version of the Kingcycle. Dailey had been put in touch with Keen through Hendry and, fortuitously for all concerned, Dailey, Keen and Boardman hit it off. Dailey, a tough competitor in his day, might have had something of the regimental sergeant major about him, all conscientious belt and braces, short back and sides and neat side parting, but, traditionalist or not, he sensed that Keen had something special on their first meeting.

The 18-year-old Boardman was equally struck by Keen:

My first tests were ordinary at best, but for the first time I came away from a test with a list of training zones, about what it should feel like in these four zones he had devised. He might well have been the first person in the world to quantify training like that, translating those physiological concepts into layman's terms. I went back home with a sheet of paper with the explanation of these zones and what sort of racing I'd be suited to. I loved his approach, because he said, 'Here's the things I think you should do and here's why.' Not to be melodramatic about it and to use that cliché, but Peter got me fascinated in the 'journey' rather than the destination. With Pete it was all about 'OK, this is where you are now, here's some evidence, in layman's terms, that suggests you can go this amount better, let's go and try it.' Brilliant! So we did that. Then we'd do the next thing. And the next thing.

Keen's early impression of Boardman was that here was a young talent who was committed to the same principles as himself – a questing, obsessive and open-minded curiosity:

What was striking about Chris was that even at that young age, he 'owned' the process; the desire to race and train came from him and nobody else, not a coach or his parents, which is often the case with young riders. Chris was so keen that he ended up driving back down a month later, on his own, in a dodgy old Renault 4, to do another test.

The meeting of Boardman-Keen-Dailey was auspicious in that it would lead, six years later, to Britain's first Olympic cycling gold medal in seventy-two years, in a roasting Barcelona velodrome. But that was still to come. In 1986, in the tiny sports science 'lab' ('little more than a large cupboard,' says Boardman), Boardman was about to put in the first of many sweaty miles, sitting on a bike, strapped to a Kingcycle, focus fixed on an 'X' hovering in the middle of a black-and-white monitor, going nowhere, watched by an impassive Keen and a curious Dailey.

Having discovered each other by dint of a casual remark, and having found themselves uniquely compatible, this threesome launched into an ambitious new venture that would lead them all much, much further than any imagined at the time. Dailey was fortunate to find Keen. Keen was lucky to find a rider as talented and coachable as Boardman, while Boardman was lucky to find a coach with new ideas that resonated strongly at precisely the right time in his life. And, in spite of some underwhelming first tests and modest international race results, Boardman got his head down and trained hard, supported by the Dailey-Keen duo, who understood and supported each other's aims. It was a near-perfect grouping, albeit that there was still no money and too much work for beleaguered national coach Dailey.

What that relationship did enable – apart from helping Boardman to a 1992 Olympic gold medal and a professional European road career – was for Keen to build his reputation while honing his methods and ideas. Although he was essentially a freelance coach, more or less precariously attached to the British endurance track squad between 1987 and 1997, Keen established a name for himself in UK coaching and racing circles.

He had stayed clear of the Tony Doyle-era 1995 BCF chaos, having briefly worked with Doyle the rider in a coaching capacity and not been impressed by what he had discovered. During one period that Keen had stepped back from the BCF turmoil, he was contacted by UK Sport to act as an independent judge of the applications that had started to arrive from various sporting organisations applying for Lottery funding. Keen read and assessed documentation sent in from the likes of the kayaking equivalent of the BCF and was not always impressed with that either. 'There was nothing from cycling,' recalls Keen. 'There hadn't even been anyone from the BCF who had attended any briefings about what was happening or how to prepare an application. I'm sure I contacted someone at the BCF about it.'

Incredible as it may seem, what with the dawn of an era of massive sports funding via UK Sport, nobody at the BCF appeared to be paying much attention. Or if they were, nobody was doing enough about it – another illustration of an over-whelmed organisation and leadership too busy fighting itself to focus on bigger goals. If nothing else, however, Keen was able to survey the terrain, see what other organisations were planning and tuck those insights away for later use.

For Dailey's part, a decade in his plate-spinning thankless job was starting to take its toll, and he began to suffer from some major stress-related health issues, so much so that he decided to relinquish the position of national coach after the Atlanta Olympic Games in 1996. 'I should have quit after the Barce-lona Games, while I was still ahead,' says Dailey, adding, 'but I wanted to bask in the glory of that gold medal.' With a decade of experience as national coach, those years of international net-working had left Dailey with a unique skill set, so, rather than walk away, he remained as British Cycling's logistics manager.

In due course, in late 1997, a selection panel comprising chief executive Peter King, Brian Cookson and two members of UK Sport anointed the 33-year-old Keen as the chosen one, with the soon to be ex-academic winning out against other candidates, most of whom assumed that the main qualification for the job of head of performance at British Cycling was to have been a good bike rider.

Keen, of course, had been a decent bike rider himself, but, much more than that, he had insights into every aspect of the task he was about to immerse himself in. And total immersion is what it was going to take.

Yet it was not a decision that Keen took lightly. The future architect of the great British cycling renaissance initially turned down the job of performance director after it was offered to him. It was his dream job, a job he was eminently suited for, yet he stalled. In fact, it took a personal visit from chief executive Peter King to convince Keen that he should take it, abandoning the security of academe for the unknown perils of running the new British Cycling show in Manchester. 'I think he was a bit dubious about what the job entailed,' recalls King, 'where it was going to go.' Considering that Keen had had a ringside view of a decade of chaos inside British Cycling, his circumspection wasn't surprising, and he had a good idea what lay in wait up the M6.

Through autumn 1997, with nobody else in British cycling seemingly willing or able to devise British Cycling's funding application, it fell to Keen, drawing on papers assembled by Dailey and studying the structure of the Australian Institute of Sport, which had been set up in 1990. After Dailey had stepped down as national coach, he worked to prepare figures and programme ideas for what would turn out to be a successful bid for funds. Dailey, with his decades of know-how and connections, was a ready font of advice for Keen and, later, Dave Brailsford.

With a combination of Keen's academic background as well as insights gained while working as an 'expert assessor' at UK Sport, there was nobody better able to prepare an application that was bigger and bolder than anything previously envisaged.

Keen's vision for cycling was widescreen and expansive, requiring a bigger budget than either Hendry or Dailey would have dared push for.

Such was the workload – and Keen's monomaniacal attention to detail – that Keen would work till three in the morning to finish the 7,000-word, twenty-five-page treatise. The document had been revised and tweaked over and over. Keen's analysis put Britain's position in the hierarchy of global cycling in context; he set medal targets and outlined goals. Keen's application contained detail that was lucid and compelling, pinpointing events in which Britain could win medals at Olympic Games and World Championships. Those targets, very clearly identified, were track cycling medals, and Keen set out 'a prima facie case for prioritising track cycling within the Cycling World Class Performance Programme on the basis of medal opportunities'. Simply put, there were more track medals up for grabs than in road racing and mountain biking combined – so track racing was where the resources would go.

The 'Cycling World Class Performance Programme' (CWCPP) presented in application for Lottery funding is still a remarkable document, particularly viewed with the benefit of twenty years of hindsight. The lessons gleaned from what was going on in the sport – the track focus, the growing specialisation of riders, the importance of sports science, biomechanics, nutrition and technology – are all present, recognised and highlighted. So too is the blunt acknowledgement that the best chance GB had of winning medals was on the track. 'Track racing presents as many opportunities to win medals as all other disciplines combined, despite the fact that total participation in track cycling is low compared to other branches of the sport. When looking purely at Olympic competition the picture is even more skewed in favour of track racing, which accounts for 65 per cent of the total medals available.' Boiled down to its bones, Keen's direction was clear. It's going to be easier to win medals on track than any other branch of cycling, even if the media profile of those disciplines is relatively small. However, if funding was going to be heavily biased towards medal-winning, then what did it matter if the media interest was modest?

Moving away from the medal-winning focus, the boldest statement in the whole document was the one that was simultaneously the most vague, the hardest to measure and presented the least likely outcome. The long-term aim and goal of the WCCP, stated Keen, 'is for cycling to be perceived by the British Public as a successful and highly respected sport, and an attractive and beneficial recreational activity. We believe we can achieve this by establishing a performance programme.'

Read decades after it was written, this sentence seems like an unremarkable ambition, given the phenomenal growth in the popularity of cycling – as recreation, sport and commuting method – in the intervening period. Forget the current blanket mainstream media coverage of the medals won over the period and realise that when Keen wrote these lines, cycling was still an obscure niche sport, and city-based bike-hire schemes and London superhighway bike lanes were pure pie in the sky. Yet starting with Keen's visionary plan, not only did GB win many medals and world titles, it's also accurate to say that cycling has moved into the mainstream of British life – and that should be Keen's real legacy. For all the travails and lurid headlines that British Cycling would generate in 2016, this vision, this plan – to turn Britain into a nation of bike riders of all kinds – was the real kernel of genius in that document.

We are, however, getting way ahead of ourselves.

When it came down to the nitty-gritty of 1997 sports funding applications, of detailing what a well-funded World Class Performance Programme would result in, Keen didn't flinch.

Under 'Goals' he wrote, 'The overall goal of the CWCPP is for the UK to be ranked sixth in the world in 2004, as measured by total top 10 results in World and Olympic championships in all Cycling WCPP-funded disciplines. On the basis of the analysis, this should result in four Olympic and ten World Championship medals.' Keen, ever the scientist, always the empiricist, wanted things to be measured.

Happily for all concerned, Keen's bid document outlining his version of the plan – the Cycling World Class Performance Programme – was well received by the Whitehall mandarins who decided these matters, and British Cycling would receive its first funding at the end of 1997. The CWCPP – which quickly became known among riders as 'the Plan' – was up and running.

Keen's good fortune – apart from that significant capital injection from the National Lottery fund – was that there were small pockets of coaches who had already worked with Keen or who were acquainted with his research. Additionally, there was a collection of sports scientists who had been building a useful body of applied research in cycling for the best part of a decade. It was a talent pool of people and principals, nurtured partly thanks to Tony Yorke's coach education programme, that Keen and British Cycling would dip into regularly.

Speaking in 2018, then president Brian Cookson was clear that for all the intelligence at the top, the wider team was crucial in the development of British Cycling. 'Once things had been stabilised and Lottery resources secured, we made sure that we recruited some excellent people throughout the organisation – and not just in the WCPP – I'm thinking here of the people who developed the talent team, coach education, development programmes, academies, and so on.' The fact that British Cycling now had a budget that was around three times bigger than any other federation also helped, enabling investment in cutting-edge clothing, equipment and nutrition, as well as funding training camps and race programmes with a breadth that had been previously unthinkable.

Whatever the specifics of funding and research in different sports, in the early 1990s, sports science was not the massive academic field it is now. Louis Passfield, now a professor of sport and exercise sciences at the University of Kent, was a contemporary of Keen's before becoming a colleague, and he explains that 'by the time I graduated in June 1990 I actually thought I knew quite a lot, because I had read most of the literature and, bear in mind, this was a period where you could do a search for published research in cycling and read it all'. However, adds Passfield ruefully, 'the fact that I knew the theory really didn't help much with any practical coaching application'.

Passfield, as lean and tanned today as he was as a club road racer in the 1980s, recalls that his interest in sports science came about by wanting to train himself and be transformed into a Tour de France winner – in other words by applying sports science to himself. 'By the time I finished my degree I expected that I would be able to pull out a spreadsheet and be able to calculate, in terms of training, what you needed to do and that the physiology of the human body would become known to me and we'd have all the answers,' reflects Passfield, laughing at his younger self. 'It didn't take me long to realise that wasn't going to happen!'

Curiously, over at Cardiff University in 1992, another road racing cyclist, Simon Jones, started to study sports science for precisely the same reason: a desire to see how far he could go as a rider. By the time he got to university, he too was trying to apply sports science theory to willing local amateurs, having reasoned that he had gone as far as he could himself. 'I was doing Kingcycle tests on riders from Cwmcarn Paragon and got an early set of SRM power measuring cranks through the university,' says Jones, who was cutting his coaching teeth with young Welsh riders in the lab and on the road. Both Passfield and Jones would go on to hold senior coaching positions under Keen at the revamped British Cycling in Manchester.

If there was a sense in which this scientific training generated by 'boffins in lab coats' using squad riders as guinea pigs to more efficiently train 'lab rats' was usurping the old order, it has to be said in their defence that Keen, Passfield and Jones had been competitive riders in their time. True, none of them had the ability of the riders they were now working with, but they all knew what it was like to train hard and race, so their interest in riders wasn't simply as detached technicians taking sadistic pleasure in measuring a rider's core temperature.

Nevertheless, in spite of their honourable sporting credentials, there was still some suspicion – indeed downright resistance – from established riders, coaches and team managers. Yes, Keen and his sports science team had competed, but hardly at a level that endowed them with credibility in the eyes of their critics. The arrogance of their youth, allied to their confidence in the science, did not always come over well, as Simon Jones remembers from his earliest days in Manchester Velodrome:

I got a job at British Cycling in 1995 after I saw an advert in the *Guardian*. I applied and was called for an interview where Louis [Passfield] was on the panel. As far as I was concerned I totally blagged the interview, talking about this relatively new idea called 'critical power' which a guy at Cardiff called Martin Lindley had just developed. I got the job on the basis that nobody really understood the concept, so they couldn't ask me any questions.

In this area too – analysing actual racing and training – British Cycling benefited from another easily overlooked but happy series of coincidences. Just as the field of 'sports science' was exploding throughout British further education, it coincided with the development of relatively cheap and portable technologies that could be fitted to bikes and riders. It meant that curious sports scientists could measure the physical demands of racing and training in ways and with detail unavailable to previous generations of coaches.

It was now easier than ever before to apply the science to the sport as it was actually practised. Could you explain to a rider what it took to win a bike race? Well, yes you could offer some sound suggestions. If you wanted to be in the lead group up Alpe d'Huez in the Tour, you needed to be able to generate around 350 watts for forty minutes – depending on your body weight. You could sit your bike on a treadmill set at an eight-degree slope and see if you could 'replicate' a Tour climb at a given wattage. Training didn't get much more specific and scientific than that in those days. What the science couldn't explain were the race craft, the psychology and technical riding skills that were essential but often overlooked components in successful racing.

Passfield has a clear idea of Keen's impact on cycling:

My biased perspective is that really Peter [Keen] was the golden child of that era, partly because cycling lends itself to the application of sports science and because Peter had worked on the development of ideas like the 'levels' of training and carbohydrate feeding and those sorts of strategies. It meant that sports science had an immediate message to 'sell' to riders and coaches, things that would make a difference to their racing and training. Additionally, the fact is that you can gather all physiological and mechanical data and use the timed track events to measure very precisely what is required to perform.

However, all things considered, it would be both unfair and inaccurate to posit 1997 as the absolute year zero of British cycling, given that much of the preparatory work that Keen and his cohort would benefit from was already in place. After all, Jim Hendry had tried to promote sports science and coaching – and introduced sports psychology in the shape of John Syer – as early as 1986.

A new generation of coaches had a basic understanding of 'scientific' coaching and the wherewithal to practise the theory thanks to the Kingcycles installed by Hendry in the nine coaching Centres of Excellence spread throughout England. Having found fellow supporters of grass roots and 'scientific' coaching in both Dailey and Yorke, Hendry deserves more credit than he has hitherto been given, his legacy still hanging on his involvement in Great Britain's 1984 Olympic shambles, an even earlier example of underfunded and underprepared British riders floundering on the biggest stage.

All things considered it would be fair to say that in many ways cycling in 1998 was, at least culturally, relatively well-prepared for the arrival of Keen's programme and the first Lottery funding that would be deposited in British Cycling's bank account. The combination of a new velodrome and a reservoir of talented and motivated sports scientists armed with a raft of new technologies, ideas and research were ready and waiting.

The new ideas which were, in Passfield's words, 'a massive disruptor', would, in fact, find many fertile and willing actors around the country, with a better educated and more receptive audience than might have been imagined.

What was required now was credible, bold leadership, a

grand plan and a truckload of cash to enable it all to happen. Who was going to integrate Passfield's 'cheeky young upstarts with totally different perspectives' into the hidebound world of British cycling, mostly run by part-timers and ex-pros, all marinated in decades of established cycling tradition?

Thanks to Chris Boardman's successes, from the Barcelona gold to the Tour de France yellow jersey, Keen's training methods had been shown to work at the highest levels – for at least one rider. Given more staff and much improved resources in the shape of Lottery money and a velodrome, could those same training methods be rolled out across a much wider field of play? For those most closely involved, the collective mood was a combination of excitement and fear, poised at the start of a new era, yet unsure if they could really pull off the plan they had devised. British cycling's recent traumatic history, as well as the totally new approach, meant that there was absolutely no guarantee of success. Whatever the outcome, the next months would be eventful, and there were less than two years till the Sydney Olympic Games.

3

US VERSUS THEM

'Resistance? There was downright hostility!'

In late 1997, Peter Keen was installed as the first head of performance at British Cycling. Near the top of his long 'to-do' list was to explain his plan to coaches, riders, mechanics and the wider cycling nation – what was this Cycling World Class Performance Programme, and where did everyone fit in?

In November, the squads had been called to a meeting at Mere Golf Resort on the outskirts of Manchester. None of the assembled riders were sure what they were going to hear when Keen stood up to address them in front of his Power-Point presentation – a technology that itself impressed some onlookers as being a step forward. Between his slides and an impassioned, eloquent pitch, Keen revealed his plan and the promise of a living wage for squad riders.

'I remember we were all excited by the prospect of getting paid. We were all like "Whoa, we're going to get money to do what we've been doing for years for nothing!"' recalls Phil West, then a first year senior on the endurance track squad.

'The money was great, but there was no training programme to take home at that point; just go back home and keep riding.' It's easy to forget now, but in that predigital era, when mobile phones were brick-sized, yuppie-owned and out of reach to impoverished bike riders, the height of high-tech communication for cyclists comprised a fax machine. Keeping track of riders, their daily training and whereabouts, wasn't possible to do via a smartphone, as it is now.

On the other side of the management fence, the tone was the same – optimistic – albeit that the excitement was tempered by the dread that comes with planning big projects. Chris Boardman recalls the feeling. 'I think to start with, when the money was announced, everyone went "Brilliant!" then in the next breath said "Shit! What do we do with it!? We absolutely don't know what to do with it."'

Given his work at UK Sport as an assessor of funding applications, and given his work as a lecturer and coach with British Cycling, coaching the talented North Wirral Velo team and with Boardman in the professional peloton, Keen was well qualified. He took what he had learned and supersized it.

'The WCPP document was based on scaling up what I had first done with Chris on an individual basis. Which is to say that you work out what the goals are, what it will take to get there and what resources you will need to do it. It was the same principle at North Wirral Velo, so the underlying ideas were the same,' explained Keen, making it sound like a perfectly straightforward and quite obvious task.

With under two years to the Sydney Olympics in September 2000, there was so much to do it was bewildering. It wasn't as if Keen was simply taking over an existing structure that required a tweak; British Cycling didn't just need switching off and on again. This was a programme that needed writing from first principles, with bolder outcomes in mind than making sure everyone had matching track suits. However, Keen's first job, on arriving at Manchester in autumn 1997, was to accompany the chief executive, Peter King, to buy some second-hand furniture for his drab office.

It would be convenient – but inaccurate – to imagine that once the money was in place that the process of reconstructing British Cycling would be a trouble-free enterprise. Under Peter Keen's new regime, British Cycling now had 'More coaches than Wallace Arnold,' according to old school road race legend Sid Barras. The problem was that, having reduced the problems of British cycling as essentially a lack of money – for coaching, training camps, race programmes, equipment and travel – many assumed that once the Lottery cash arrived, British cycling's problems would be over.

Keen understood that the changes required were far more radical than opening a new bank account; it wasn't simply a matter of distributing money throughout an organisation that was skint but otherwise healthy. Writing cheques was the easy part; hiring new staff as well as integrating training methods while nurturing a profound cultural shift was much trickier. It wasn't as though, having built this gleaming new Jerusalem in a Manchester Velodrome, believers in the religion of 'scientific' cycling flocked to the reborn British Cycling, supported by coaches converted to Keen's commandments.

Of course it didn't develop like that, and flashes of Keen's arrogance – his insistence that he knew best – often rubbed people the wrong way. 'Oh, you couldn't ask him silly questions or he'd just walk away from you,' said one former British Cycling staffer, laughing as he recalled the young academic's approach to interpersonal relationships. Keen, aided by Dailey and Jim Hendry, had written the plan, but could he convince the agnostics and non-believers, people whom Keen needed onside to help him implement the WCPP?

Keen's early months were complicated by the recently abolished differentiation between professional and amateur riders, who had hitherto raced different events and calendars, rarely competing against each other. There had always been a prickly – at best – relationship between 'professional' and 'amateur' riders in the pre-unification era, prior to the 1996 rule change, which dissolved the distinction between the two classes. Essentially, after the age of 23, riders were required to compete in the 'Elite' class. Thus, full-time British amateurs – or part-time UK pros racing domestically – who were aged 24 would henceforth compete in the Elite world road race championships, against full-time World Tour professionals who raced in Grand Tours. Equally, from 1996, the Olympic and Commonwealth Games, which had been strictly amateur-only affairs, were now open to professional riders.

Before the rules dissolved the difference between 'pros' and 'amateurs', the enmity between the two classes would often result in 'robust' riding and dubious tactical alliances in pro-am Open events. Professionals would invariably band together to ensure prize money was won by pro riders, put in a communal pot and split between them. Very few 'Open' races were ever won by amateur teams or riders, and there was an obvious divide between 'them' and 'us' in cycle sport.

It was clear from the outset that Keen was intent on streamlining the new organisation, both in terms of squad number as well as concentrating resources in areas he was confident they would make a difference. Hard choices were going to be made by Keen's new WCPP, and the former professional class was about to lose out to this new organisation that was, as far as the pros were concerned, being run by some failed amateur in a lab coat.

Crudely speaking, Olympic track events would be singled out for special treatment, while Britain's domestic professionals, who almost exclusively raced on the road, were about to be sidelined. Like any lottery, there were winners and there would, self-evidently, be losers. And the losers, with their grievances and hard-luck stories, always outnumber the winners. Nonetheless, British cycling, with its long tradition of hardmen road racers, was about to undergo a track-based revolution, whether it was ready for it or not.

It's not that road racing and endurance track racing were incompatible, far from it. In terms of the physiological demands, training and riding skills, racing in pursuit, points, scratch and Madison track races is universally recognised as benefiting road riders. However, in a country with only two properly banked roofless tracks (Leicester and Meadowbank) combined with a northern European climate, track racing had, historically, enjoyed limited appeal. Following the opening of the facility at Manchester Velodrome, those issues would disappear, and track racing was about to be taken much more seriously by a new generation of riders as well as the governing body. The 'fit' between road and track, as well as between established professionals and young amateurs, was not a neat one, and it's hard to understate the resentment felt in 'old-school' networks.

The winnowing of what Keen considered the wheat from the chaff wasn't exactly cycling's night of the long knives, but plenty felt they had been stabbed in the back, or at least elbowed into the gutter, by the new regime. John Herety, the ex-pro and team manager who had been employed as WCPP road coach, had a foot in both camps – the new Keen organisation and his career and contacts in pro old school:

> The hardest thing for me in that era was the fact that we had to cull, basically, all the best riders in the country when that performance plan started. We couldn't look after John Tanner or Chris Lillywhite or Mark Walsham.

They were – no question – the best riders in the country at that time, but the government's brief for that programme was very, very simple: if you weren't an Olympic prospect then you couldn't be funded. It wasn't particularly nice to work there; there were a lot of older guys who just didn't like Pete.

Although they didn't 'blame' me too much, it was more a case of 'I can't believe you're working for him,' though I wasn't afraid to say to them that I thought they were wrong. I was happy to fight my corner if I had to. I believed the track-based idea was the right way to go. The Australian Institute of Sport 'system' was already running, and Australian ex-track riders were already trickling into European pro teams. So the dyed-in-the-wool road guys had been coming up against Australian road riders who had come through a track programme similar to the one Pete was developing.

There was clearly some resentment that this middle-class university lecturer had set up a regime that sidelined a generation of riders. For all that the new leadership and the 'old' grass roots shared the same broad goals, the integration of these groups was far from assured. There were hearts and minds to be won, and Keen wasn't necessarily the best man for that particular task.

In some ways – rather paradoxically – the timing of British Cycling's financial windfall didn't help either. By the mid-1990s the previously healthy domestic British professional scene was struggling as economic recession bit. The Milk Race was long gone, the Nissan Classic Tour of Ireland had vanished in 1993, the Kellogg's Tour of Britain had folded in 1995 and the city centre criteriums were vanishing as quickly as sponsors were departing the road racing scene.

In the mid-1990s road bikes were not selling; it was mountain bikes that were flying out the shops as road bikes gathered dust. Viewed from the perspective of the UK professional class, UK Sport had just awarded millions of pounds to competitive cycling, and the riders who had helped build the sport's profile, riders who had up to now been regarded as the best of British, were being told there was no room inside that flashy new velodrome. Here was the biggest prize fund British cyclists had ever seen, and professional riders were being excluded from divvying up that pot of Lottery money.

Another layer of experienced volunteers who had also functioned as an essential spine for elite British cycling were also left out, although their decommissioning was less evident. Since its earliest days the old BCF had relied on volunteer, unpaid team managers, soigneurs and mechanics to fulfil race invitations from foreign events as prestigious as the Peace Race, the Giro delle Regioni and the Circuit des Mines, to name only three. As the new British Cycling sought to professionalise itself, what place was there for those long-established associations of support staff and managers? Essentially, there was none.

In an era where there were no police background checks, no register, where the skills involved in being a cycling team soigneur were learned 'in the field' rather than in further education courses in physiotherapy, work experience and worth were measured in word-of-mouth recommendations and long friendships. It was the same with mechanics – there was no B.Tech qualification, no Shimano-accredited mechanics courses or City and Guilds courses. Needless to say, competences in these important areas varied wildly. And, in as much as people filling those roles were doing so voluntarily, what could a rider expect, and what could a manager reasonably demand? If someone is working for free – a friend of a rider or the team manager – the bar is inevitably set low.

The fact is that with the arrival of money, the federation was undergoing a process of professionalisation. As much as possible, in the future, GB staff and riders would be full-time employees of British Cycling. It was inevitable and unavoidable, since there was government money involved and accountability, screening and qualifications would be required. The road and track teams would have a manager, full-time mechanics and soigneurs, so the days of managers and staff being selected on the basis of the size of their estate cars and ability to get time off work – as had often been the case throughout the 1980s – were over. If the move towards a more professional set-up was a step up for British Cycling squads, then the loss of the good will, experience and international contacts held by those discarded volunteers was a blow for both sides.

After Keen made his 1997 presentation at Mere Resort, he invited mechanics, managers and soigneurs to Manchester to hear his sales pitch and apply for full-time jobs. Alex Jaffney was one of the volunteer mechanics sitting in the audience that day. 'I'd been working on British teams from 1996, and there were usually three people – a manager, mechanic and soigneur – to look after the riders; that was it. But it was good, everyone pitched in, you just got stuck in to whatever needed doing. So when Peter Keen said there would be full-time jobs available, it was a big change.'

Jaffney spent the next twelve years working as a Team GB mechanic. As the money and glory arrived, the fun of those earlier volunteer days was eroded. 'It's just not the same when there's money involved. It can't be. When you are working as a volunteer, you all muck in, but with more money and more people around, attitudes change.'

Jaffney's observation is an indication of a shift in British Cycling's culture and, from a wider perspective, what began here was a battle for the soul of the organisation as it began its transformation from modest amateur enterprise run by friends to professional global superpower. The rejection of people and culture that had underpinned the sport for years was a buried grievance, a repressed trauma that would resurface nineteen years later, played out in the media. Was British Cycling too focused on winning Olympic medals at the expense of its grass roots and any sense of proportion, abandoning its role at local club level?

The thing was that when the BCF was a small, penniless, amateur-run organisation, there wasn't much room for rivalries or ego-clashes. Everyone was more or less in the same leaky little boat. But with bigger budgets to be shared out, fiefdoms were established and minions accumulated inside the WCPP, causing cliques to be formed. The split between 'them' (the well-funded and high-profile WCPP) and 'us' (the backroom British Cycling staff occupied by school talent spotting and membership-drive targets and initiatives) was almost inevitable. The British Cycling family might all have been living in the same house (Manchester Velodrome), but not all were equal.

If the focus was on the elite, then what of those who weren't *quite* elite enough – good enough for Centre of Excellence assistance but not national squad? What, indeed, about the grass roots weekend warriors who were nowhere near elite, but still needed a federation that supported them and fought their corner with police and government seeking to restrict racing on public highways?

The split between the restructured British Cycling – with its coach training, talent scouting, advocacy and infrastructure projects – and the WCPP was never considered a big issue during the helter-skelter early days of rapid progress and too much to do. Or if relations between the WCPP and the workaday departments were problematic, those who were concerned about a 'them' and 'us' culture developing inside Manchester

Velodrome did not voice their fears loudly enough. Yet the glamour, the money, the headlines and the medals would more easily attach themselves to Keen and the Olympic champions and coaches rather than British Cycling staff manning the phones. The WCPP basked in media glory. The staff running the membership services, the nitty-gritty of the sport week-in, week-out? Not so much.

The still bigger picture – setting out an overarching ethos, embedding the values of the 'mission statement' in this new British Cycling – was something that would mutate over time, though any clarity of vision would be muddied even more by the arrival of Team Sky and its early incestuous links with British Cycling. If the sense of 'them' and 'us' already bubbled away, the presence of Team Sky – with its glamorous profile and the wages it paid to seconded or poached WCCP staff – did little to foster togetherness.

Apart from low-level resentment of the WCPP inside Manchester, even in its early days, there were sizeable areas of cycle sport that would remain marginalised by that elite department. For example, Britain had been producing remarkably talented downhill mountain bike racers from the early 1990s, but because 'DH' was not an Olympic sport, it was all but ignored. Britain produced world champions and medallists throughout the 1990s – notably Steve Peat and Rachel Atherton – but the WCPP support and funding for this UCI-regulated sport was derisory.

The grim fact is that mountain biking still struggles to be recognised inside British Cycling. Predictably, in the scramble for the Lottery money flowing in to British Cycling, there would not be equal shares for all and, both individually and collectively, mountain biking has lost out.

Ironically, in the 1990s British cycling needed fresh blood, but it never looked like it was going to get it – or even try to get it – from the swelling pool of mountain bikers. What did British Cycling have to offer these riders? The answer was: not much. Interviewed in 1994, the then BCF president, Ian Emmerson, had said, 'The kids are not coming in [to the BCF] because they are not buying the right bikes, I believe that since 95 per cent of the bikes sold now are more mountain bike design.' With a leadership either unable or unwilling to see the opportunity presented by mountain biking, the terms of a tetchy relationship between 'them' and 'us' were established from the outset. Ironically, in the light of the number of high-profile road professionals who started in mountain biking, this rupture between the two branches of the sport helped no one.

Simon Burney, who went on to work at the UCI mountain bike commission, had been a long-term supporter of both cyclo-cross and mountain biking. In the 1980s and 1990s, Burney was an influential mountain bike race organiser, coach and team manager as well as the GB team manager after the first incumbent, Ed Nicol, left. He recalls his frustration at the time. 'I was hired by British Cycling in 1999 through to 2007 and my budget for everything, for men, women, juniors, training, racing, travel, support staff, equipment, the lot, was £196,000. In Manchester, I had to watch as the track squad spent more than that developing new handlebars which, in the end, they decided they didn't like.'

Even in the years after the Sydney Games, as more young or inexperienced riders found their way into cycling through mountain biking, it seemed aberrant, to say the least, that there were no pathways to scoop up any nascent talent. The residual distrust of the mountain biking fraternity was compounded by the thinking inside Manchester. British Cycling's logic framed the 'problem' of mountain biking by explaining that it simply wasn't quantifiable enough in ways that fitted with the dominant thinking at British Cycling. Compared to track events like pursuit and team pursuit, cross-country mountain bike racing was chaotic, full of those baffling 'known unknowns'. Additionally – crucially – there were only a total of six medals up for grabs: three each in the men's and women's cross-country races. Mountain biking would never be a big part of British Cycling's plans; the focus was on developing track endurance talent, though even that was a fraught enterprise.

'Some of the coaches that Peter hired in those early days were rubbish,' states one former rider turned coach, bluntly. 'They knew about the principles of physiology, they knew the science, but they couldn't spot talent even if it was in front of them, and there was such an over-reliance on "the numbers" and performances in lab tests when it came to making decisions about who got on the squads it was scary.'

A first-year track squad senior in 1998, Phil West recalls the relative chaos of the time, even though he and others were the happy recipients of a 'wage' for the first time ever. 'I was given a cheque for twelve grand and I thought, "That's brilliant", but then, I wasn't given a coaching programme, which was a bit weird.'

Another early, happy recipient of funding in 1998, agrees with West. 'At the time, you were given funding, told to keep all your receipts, but there was no coaching support or hands-on coaching; that wasn't there at that point,' says international roadman Russell Downing. 'There was a programme of races to do, but that was pretty much it. I got the feeling they were making it up as they went along back then.'

It's clear that the early approach to coaching and rider and trainer relationships at the new British Cycling was based on the Boardman-Keen model, even if working with a tightly knit group was always going to be more comfortable for Keen than leading a national federation. Scaling up the working method he had employed with Boardman was one thing, but the bigger enterprise in Manchester would, inevitably, bring additional problems. Keen had always been capable of winning any argument by dint of his impressive intellect; he could always manoeuvre himself into a winning position. At British Cycling, that approach would be more problematic, rendered more acute by Keen's brutal, clear-eyed focus. Keen was never one to sugar-coat a bitter pill.

Those sports scientists, coaches, riders and physiologists who gathered around Keen weren't blind to his idiosyncrasies either. If there was a cult of personality developing around Keen, it wasn't comprised entirely of adoring supporters lacking critical perspective.

Inside cycling circles, Keen's bristling intelligence intimidated some and impressed others. As early endurance coach Simon Jones put it:

> I think Doug [Dailey] was really progressive, as was Jim [Hendry], they were both ahead of their time, but Doug knew that Pete [Keen] was the future. I think because of Pete's style and the way he comes over, not taking anything away from him because the guy is a genius, but had he had a bit more of a 'people side' then I think things might have turned out different. Building relationships was not his strong suit.

Make no mistake too that in the late 1990s hearts and minds needed to be won. In the words of road team manager Herety, there were plenty of grumpy old men ready to brand the fresh-faced college-boy Keen 'an idiot who doesn't know what he's doing. He was well-spoken and not from their world whatsoever and there were older road team managers who were completely against it. When Pete brought in using heart rate monitors in training, that was the end of the sport as they knew it.'

A key early sports scientist turned coach promoted by Keen, Simon Jones, agrees with Herety's assessment:

> I'd say – simplistically – that you could split people into those who were early adopters and late adopters, or sceptics; there were two schools. There were people like us with our 'four levels of training intensity' and we really needed to get off of our high horse and listen. Training was much, much more complicated than four training zones and plenty of hours of level two. We came in and we thought we had the answers, but there was a clash of cultures and some riders really didn't like the methods we were advocating. In the end I think we sort of grew up and everyone moderated their attitudes; both sides started to listen.

According to Jones, that process took somewhere more than five and something less than ten years.

The numbers-based sports science that was to form the bedrock of the revamped coaching regime at British Cycling was a common source of friction, but it was going to take more than a rigid application of cold, hard science to get the best out of riding talent.

Another rider who would go on to have a fine professional career and, in due course, win Sky Procycling's first ever European race, also fell foul of the Kingcycle lab test. Russell Downing had been an eager and committed roadman and had been one of the first intake of WCPP-supported riders in 1998.

> I remember I had got my funding and went to Manchester for a test on the rig and my power numbers had been nothing special. A few days later I got a letter from Peter Keen saying, in not so many words, I had better buck up

my ideas or I would be losing my funding, because the test wasn't good enough. A month later we went to the Tour of Morocco with GB and I won two stages and did pretty good on the general classification and they went 'Ah, right, we'll keep funding you then!' It's been said before, but some guys are just 'racers' you know? Maybe if I had been getting fourth or sixth places in those international races I would've been let go?

To be fair to Keen, part of the reason for the significance of performance power data was to avoid the possibility of riders suing the federation over non-selection. Keen had been inspired by the influential – and successful – Australian Institute of Sport when he had been drawing up his blueprint, and he wanted to make sure that the selection processes were lawyer-proof, as well as being grounded in realistic performance parameters. Even the best barrister in the Inns of Court would have a hard time arguing with SRM Power Meter data and a stopwatch accurate to a thousandth of a second.

If Peter Keen was the man with the vision and the plan, the head of performance who set the tone, then it became obvious relatively quickly that the emphasis would be not just on track racing, but, more specifically, on the pursuit events. While the bunch track racing events – the two-man-team Madison and the Points race – were still Olympic and World Championship disciplines, there was a tangible feeling that those were put on the back burner. In the words of Phil West, 'they just weren't quantifiable enough; they couldn't be won by the numbers. The pursuit was a "safe" event, while other coaches couldn't have ridden a Points race if their arse had been on fire and, more to the point, they couldn't coach those riders either.'

If there was a battle for the hearts and minds of riders, coaches and the cycling fraternity, then Keen needed results on road and track, in sprint and endurance events. Characters like Herety and experienced pro roadman turned pursuiter Jon Clay, with their roots in the old school, were crucial opinion formers, and when Clay was part of a medal-winning Olympic pursuit squad, Keen and his coaches had some evidence the new method and track focus was paying off. Brits were winning Olympic medals, even with hitherto traditionalists like Clay.

'Well, there was logic there. If you are going to pick on certain disciplines, you pick the ones with less variables, and the timed events on track fall into that category,' suggests Clay now. 'I think it was right to take that kind of decision, although the likes of Simon [Jones] and [track manager] Steve Paulding probably were feeling their way back then. It was a big change, a steep learning curve.'

The other reason for Keen's clear preference for pursuiting was obvious. 'I thought it was our best chance of winning medals at World and Olympic level, and I was right,' he states, brightly and with the conviction of having been proved correct over and over. 'It worked.'

If it was obvious that the endurance riders were the chosen sons of Keen's programme, then the track sprinters, those impressively muscled gym bunnies whose efforts rarely lasted more than ten seconds, had at least, at last, been provided help in the shape of French-Canadian coach Martin 'Merv' Barras, who was recruited from the Western Australia Institute of Sport. Barras arrived having coached a fine group of Australians, including world champions, so his bona fides were solid. By January 2000 Chris Hoy, Craig MacLean and Jason Queally had extracted what they could from Steve Paulding, so the arrival of Barras was a huge boost. For Britain's sprinters, who had long endured 'outsider' status inside British Cycling, Barras' appointment was significant both in terms of morale and actual training advice.

As Hoy now puts it:

The thing is we had been going to World Cups and not even qualifying, so we would go to World Cups, do the time trial qualifier, get knocked out and come home. You could see how Doug [Dailey] and British Cycling didn't really have much interest in the sprinters; they only had a small pot of money, why not give it to riders who had a small chance of doing something? In terms of our approach we were a bit different. People who tended to be good at sprinting tended to be one-offs, so I don't think British Cycling knew how to handle us, but they knew we were miles away from winning. We laughed about it later but we were a bit militant, a sort of marginalised group who always wanted their point heard.

In light of the subsequent stellar successes of Queally, MacLean, Hoy, Victoria Pendleton, Jason Kenny, Callum Skinner, Becky James and the men's and women's team sprint squads, Hoy's recollection of those early years of their near pariah status inside British Cycling is striking. Yet again, the talent was there, happy to survive on their £10,000 grants that covered the rent, but the back-up resources were simply not in place, not until Barras arrived a few months before the Sydney Games.

The 'individualism' that appears to be a required component of every track sprinter's make-up meant that not all the riders took to Barras' approach with the same enthusiasm, with Queally and MacLean in particular needing some convincing. Hoy, the youngster of the group at 24, was happy to listen. 'I was still quite young and just desperate for advice and ideas. When I look back at my old training diaries, before Martin arrived, I would do so much, ridiculous amounts. To get a coach on board who was world level and knew what it took, was huge.'

With Barras' guidance, Hoy tackled training with greater appetite and conviction as Sydney approached. 'Suddenly we had someone who had coached riders at World level and we had structure, planning and proper guidance. It was a turning point for me; that was when I started thinking, "Wow, we've got a chance here."'

While Hoy and the sprint group were receiving some belated coaching 'love' from Barras, eighteen months out from the Sydney Olympics, that first WCPP track endurance group was being groomed for the team pursuit event. By the time the squad was getting on the plane for its pre-Games training camp in Australia, only Bradley Wiggins and Paul Manning from the original group would be on it. Riders had walked off the programme, picked up injuries or failed to meet performance criteria. It was a far from smooth run-up to a major goal, and it's clear the unity of purpose the new programme needed was not yet embedded inside Manchester.

Less than two years into Keen's programme, WCPP staff and riders were about to face their biggest test in Sydney. Squad riders had been put on a wage; coaches, soigneurs and mechanics were full-time, as were managers and sports-science support teams; and this new configuration was set to compete in its first Olympiad. Sports science-based trainers who had learned the art of coaching on the job, a near constant state of flux of ideas and a fiendishly steep learning curve for all participants, those were the way markers on the road that pointed to the 2000 Sydney Olympic Games. How would they fare?

Happily for Keen and his supporters, the Sydney Olympic results provided reasons for optimism, thanks in part to the explosive effort that won Jason Queally a gold medal in the kilometre time trial on the opening day of the track events.

British Cycling president Brian Cookson, sitting in his office in Manchester Velodrome, summed up the impact of Queally's gold to journalist Richard Moore: 'It took 61.606 seconds for the perception of this place to change from white elephant to gold medal factory.'

In fact, the Games hadn't been an unqualified success, and judged by later Olympics the medal tally looks meagre, but at the time, they had a significant impact inside British Cycling. If international results between 1998 and early 2000 saw the tentative steps of an organisation finding its way, after Sydney it was clear that the restructured organisation had attained a new level.

With a gold medal in the kilo, a silver for the team sprint trio, bronze medals in the team pursuit and women's individual pursuit, as well as a fourth place in the Madison for Rob Hayles and the 20-year-old Bradley Wiggins, there was plenty for British cycling fans to smile about in September 2000.

The medals won at those Australian Games had a psychologically significant impact, and they would be fondly recalled by riders who henceforth started to believe in their potential. It was felt by staff too. Mechanic Alex Jaffney recalls the events clearly:

I distinctly remember being with Jason [Queally] before he went up for his kilo ride and he had watched Rob Hayles qualify second in the individual pursuit earlier in the day. He turned to me and said, 'OK, you know what, I think we can do this' and he went up and set the fastest lap. We had gone to the Games thinking if we came back with a bronze that was realistic. Suddenly, we had a gold medal. We were stunned. But the next day the momentum kept going and we won medals in the team pursuit and team sprint.

Nobody realised it then, but British riders were on a roll that would run for sixteen years.

Obviously the results posted in Sydney weren't simply down to two short years of Lottery funding, but those involved are happy to acknowledge that that funding played a big part. 'I'd be happy to say that nobody in Sydney would have got a medal if the Lottery money hadn't been there,' states Simon Jones, head endurance coach at those Games.

Chris Boardman, whose work as a consultant at British Cycling would shortly change when he joined the senior management team, sensed the change in attitude. 'There were riders able to go into every session and measure themselves against the best, so they could say "I've just gone faster than him and he's got a gold medal" and you create a very different coaching environment, one that's grounded in success, where success is the *norm*.' The process of normalisation of winning Olympic medals had begun. The squad's old ethos of 'being chuffed to do all right and finish sixth' was dead.

The revolution in attitudes and establishment of a winning mentality that would underpin much of British Cycling's future successes achieved 'escape velocity' after the Sydney Games. Almost overnight, riders who had underperformed – or performed to bars set historically low – were surrounded by people with different attitudes and better results.

'Jason's gold medal was the real changing point. All of a sudden, Jason was Olympic champion, and it just struck home that, well, if he could do it, so could I.' These are the words of Chris Hoy, who clearly felt the beneficial impact of Queally's Sydney gold – and he was not alone.

You can always quibble about the fuzzy impact of a 'feel-good factor', but a medal tally brooks little argument, and the Sydney Games was GB's most successful cycling Olympiad to date. Those looking for evidence of the importance of the psychological component in performance could look at the names who were now part of medal-winning teams and note that they had been there all along.

The happy gloss that Sydney successes had provided turned out to be slightly deceiving, however, as Keen revealed he wasn't entirely convinced that the culture his plan rested on was the right one. In fact, it turned out that the architect thought the medals and performances from Sydney weren't an indication that all was well after all.

Post-Sydney, the organisation and approach was toughened up again. Having dropped riders, hired new management or offered contracts to existing staff in the first two years, Keen instigated a cull of staff and riders who, he felt, weren't 'with the programme'. 'There was no point in funding and supporting riders with coaching, in putting resources into athletes who were simply not going to be able to perform at World and Olympic level. It was a very difficult thing for a lot of people to accept, but I felt it was required if we were to progress after Sydney,' says Keen.

Keen's rationale was that British Cycling wasn't there to help athletes be 'the best in Britain' or 'the best they could be' but rather be the best in the world, and if they weren't able to operate on that level, there was no longer a place for them at the Lottery-funded British Cycling on its *World Class* Performance Programme. The clue had been there all the time, staring everyone in the face.

Although the funding of the revamped British Cycling had brought benefits to many riders, there were casualties too, and some didn't simply walk away. Among the riders culled was women's sprinter Wendy Everson, who, on failing to be selected for the Sydney Games and having her funding ended, took British Cycling to an employment tribunal, claiming unfair dismissal.

Everson lost her case on the basis that she was not actually *employed* by British Cycling to produce goods or services, and neither was she paid by them – that was UK Sport – and the judgement would enter the statutes as precedent in similar cases where a government-funded sports federation had a relationship with an athlete. In light of future problems with riders, the Everson case was a hint of what lay ahead, though at the time it caused barely a ripple.

When cycling was an impoverished niche sport, the concept of a 'duty of care', an examination of selection processes or the position of women's sport more widely never gained any traction in the mainstream media. The 'cost' of sport and medals won was tallied in terms of training camp and equipment budgets, salaries for staff and riders, not the psychological price paid by all those involved in the drive for gold.

However, in 2017, Keen insists that the Everson case was crucial in establishing what British Cycling's World Class Performance Programme was about. 'You can't fund mediocrity,' states Keen flatly. 'The fact was that she wasn't performing at world level and there was no realistic prospect of her doing so.' That being the case, Everson was dropped from the programme, losing her £23,000 tax-free 'salary' in the process.

There were many echoes of Everson's case in the 2016 furore over fellow track sprinter Jess Varnish and her deselection prior to Rio 2016, yet it seems lessons learned in 2000 had been forgotten. The broad strokes of Varnish's story of a rider who was unhappy at the circumstances around her deselection prior to the Olympics, goes public and instigates legal action would sound familiar to those who recalled Everson's complaints, even if the ruling had slipped many minds. Less obviously, too, if riders were not employees, what sort of 'duty of care' did British Cycling have to those racing for GB?

Nevertheless, back in 2001 UK Sport clearly saw the

outcome of the Everson case in a generally positive way. The UK Sport funding model used to support athletes in many different sports now had case law and a precedent to refer to in future arguments. At the next funding round, British Cycling's budget was increased by £3.2 million, with the WCPP awarded £8.6 million to prepare for the 2004 Athens Games. It was a strong vote of confidence in an organisation that, a few years earlier, had been on the brink of bankruptcy and the subject of questions in Parliament.

The expansion of the programme, the increase in budget and, post-Everson, a clear need for clarity and transparency focused many minds in Manchester Velodrome. Those issues that would plague cycling – and many other sports – in the decades ahead, concerning young athletes' welfare and a federation's duty of care to them, were already manifesting themselves. At the time, however, given that cycling was a niche sport and the ramifications of government funding had yet to be fully appreciated, very few outside of Manchester Velodrome noticed.

In fact, throughout the post-Sydney period there were a series of painful changes in staff that saw mountain bike manager Dave Mellor leave and Steve Paulding sue British Cycling for unfair dismissal (British Cycling settled out of court, with the inevitable confidentiality clause), while former GB men's road coach, women's endurance manager and GB Paralympic manager Ken Matheson also left in December 2002 under equally fraught circumstances. Matheson would later claim he had been bullied and forced out by future performance manager Dave Brailsford.

In as much as anyone at British Cycling would comment, it was pointed out that a number of coaches had formed relationships with female athletes, which British Cycling felt was not compatible with best practice, even though none had hidden their emotional involvements. Such was the level of disruption of these various affairs of the heart that a 'relationship proto-col' was written up to try to clarify what constituted acceptable behaviour inside the Performance Programme. When Victoria Pendleton and coach Scott Gardner started a relationship that generated headlines in 2008 ('The affair that nearly destroyed Queen Victoria, how her love for her coach cost him his job'), it's against that protocol that its handling by British Cycling should be seen.

The transition from good-natured, do your best, mud-dle-through amateur BCF to a well-funded federation with full-time staff, clear goals and a thoroughly professional 'winning' approach was never going to be painless. Attitudes that in a basically volunteer-run organisation had been over-looked or indulged could no longer be tolerated. Things were getting serious – in every department – except that, as in all walks of life, the old culture takes time to catch up with the new approach and rule-makers.

Clearly, not everything was sunshine and roses when the Sydney Games results were examined in more detail. If Keen's emphasis on track riders had paid off, he was wise enough to see that those Sydney medals shouldn't mask deeper prob-lems – his post-Sydney cull was recognition of that, while the relative 'maturity' of some of the Team GB riders – Jonny Clay, Bryan Steel – was a concern. Quite simply, there was a dearth of young talent behind the old guard. Where was the new wave coming from? 'We recognised that there were some big gaps in the pathway to the top,' admits Jones, 'and we got rid of the performance times and time-based criteria. I think we recog-nised that we needed to invest more in the long-term talent.' The absolute tyranny of the clock and the watt were ques-tioned, and it was recognised that some flexibility in coaching and selection was also needed. Both developments repre-sented philosophical tweaks of the plan – an end to over-rigid adherence to brute, number-crunching sports science, as well as the need for a more humane style of coaching. Clearly, both elements were connected and, over time, they were better integrated by coaching staff.

The Sydney medals had been a major boost, both in terms of rider attitude and public relations, while there were other signs of progress at the 2001 (medals in the men's team pursuit and team sprint) and 2002 world track championships, with three golds, a silver and bronze won by the men's squad. These international track results demonstrated that the Keen-specification Medal Factory was capable of producing the goods, yet Keen was clear this was still a work in progress.

Coaches were shuffled, new staff recruited and Dave Brailsford, an erstwhile consultant equipment supplier, began his rise to prominence. But Keen was still not a happy man manager, and he threatened to resign on a number of occasions, stung by criticism from the likes of Sid Barras and his traditionalist allies in the media. Keen was hurt and angry. How could they be giving him such a hard time when they were, in the end, all wanting the same thing: winning British riders? In the end, to take the pressure off their prize boffin, the British Cycling Board decided to offer Brailsford the post of performance manager, thus enabling Keen to busy himself being head of performance, focusing on topics that really fascinated him.

'Pete and Dave got on like a house on fire; they were thick as thieves, the pair of them,' reflects Doug Dailey. 'Pete had all the coaching skills, but he needed Dave to work on the business side. That was what was causing Pete problems, that financial responsibility wasn't his thing.' If the preparation in the run-up to Sydney had been driven by Keen, then the Athens Games in 2004 would – eventually – see a new man at the helm, as David John Brailsford began his ascent to the top of British cycle sport.

4

NEW MAN AT THE TOP

'I said, let's have a laugh in Sheffield.'

If Peter Keen had been the architect and planner of the new, Lottery-funded British Cycling, then Dave Brailsford was the project's site manager. Brailsford was the man who ultimately helped ensure Keen's original Cycling World Class Performance Plan would be completed, on time and delivered as per specification. More importantly still, Brailsford would be the person who would take over when Keen left, establishing himself as a pivotal figure in British cycle sport.

Brailsford's initial arrival in Manchester had been decidedly low-key, when he was offered a modest logistics role, on a consultancy basis. For a man who would ultimately direct the greatest successes in British cycling, Brailsford was simply one of a number of important personnel who arrived on Keen's coat-tails, hired or promoted in the aftermath of Keen's post-Sydney Games rethink.

While the first two years of Keen's Lottery-funded WCPP saw improvements in results, coaching and processes, it was the period between the Sydney Games in 2000 and the 2004 Athens Olympiad that saw significant developments. This was when several key staff and departments who would go on to shape the culture and mould British Cycling and, later, Team Sky, began to assemble in Manchester. Apart from Brailsford, the nucleus of the crucial senior management team would coalesce, with Shane Sutton, Dr Steve Peters and Chris Boardman all filling new positions inside British Cycling. Influential German coach Heiko Salzwedel – who had also been instrumental in building the Australian Institute of Sport (AIS) cycling department – would also join the senior WCPP management team. Salzwedel, from the former East Germany, had been poached by the AIS after the fall of the Berlin Wall, and his work with the East German track squad had been a major influence on Keen in the late 1980s.

Of that cast of characters, the one who would have the biggest impact was Brailsford, who had actually first been hired in the earliest days of Keen's WCPP project. However, rather than being recruited on the basis of his management drive or vision, Brailsford's entry into British Cycling was much more mundane. It was Keen's immediate and pressing need for equipment that enabled Brailsford to gain entry to Manchester. In fact, it was the then WCPP road team manager John Herety who 'found' Brailsford and made the introduction between the current and future heads of British Cycling performance. Keen interviewed Brailsford in November 1997, though Herety and Brailsford's relationship went back much further, to somewhere near the grass roots of British cycle sport.

'Dave had raced in France, come back and went to university, finished that and worked for me as a masseur on the Neilson-Tivoli team,' explains Herety.

He was living in Chester just going out on his bike with the lads I worked with, out of university and looking for a bit of work. So I asked him if he wanted to drive for us and maybe do a bit of leg rubbing with the British team at the world road championships in Oslo in 1993. It wasn't anywhere near as professional as teams are now. In fact, we were so poor, Dave was washing used bottles in a bath before the Norway worlds that year.

Herety stayed in touch with Brailsford, and when Herety started work with bike brand Muddy Fox, running its pro team and helping with marketing, he threw Brailsford another lifeline. 'I heard Muddy Fox were looking for an area sales manager, so I said to Dave I can get you an interview if you want. He went in for the sales manager job and came out with the European marketing manager job!' Herety laughs at the memory, recalling Brailsford's chutzpah and this early example of 'Dave B's' powers of persuasion, the Welshman's Celtic gift of the gab.

Brailsford dived into the Muddy Fox role, working with a seminal UK mountain bike brand that was past its best, overtaken by American names that would dominate the market. What his European marketing manager job did enable Brailsford to do – if not promote Muddy Fox – was to make connections with the European bike trade that would become useful in the future.

It was at this point that Herety introduced Brailsford to Keen, which, as events transpired, would be a meeting of consequence. It would see Brailsford installed inside British Cycling as an equipment procurer and lead, ultimately – ironically – to Brailsford eventually sacking Herety in 2005.

While he was employed at Muddy Fox, Brailsford had come into contact with charismatic Sheffielder Dave Loughran, the man who would found Planet X, a bike and component brand whose 'core values' were fair price and quality, wrapped up in a tough ribbon of northern piss-taking humour.

History shows that Loughran has been a long-time supporter of the best talent on the British road racing scene, sponsoring Paul Curran, John Tanner, Wayne Randle, Kevin Dawson, Ray Eden, Jamie Burrow, Mark Lovatt and many others during the pre-Lottery years. Loughran, a bike racing entrepreneur with his senses finely tuned from having spent years selling into bike shops around the country, was 'right on the curve' with Planet X components 'so we had it away,' recalls Loughran wistfully. 'By this point Dave was working for some French perfume company and I said, "Oh Planet X is going well Dave, why don't you come and work for me? I'll give you two and a half grand a month and let's have a laugh in Sheffield," which is what he did.'

Throughout 1996 the dynamic Loughran-Brailsford duo set about learning the trade, making contacts, building Planet X by day and riding home from work. Recalling those less complicated pre-millennial, predigital times, Loughran makes several observations about the bike industry that mirror the changes in the UK cycling culture that British Cycling and local clubs were about to confront:

> Back then, the bike market and bike shops were different. You'd visit them, tip your bag of stuff on the floor and ask what people wanted. You'd take £500 in orders and then go for a bike ride with them. Now the big players are owned by venture capital and nobody is asking you if you want to go for a ride or stay at their house.

The cycling trade, like the sport it was symbiotically linked to and the federation that ran it, was essentially amateur, friendly, more about handshakes than spreadsheets, and there wasn't much money in it. The only cycling 'chain' was Halfords – and club cyclists didn't shop there – while mail order bargains were sourced via the small ads that had helped make *Cycling Weekly* magazine the club cyclists' almanac for decades. Venture capital, online retailing, sportive rides, mountain biking, Lottery funding, corporate sponsorship, World and Olympic medals as well as Tour de France successes were yet to transform UK cycling.

The story of Brailsford's entry into British Cycling is effectively a microcosm of British cycle sport in the 1980s and 1990s. A sport, from grass roots to World Championship level, that was essentially organised and run via word of mouth, dependent on networks based on friendship, underwritten by cut-price amateurism and local resources that would be turned upside down by Keen's WCPP, Lottery funding and subsequent Olympic successes.

At so many levels – races, training, communications, marketing, bike and component technology – cycling was still bargain basement. The BCF finances came mostly from amateur race and club levies which were added to membership fees and race licences (£22 a year in the 1980s). Cycling was organised in an artisanal fashion, underpinned by the bike shops Loughran and other small companies were supplying, who in turn supported local clubs and casually employed talented riders who enjoyed discounted kit and generous 'flexitime' to train.

Many international riders were funded by a combination of weekly Department for Health and Social Security 'supplementary benefit' cheques – the dole – and cash-in-hand casual work. There were three or four big UK clubs, sponsored and backed by wealthy benefactors who would offer expenses and win bonuses for their riders, but that was as 'professional' as backing for top UK amateurs got. That 'funding model' – local shops basically subsidising GB squad riders – was about to be overturned, in part by a Lottery-funded British Cycling and by the explosion of cut-price internet shopping. Not forgetting Social Security reforms ...

Those seismic changes were still several years off though, as Loughran and Brailsford continued to improve their trading skills at Planet X throughout 1997, until the phone rang in November of that year. It was Herety, looking for some practical sales help for British Cycling's nascent World Class Performance Programme.

Herety correctly reasoned that the combination of Brailsford and Loughran could find the bikes, parts and clothing required at a good price and – importantly – in quick order.

> I said to Peter [Keen], 'Look, I think I know somebody who will be able to bypass all the big dealers in the UK who all have their own personal interests and axes to grind, so you're best to go directly to Europe, where we'd get a better deal anyway.' So we brought in Dave Brailsford, which is how he got his foot in the door at British Cycling.

Loughran takes up the story: 'I said, "OK, tell you what, I'll subcontract Brailsford out, you pay his wages and pay us a little bit of a bonus on what we save you on budget," and that was how it started. Dave went to Manchester.'

That first Brailsford and Keen meeting engineered by Herety turned out to be an important one for all concerned. Keen, still in evangelising mode, explained his plan to British Cycling's new equipment procurer, Brailsford. 'That was the first time I met Pete, who told me all about the Lottery funding plan, and it sounded fantastic,' recalls Brailsford.

In truth, it did more than simply sound fantastic. For Brailsford, it was something of an epiphany:

It was the moment that I had been waiting for, though I didn't quite realise it at the time. I had gone over to France as a young lad, to race, and didn't quite make it as a cyclist, came back, thought I'd better do something, so I did my first degree. I wanted to be a sports psychologist at that point, but as a profession, back then, it didn't really exist; it didn't look like it was being taken seriously in professional sport.

Brailsford also had an MBA from Sheffield University and that, combined with his love of cycling, his interest in sports science and psychology meant that Keen's explanation of a 'plan' for British cycling was a lightbulb moment – a near perfect and quite fortuitous meeting of minds. 'He sort of explained, "OK, this is the idea, this is how we are going to make it work, this is the funding, we're looking at the Olympics." I just thought, "OK, this is unbelievable, this is the opportunity I've been waiting for, and I just wanted to be part of it."'

And there, from that meeting in autumn 1997, was the key partnership between Keen and Brailsford, the architect with the visionary plans and the builder with the drive, the sales pitch and people management skills. Even in early meetings, Brailsford was impressed by Keen's intelligence and attitude, and by all accounts in those first months they worked well together. Brailsford was a calculator and thinker, assuredly no shrinking violet, but he also had the intellectual wherewithal and the confidence to engage with Keen. Brailsford explains that

Peter was brighter than a lot of the people in the sport, and he wasn't scared of demonstrating his intellect either. For me, that attitude was impressive, though the thing I liked most about him was that visionary side of him, the fact that he could see the potential of what could happen, the way he talked about what cycling could be and how it would work. There is nobody else who could have written the plan, there was nobody else who had the vision he had. That was his gift, absolutely. You have to give credit where credit is due.

Although Brailsford's initial job had been as an equipment procurer, his influence and usefulness to British Cycling grew. It quickly became obvious – particularly to Keen – that Brailsford's talents stretched well beyond getting a good deal on Italian Lycra and Dutch frames.

By general consensus, the pairing of Keen and Brailsford in those early years was a match made in sports management heaven. While Keen got on with the business of refining and developing the WCPP, Brailsford was 'front of shop', dealing with people and implementing Keen's programme, which, in the early days, included hacking out the dead wood in the squad of 120 riders that Keen had inherited. There was no way to soft sell the fact that riders were being dropped. Keen was ruthless enough to see the need for trimming the fat, while Brailsford was well capable of wielding the flensing knife. In due course, Brailsford would be given the title of programmes director, with oversight over the various road and track squad projects and developments.

In the months following the post-Sydney shake-up, with new staff being recruited, Shane Sutton, then head coach at Welsh Cycling, was discussed more frequently, championed, in particular, by the new performance manager, Salzwedel. It seemed there was a place for Sutton in Manchester, although there were dissenting voices, with former national coach Doug Dailey and road manager Herety among those counselling caution. Nevertheless, Keen and Brailsford decided to hire Sutton, aware of the risks that came with his fiery temperament, but certain that – in particular – the 'bolshie' men's sprint group needed someone like Sutton to manage them.

Sutton, from the famous Australian cycling town of Moree, close to 'the middle of nowhere' in northern New South Wales, was part of an illustrious and talented cycling family, a clan that included brothers Gary (who would coach at Cycling Australia and the US national squad) and Steel, as well as a nephew, Chris 'C.J.' Sutton, who would ride for Team Sky for six seasons.

Sutton had won a Commonwealth gold medal in the 1978 Games in the team pursuit (with brother Gary), and the talented road and track rider eventually found his way to England to become a prominent fixture on the burgeoning British professional scene, arriving in 1984.

With his strawberry-blonde hair fashioned into the modish 'sport mullet' of the era, a dubious moustache playing a supporting role and a suspicious scowl in every team photo, the wiry Sutton was a bona fide character. And that 'character' already divided opinions, depending on whether he was riding for you, or against you. By his own admission, he was 'pretty wild in them days', a man who enjoyed a beer, and it took him a couple of seasons to settle in to the British scene.

Sutton enjoyed one ill-fated start at the 1987 Tour de France with the chaotically organised ANC-Halfords team, before winning the Milk Race on the Banana-Falcon team led by manager Keith Lambert in 1990, who Sutton had raced with on various team incarnations. Rob Holden, who rode as part of the Banana-Falcon team with Sutton in 1990 and 1991, during which time the Australian won the Milk Race, says

There was a 'Good Shane', who was just phenomenal, [who] you'd walk over hot coals for, who you would do anything for and who would do anything for you in return. Then there was a 'Bad Shane', who'd give you such a hard time and you'd think, 'Why the hell did I turn myself inside out for you?' But I used to ride a lot on morale and Shane was like Mr Motivator. When he was 'on' he was amazing, but I think he used to get frustrated with us at times, because there were some young guys in the team who he felt had talent but weren't working hard enough.

Being part of 'Team Sutton' clearly required total commitment, even then.

Sutton stopped racing in 1993. As he puts it:

I had had enough by then. I was 38 and time had caught up with me. I had a young family and I needed to make a living, though I didn't really have any plans when I stopped. I was actually fixing forklift trucks for a mate in West Bromwich, doing that while I decided what I was going to do. Then I got a call from Bill Owen in Wales, asking me if I fancied doing some coaching.

Bill Owen is yet another name from the pre-Lottery era of British cycle sport who deserves more recognition than he has been given. As chairman of Welsh Cycling, Owen was one of the prime movers behind the drive to get funding for a velodrome in Newport, a facility that boosted Welsh cycling enormously when it opened in 2002.

'We [Wales] did pretty good in Manchester at the Commonwealth Games,' says Sutton, 'I think we surprised the other Home Nations that year, on the road and track, especially since at that point we didn't actually have a track in Wales. After those Games I was thinking of moving on, though.' And then the call came in from Manchester. There was a job that suited him at British Cycling.

The further background to Sutton's appointment at British Cycling was that Brailsford and Keen had decided that the sprint riders needed a strong character installed as a kind of overseer. It was agreed that the then sprint coach, Iain Dyer, would benefit from help to keep the more strong-willed elements of his group in line. Sutton wouldn't be a hands-on sprint coach – it was never the plan for him to run sessions in the gym or the track – but he would be a manager, able to get inside their heads, work on tactics from track centre, offer support and instil some discipline.

On the face of it, the appointment of Sutton to, however you want to interpret it, 'sort out' the track sprinters seemed either inspired or insane, like adding a highly combustible fuel to an already crackling bonfire. Predictably, given the attitude of the sprint group as well as Sutton's character, sparks flew when these two worlds collided. It wasn't what you'd call love at first sight.

'First of all, the sprinters were angry because our coach Martin [Barras] had left to go back to Australia,' recalls Chris Hoy.

His wife hadn't really settled, and he said that he was moving back to Australia and hoped we'd understand. He told us he wanted to fulfil his promise to us to take us through to the World Championships in September 2001. But then, basically, he was told to pack his bags and get out right now. We had all become really loyal to Martin and we were so angry with Peter Keen and the management. I mean, how dare they do this to him and to us?!

Hoy isn't spicing up his recollection for dramatic effect. Brailsford was the man who was tasked with delivering the news. 'They went apoplectic at me, they really did, big style,' chuckles Brailsford, recalling the incident from the safety of seventeen years' distance. 'They were not happy.'

Hoy continues, 'Their explanation was that he wasn't showing any loyalty to us, he was leaving to go back to Australia, our "enemy", he's going to help them. Basically, we got left in the lurch and we were very angry. It wasn't a great time.'

The sprinters were revolting. Into this testosterone-powered team, seething with a sense of betrayal and angry with a management team it felt had never supported them, walked Sutton, a man with as much experience of shearing Merino sheep as track sprinting. He'd seen it done, but never tried it, not even in his early racing days on Moree's concrete track. What could Sutton bring to the sprinters' party?

'I remember seeing Shane for the first time in the canteen in Manchester and I really took an instant dislike to him because he said something harsh about Martin and I said, "Who the fuck are you and what do you know about it?"' laughs Hoy.

Sutton recalls the moment. 'Well, for them to accept me was always going to be difficult, but bike racing is bike racing and in time we got on well. At that point it was all about building relationships with the sprinters. It was a fun time, and apart from Vicky [Pendleton], who's drifted away, we still keep in touch.'

Hoy continues,

> From that moment to this day, sixteen years on, he's been the same, and initially, always, you'll be taken aback by his bluntness. But then within a couple of days of working with him, you realise that he'll tell you to your face, immediately, exactly where you stand. There's no hidden agenda, no two-facedness. Obviously he had rough edges, though I'd defend him on most things.

For all the bad blood as well as the ferocity of the initial introduction, Sutton won over Hoy and the other sprinters by demonstrating a willingness to learn:

Shane just got stuck in, pumping up tyres, helping to change gears and chainrings, pushing you off. He was getting his hands dirty; he wasn't the sort of manager who sat behind a desk, monitored you and then sent emails. OK, he wouldn't take any messing around, but at the same time, if you gave 100 per cent, he'd give you 100 per cent support back. That was Shane.

Sutton's arrival and his impact on the sprint group was significant, since it signalled a new approach to coaching as well as the installation of a character who could 'tame' the sprinters – and get results. If the cultural landscape that Peter Keen had designed at British Cycling tilted more towards sports science, evidence and caution, then under Brailsford's influence the balance would shift towards a more flexible 'real-world' interpretation of bike racing. The mind would no longer rule the cycling body; rather the heart, soul, blood and guts would come roaring back, albeit tempered by in-house psychiatrist Dr Peters. The arrival of East German disciplinarian Salzwedel and the installation of Sutton were signs of a change in approach.

Endurance squad head coach Simon Jones notes that the make-up and balance of the management group is best understood from a distance. 'Maybe it needed a bit more flair, a bit more character at that time,' is his explanation for Sutton's chair at the top table. Also significant were Salzwedel's presence as well as young coach Rod Ellingworth's growing influence within the under-23 men's endurance squad and the setting up of the academy. 'Rod is close to the opposite of a sports-science-based coach. He comes at coaching from a leadership perspective, with high standards [and] could be pretty hard on the lads and I think they respected him for it.'

Hoy and Jones' observations highlight that Sutton's talent – the embodiment of a 'tough love', hands-on coach – was, in fact, more than just as a motivator of riders on track. Thus, in 2002 Sutton (then on his best behaviour) was hired partly as an essential link between riders and management, to 'translate' ideas, as well as a motivational coach.

If Sutton's 2002 appointment had raised some eyebrows, they were soon calmed, as Sutton gelled with the track sprinters, particularly Hoy and Victoria Pendleton, as well as starting to develop a paternalistic relationship with the 22-year-old Bradley Wiggins, who was then struggling to find his role as a European pro with the Française des Jeux squad. Wiggins, a former junior world pursuit champion (in 1998), had risen through the ranks and won Olympic track medals at Sydney as well as world track medals at successive championships in Manchester, Antwerp and Ballerup. On the road, however, his talent lay dormant, his potential untapped; but as Sutton established himself at British Cycling the pair would 'click' in a way that would ultimately lead Wiggins to a Tour de France victory and much more besides.

As their relationship developed throughout the course of Wiggins' track-focused years, there was nobody else who could talk to Wiggins the way Sutton could. Of course, Brailsford could administer human-resource-style dressings-down in his office, but when it came to a bit of Aussie rules cursing and cajoling, Sutton was the man. None of Wiggins' other coaches, not Simon Jones, Matt Parker, Ellingworth, Salzwedel nor, later, Tim Kerrison could – or would – tackle Wiggins with the bluntness and efficacy of Sutton. Somehow, the pair hit it off.

Sutton made an impression on everyone who worked with him and everyone had a Shane Sutton story – even those who found his manner brutal would almost all admit that he was highly effective as a motivator. 'If you didn't know him, then he could be intimidating; he had a hard exterior,' reflects his former team manager, Keith Lambert, the 69-year-old former national pro road champion who would eventually join British Cycling as road team manager in 2009:

> He was the sort of guy who, once he accepted you and trusted you, would do anything for you, absolutely anything. And sometimes, some people need to be treated hard. There's no point pretending we're going out for a game of tiddly-winks. It was like one of the under-23 riders I was working with last week. He said, 'Oh are we going out, it's pissing down', and I turned to him and said, 'Yeah, it's pissing down, and what? If it's pissing down when we go to Belgium are you going to say you're not starting? Tell me now and I won't bother taking you. You're in the wrong game boy!'

Just prior to the raft of senior appointments, the Commonwealth Games of 2002, hosted in Manchester, had seen England and the other Home Nations scoop up more medals than ever before in track events – twelve compared to six just four years earlier in Kuala Lumpur. The sense of momentum that had begun rolling at Sydney was picking up pace, and the feeling of excitement and potential inside British Cycling was palpable. Having said that, the post-Sydney rider cull and the loss of Martin Barras had caused some tension inside the organisation, and it was clear that a winning methodology hadn't been settled on just yet.

It wasn't like all was well with the road racing and endurance riders either. An examination of the junior and under-23 riding programmes had revealed that the route to success needed some new signage. Post-Sydney, as Simon Jones noted, there had been a recognition that the 'pathways to performance' weren't clear, that the reliance on performance time standards for kilometre time trial and pursuit efforts as well as lab-generated data was far from ideal when selecting riders – training in a lab isn't the same as racing. There was a need to identify young talent, and urgently too, given the ageing senior squad.

For coaches whose inclination was to assess a rider's potential in terms of actual race results rather than in power outputs in numbers of watts and VO_2 max laboratory figures, there was unease at what was described by one squad rider as 'a terrifying reliance on numbers when it came to talent spotting and development'. The blend of coaching art and training science had not yet been achieved.

Keen's early inspiration, now installed as performance manager, Heiko Salzwedel, recalls furious rows with Keen during this period.

> Oh, Peter was a number cruncher. We had a very different approach there. I mean, he had numbers – the power output required for qualification in every event – in every track temperature and rolling resistance for every tyre, it was very complicated! I remember I had a major argument with track coach Marshall Thomas over two riders who just couldn't do a good test: Mark Cavendish and Ben Swift. Maybe if we hadn't had that argument then Mark or Ben wouldn't have been on the academy, so we made a special concession for them. But Peter would always listen to people. Yes, he was very much into numbers, but he would listen very carefully too, he was an intelligent guy – in fact, still one of the most intelligent guys who worked in cycling, and to be fair, the models he calculated

were always excellent. But he lacked a bit of that other part of the equation, the *mentality* of a rider. And one theory does not work for every rider, just because it worked for Chris Boardman doesn't mean it will work for every rider. That was a little bit the flaw in his system.

In his quest for medals from what he perceived as 'low-hanging' fruit, Keen's programme was centred on timed endurance track racing, with its focus on a rider's track time trials and ramp test power meter figures, though there were dissenting voices within British Cycling who felt that a road racing component should feature more prominently. One of the younger coaches agitating for that road racing element was Rod Ellingworth. Then a 31-year-old assistant coach working with Simon Jones, Ellingworth was more comfortable with the cut and thrust of racing than lab rat tests and stopwatch-calculated outcomes.

In fact, the British Cycling under-23 academy programme that would ultimately lead, in 2006, to a training base being set up in Quarrata, Italy, started to emerge in late 2002 because of Ellingworth, talent team coordinator Simon Lillistone, Salz-wedel and Jones. They realised that watts, maximal oxygen consumption and blood lactate measurements don't accurately calibrate desire, and the psychology of a rider is as important as the physiology in generating performance.

Throughout 2002, with Lottery funding guaranteed and growing, Ellingworth and Lillistone detected an air of compla-cency and entitlement among funded riders inhabiting Keen's WCPP. Ellingworth, among others, was sure neither of these attributes was helpful in developing athletes with a winning mentality. Attitudes and processes – as well as some riders – needed to change. The Lottery-funded gravy train that some squad members were riding – some without an actual race win to their names – was about to be derailed, stripped down and retooled.

Lillistone sets the scene.

> It was all about changing the mindset, because up until then you'd had other under-23 riders living at home, cruising into the velodrome with their twenty grand a year tax-free grant, driving in in their new cars, all designer jeans and mobile phones. And none of that is helping you be a better bike rider and you are begrudgingly coming to Manchester once a month for a couple of days?! That had to change.

Ellingworth too was as firm a believer in the importance of racing-as-education as Keen was in calculations of optimal power outputs for pursuit performances. There were skills, reflexes and attitudes that simply couldn't be learned anywhere else but in the stressful racing arena. Ironically, Ellingworth had come to the attention of Brailsford and Keen thanks to his innovative 'coach-led' track racing sessions. Ellingworth designed bunch races on the track – points or scratch races – inviting talented young riders from around the UK regions and video-recording the proceedings:

> I'd give riders specific tasks – to attack non-stop, to ride at the back or the front, to try to break the group up, or to keep the bunch together or ride for a sprinter, whatever – and we'd video the race and get them straight into track centre and study what they just did. The point was to try to get them into the habit of thinking about *racing*.

Ellingworth was a more instinctive coach than most at British Cycling and at Sky, where he remained until 2019, when he left

Brailsford's team after 18 years to become general manager of Bahrain McLaren.

With the benefit of hindsight, it's easy to say that a specific under-23 academy looks like such an obviously good idea, yet at the time, there was some resistance to the project. 'I was only looking for a tiny amount of budget, I had it all planned out. But Pete just kept saying, "No, it wasn't going to happen, not in the run-up to an Olympic year, in Athens." I kept on at them and eventually it got off the ground,' remembers Ellingworth. The green light was given in January 2004 and six riders, including future superstars Mark Cavendish, Steve Cummings, Ed Clancy and Matt Brammeier, were selected to live in Manchester to train and study.

For all that, the expectation was that it would take years for the academy alumni to deliver results. Ellingworth's 'tough love' coaching style saw 19-year-old Cavendish win a World Madison title in 2005 and a just-turned 20-year-old Ed Clancy win team pursuit gold at the same Los Angeles world track championships. Ellingworth was a no-nonsense coach, and any deviation or shirking would have consequences and punishments involving mundane tasks or grim long-distance efforts for his young charges. Yet, looking at subsequent results and careers, those soggy, five-hour punishment rides and British Cycling staff car-washing reprisal sessions clearly paid off...

It was ironic, to say the least, that as Wiggins and other senior British riders were really hitting their stride in the run-up to future successes in Athens, Keen seemed to lose interest. But it seemed that Keen had a plan – he was after all the author of the plan – as some of those closest to him deduced that his character and ambitions would lead Keen beyond cycling. And those colleagues were proved right, first, briefly, when Keen fronted a sports science project funded by GlaxoSmithKline and then to head UK Sport.

Months prior to his final departure, he had been seen less and less in the velodrome, to the point that he wouldn't be at senior management meetings, and when he did appear, he seemed stressed. As one manager recalled,

> He was such a smart bloke, so intelligent, but he would struggle with the idea that he needed to tell people to do things more than once, like he'd need to remind a mechanic to do something a couple of days after he had first asked. He struggled to deal with people at that level; it stressed him out more than it should have. It was pretty clear that all was not well.

Add to that the fact that, as his fellow sports scientist and colleague Louis Passfield suggests, Keen

> had done the exciting bit, written up the plan and then when he could see that it was sort of working, he said, 'OK, I've done that now, we've got some gold medals' and after Sydney I got the impression that he was on to the next thing. The thing with Pete is, I would say he was a disruptor more than a stayer. And you need those disruptors in an organisation.

Those who thought they had detected a restless Keen through 2002 had their impressions confirmed when, in winter of 2003, the great architect and disruptor had gone, leaving British Cycling with little fanfare. Almost no one outside of his innermost circle saw it coming. 'It was his baby, he had worked so hard on it and he was gone,' recalls Herety. 'It was a massive shock.'

In the five years since Lottery funding arrived at British Cycling, the organisation had been transformed from one run by three full-time staff and well-meaning volunteers to a multi-million pound business and forty staff and 'salaried' squad riders, with its attendant challenges. Keen was more than capable of working out strategy, happy with the sports science and distilling complex ideas, but when it came to dealing with disappointed riders and parents unhappy with selection decisions or untangling romantic liaisons, his intellect was less helpful.

'I wouldn't say that I was unhappy in those situations,' demurs Keen, 'but I did spend a lot more time in the office rather than at the trackside or coaching. In the end I was just burnt out. You know, no matter what job you do, when you've had enough and you need a break or you need to stop, you recognise it. I had to stop.' It was time, then, for another man to start.

5

STEADY EDDY AND CAPTAIN CHAOS

'Right, fuck it, I'm gonna do this.'

In much the same way that Peter Keen had nursed doubts about his ability to set up and run a World Class Performance Programme – recall he had to be persuaded to take the job – Dave Brailsford harboured similar misgivings. For two men often accused of unswerving self-confidence and a near sociopathic lack of doubt, their reticence reveals a curious symmetry.

Nevertheless, the departure of Keen and the installation of Brailsford as head of performance was another step change in the history of British cycling. Brailsford recalls the moment:

> I remember we were getting together for a management meeting and someone said, 'Oh, Pete's not coming, so maybe we should reschedule', and I said, 'No, no, come on, have the meeting, keep going, there's not a problem, I can run it,' and I kind of felt, 'OK, this is my chance', you know? If I'm honest that's sort of how it seemed, one of

those moments where you see a chance and you get your elbows out: I'm going to go through that gap there.

After that meeting, Keen telephoned Brailsford to tell him that he couldn't see himself carrying on, certainly not to the Athens Games a few months hence. 'Pete said, "You do it, you can lead this", and I said to him I needed to think about it,' continues Brailsford. 'I was surprised, since myself, Pete and [chief executive] Peter King had all agreed we'd stay till after Athens. The three of us seemed to be working pretty well together.' The plan – that all three would remain in post – was torn up.

Sharing a car on his work commute up to Manchester with Ian Drake, who was then heading the recently formed British Cycling talent team, Brailsford weighed up his options, bouncing ideas off Drake. Should he take up the challenge? After all, Keen had been an intimidating presence with a blazing intellect, and the pressure of the performance job had seen him off. Keen the visionary was a hell of an act to follow.

I remember chatting with Ian and then thinking, 'Right, fuck it, I'm gonna do this – but – but, I'm going to change a few things.' I thought if I'm going to do it, I want to be able to say I gave it the best shot in the way that I thought it should be done. I'm not just going to carry on with what someone else started.

Brailsford's years working at cycling's coal face, racing as an amateur in France, driving team vans, working as a soigneur and washing bottles with Team GB, visiting bike shops and negotiating deals with Planet X, all of this would all be useful for him in the years ahead. With relevant academic qualifications also tucked away – his MBA and Sports Science degree

– Brailsford's 'field work' had enabled him to hone his people skills and work his considerable charisma. After five years of observation and in-house training beside Keen, at the end of 2003 Brailsford was assuredly the ideal candidate to take on British Cycling. Although other candidates were interviewed, Brailsford got the top job.

So what was the impact of this change at the top of the World Class Performance Plan? Even if Brailsford had travelled far in Keen's slipstream, he was determined to bring his own ideas and style to the organisation. Helpfully, the rise to prominence of other British Cycling staff around the same time accelerated the changes Brailsford was determined to make.

Former national coach Doug Dailey, then head of logistics and stalwart of the pre-Lottery era, remains an unstinting Keen supporter, yet his analysis is delivered without a hint of doubt:

> Peter couldn't have done what Dave Brailsford did. Dave Brailsford was much more driven and also Dave could take hard decisions – really hard decisions. I'd say that Dave could handle the stress of it all. I mean, let's face it, any guy who can sack his head coach just before the Olympic Games – as he did with Simon Jones in 2007 – is a hard man. Any guy who can decide to hire Heiko Salzwedel three times and sack him twice is a hard character.

Hard he may have been, but Brailsford's confessed nervousness about taking on the new job was real. In the eyes of one senior management insider, Brailsford

> was wetting himself, because the job was so big. He was like, 'Christ, I'm now in charge, what the hell am I going

to do?' Straight away he started to pull as many people around him as he could. He started off in a way that he carried on, which was to grab all the ideas and people that made him feel better and think they might be useful.

With few in cycling as level-headed or experienced as Chris Boardman, Brailsford, at his flattering best, grabbed him too, offering the Olympic medallist and ex-pro a post as head of research and development and a place on the senior management team.

As Keen had discovered in his years at the head of the WCPP, there are situations when managers need to be ruthless, and Keen had been less comfortable engaging that part of his personality. Brailsford had far fewer qualms in that regard, and in Shane Sutton – the man who had helped rein in the raucous sprinters – he had found a fellow traveller, while coach Salzwedel was no shrinking violet either.

If the original WCPP had been Keen's, and if the first three years had also been Keen's, the new leadership that would help shape the culture at British Cycling would be set by Brailsford, Boardman, Sutton and psychiatrist Dr Steve Peters from here on. The sports science would remain, but with more flexible coaching, backed, ironically, by more science, in the shape of a more assiduous developing of equipment, clothing and nutrition. Brailsford was happy to invest in people and projects in a way that would have given Keen more pause for thought.

If the post-Keen Brailsford shake-up inside Manchester Velodrome wasn't seismic – there was no massive staff clear-out after all – it was profound enough to have an impact. As far as Brailsford was concerned, the WCPP had been more about top-down management dictating terms to coaches and riders, with a selection policy that was too reliant on punching numbers into a computer and, if the computer says 'No', well, you can take us to court if you disagree, as Wendy Everson had done.

'Overall I'd say it didn't feel enough like a team,' reflects Brailsford on the WCPP he inherited:

I thought, 'What are we actually meant to be doing here?' Back then, it seemed we were focusing on running the organisation, and it felt quite bureaucratic, maybe a little bit dictatorial, run by policy, and it struck me that that's not going to get us success. We need to make it more human, a bit more like a sports team. What's going to get us success are individuals who feel fantastic, who feel supported and who can perform at the very top level. We'll be judged on whether or not they win medals, not on how well we run British Cycling. I'm never going to be able to win medals, so I better get pretty damn good at thinking about the things that can make a difference to the people who *can* go out and win. That's how I saw it.

Boardman, as part of the four-man senior management group, had a grandstand view of the transformation of British cycling from the point at which Brailsford assumed control. Additionally, having worked so long with Keen, he was well-placed to compare them:

From early 2004, [Brailsford] took it to the proverbial next level, and I don't think Pete could have done that, because Dave had different skills and was better with people. He surrounded himself with people who didn't think like him, who made his life very difficult, so there was lots of squabbling and fighting, but that meant you've got that much broader perspective of things.

97

With the benefit of hindsight, Boardman offers a clear-eyed analysis of the differences between Peter Keen, his original coach, and Brailsford:

> When I was working with Pete I was a very similar char-
> acter and we did really well, but we only looked at any
> problem from one angle, which meant that there was lots
> of stuff that we *didn't* do, stuff that [maverick Scottish
> track champion] Graeme Obree would have done or info
> that Mike Burrows had from the 1980s on aerodynamics
> that we just ignored, because, 'He was a nutter' so we'd
> keep him at arm's length. Whereas, in fact, *because* he was
> a nutter, the fact that he was different from you made him
> useful and it took us years to work that out. That attitude,
> in the end, was the main reason why Dave was the better
> person to be in charge than Pete.

It's curious, in the light of later criticisms levelled at Brails-ford – that he found it hard to deal with dissenting voices – that so many insiders testify to his early unwillingness to surround himself with like-minded souls. If Brailsford was intent on refashioning British Cycling in his style, then that image was one of trial and error, tough debate, argument and 'chaos' rather than uniformity and regimentation.

Brailsford was a man who was 'relaxed' about disruption – more tolerant of it than Keen – seemingly happy throwing things up in the air and resisting the comforts of institutional complacency. If Keen's disruption had been focused on aca-demic or coaching paradigms, Brailsford was unconcerned about ruffling everyone's feathers. 'I think you could describe Dave as an innovative disruptor,' suggests Louis Passfield now. 'That was certainly his pitch when he took control at British Cycling – and he'd go on to claim the same philosophy at Team

Sky. In the end, maybe things weren't that different from other teams at Sky, but what Dave *wasn't* willing to do was simply embrace the existing culture. He had a willingness to look beyond the dominant culture.'

Nearer the shop floor, working with riders and other coaches, Olympic pursuit medallist turned British Cycling track coach Paul Manning offers this:

> I'd say that Dave was more comfortable just allowing things to happen, happier to give coaches more autonomy and trust them more – actually trust isn't the right word. During the Dave and Shane era we were given more autonomy and freedom. We were left alone to plan in a way that was appropriate to the world we work in. Plans are fine, but people crash, you know?

The experiences Brailsford had garnered in 'the real world' were what helped shape the culture that developed at British Cycling under his leadership, contributing to the new attitude. Keen, the academic and sports scientist, had laid the foundations of a plan written on a blank sheet of paper. Brailsford, the driven, intense character, the charismatic seller of big ideas, was about to build something still more impressive when it came to winning bike races.

In the words of one former coach recruited early on by Keen,

> With Dave, it was simply, 'We're going to fucking win.' He'd put a stake in the ground, way over in the distance, saying, 'OK, that's what we want to get to,' an Olympic gold or whatever, and then gather people around him and say, 'OK, how do we plot a course to get over there?' and then go and do it. He was great at rallying the troops, and

during that period after he took over, he learned how to be a leader as well, and he made you feel like you were the best in the world. Pete would make you feel that you always had to prove yourself to him. Dave was the opposite; he came in and made people feel like they were great at their jobs.

Having said that – and it's a notion echoed by many others from that era – there was also a sense early on that Brailsford was winging it, giving those he trusted real freedom. Brailsford was moving quickly with restless energy, partly motivated out of fear of getting it wrong and partly because he was driven to surpass Keen's achievements.

When asked to describe Brailsford's management method, compared to his predecessor Peter Keen, the then head endurance coach Simon Jones laughs.

Ah, Dave was pure 1980s management style. I'd say his approach was 'Fake it till you make it'. That sums up Dave in that era. He didn't have a clue, but then *none* of us had a clue, because it was still a new organisation. But the drive that was there in Dave, that intent and intensity that he brought, that had an impact. The thing is that people like John Herety, Pete [Keen], Marshall [Thomas], me and Doug [Dailey] were all obsessed, and that was amazingly important in setting the tone. Back then we didn't know exactly what it was going to take to develop a high-performance cycling programme, but we all went away and thought about it all day, every day. We worked out what needed to be done by working things out and innovating. Looking back, when you see British Cycling's successes presented as the execution of some carefully constructed master plan, well, sometimes I think a bit of humility would be good. Maybe we should recognise that chaos theory played its part; things happen in a much more random way than most are prepared to own up to. But then the important thing is to have clear goals, be agile and quick to adapt.

In light of subsequent developments – talk of marginal gains and no stone left unturned, a focus on details and process, as well as accusations of number-crunching and soulless cycling – Jones' observations run against the narrative that was spun over a decade later. He states a fact that is easily overlooked following the multiple triumphs of British riders – nobody in that senior and influential management group had a clear idea what they were doing. Given the lack of a road map, they were finding their own way, mixing their decades of cycling experience with new sports science and Lottery money. As it would turn out, this mix of cultures and old ideas was not always perfectly in tune with the more nuanced considerations of modern sports organisations, with their duties of care, their sensitivities and demands for inclusivity. More than anything else, this management group was determined to work out what it took to win and little else, inculcating a culture that was focused on Olympic medals and driving the sport forward.

Where Keen had been cautious in his thinking, Brailsford was more intuitive, more likely to take a chance, although deep down he had a belief and a confidence in those working around him. Brailsford was also a chance-taker. Compared to the inherently analytic and risk-averse Keen, Brailsford was a street-smart fast-talking cowboy, Captain Chaos to Keen's fussy Steady Eddy.

And make no mistake, those early days with Brailsford leading the outfit could be chaotic. Simon Jones says:

I remember Dave came into my office one morning – and he'd deny it now, I'm sure, but he came in and said, 'Jonesy, I've just lost £350,000, I can't find it, I don't know where it is, I'm going to have to hire a forensic accountant to sort this', and then a couple of days later he came back and said, 'Oh, I found that money.' And that was Dave back then.

If Brailsford had drive to spare and his own vision for British Cycling, he was also fortunate to become head of performance when he did. It had inevitably fallen to Keen and his first staff intake to make mistakes, before finding the blend required to make this new elite division of British Cycling work. When Brailsford took over, he was leading a very different organisation to the one that had first seen the light of day in January 1998; rather this was one in which a number of staff and strategies had already been tested, found wanting and discarded.

In the flux of people whose stature changed during this period, Dr Steve Peters became a permanent fixture, his rise encouraged by Brailsford. The senior team and coaches had all seen the benefits that Peters' method had brought inside British Cycling. In his own efforts to clarify his thinking, Brailsford too approached Peters. 'Steve wasn't like other people who I had encountered working in more or less the same area,' recalls Brailsford.

Instead of some sports psychologists who are a little bit fluffy and vague, saying, 'Oh we could do this or you could encourage them to try this or that', but when you try to pin them down they sort of go, 'Yeah, well, hmmm …' and Steve came in and he just went – 'Whack! OK, here's the basics,' with such astonishing clarity and intuition.

Dr Peters is invariably – justifiably – cited as a key player at British Cycling as well as, later, at Team Sky. As with so many instances of recruitment and partnerships at British Cycling, Peters' arrival owed much to chance. In this case, a rider had approached the then British Cycling doctor Roger Palfreeman with problems that Palfreeman recognised were more psychological than physical. At which point Palfreeman got in touch with an old contact who was undergraduate dean to the medical school of nearby Sheffield University, Dr Steve Peters.

Peters, with no background in cycling, decided to help Palfreeman and his troubled rider, turning around what had seemed like a very serious problem, getting the rider quickly (literally) back on track. Impressed, Brailsford recognised the value of Peters' insights, given the efficacy of the help he had offered the troubled Olympic medal-winning rider and, using his fabled powers of persuasion, 'poached' the psychiatrist from his other post with the NHS at Rampton Secure Hospital. Brailsford knew that Peters could help his riders.

Peters – a forensic psychiatrist rather than a sports psychologist – would claim his starting point was assuming that all athletes were unbalanced, that they were all more or less crazy, and his skill was in helping them understand and control their impulses. Peters reasoned that if a rider could control their emotions more effectively, they could perform better. That model appealed to Brailsford, partly because emotions had been running riot inside Manchester Velodrome.

The early years of the WCPP had, for whatever reasons, been plagued by romantic liaisons between staff and riders. There is no suggestion that anything particularly unsavoury was happening, but with three male coaches involved with women squad members in three years, boundaries were being stepped over. Inside the velodrome, gossip and jealousies were undermining squad cohesion. It would be impossible to totally refute accusations of favouritism when there are romantic connections in the mix or if a rider on the programme is paying rent to a coach and staying in their house.

In any case, given that these liaisons were extracting a heavy price from Keen, this was an area that needed clarification, and Dr Steve Peters was just the person to deliver the message, as one staff member recalls:

> After another 'scandal', senior staff were called in to a meeting room and Steve stood up at the start and said, 'OK, which of you has never had a sexual thought about any of your athletes?' and of course everyone shuffled uncomfortably, because, at some fleeting moment, we all probably had. 'See? The problem isn't the athletes and it isn't rare either. The problem is you.' It was a bit of a shock, but he was right.

Peters was a smart man and a straight talker with an ability to 'command' the floor. 'The thing with Steve,' says Chris Boardman, 'is that when he comes into a room and starts off his presentation by saying that he usually works with psychopaths and mass murderers, people stop and pay attention.' The hiring of a polymath with startling insights was a useful addition to British Cycling's talent pool, and another (small) reason why Team GB riders' performances started to improve in the post-Keen era.

The Brailsford version of British Cycling was starting to take shape. In an organisation where a skilful psychiatrist was using his brief to good effect, where Shane Sutton was fostering and inculcating a sense of belief among newly empowered and autonomous coaches, British Cycling was changing. There was money, there was equipment, a sense of belief and growing momentum and, although there had been departures, the new senior management team was getting into its stride, bolstered by results.

Brailsford's key new 'partner', head coach Sutton, was a much more emotional and impulsive character than his fellow senior managers, and Brailsford often reined in the Australian's more outlandish flights of fancy, though Brailsford insists that Dr Peters – and Sutton himself – put in a lot of effort in corralling the Australian. 'I'd say Steve helped Shane a lot,' says Brailsford, 'because Shane really bought in to Steve's "inner chimp" model.'

The Peters model, brutally condensed, is that we all have a wilful, impulsive and highly emotional part of our make-up – our 'inner chimp' – that needs to be listened to, controlled and sometimes let out to make its feelings known. Some have their 'chimps' more or less under control, sitting quietly and waiting to be exercised, while others are 'ruled' by their overeager inner primates. As Brailsford puts it:

> When you look at Shane, you've got the real person who is actually a kind, caring and very, very generous person, but also very volatile, so when Steve [Peters] went through his chimp model, it was pretty clear that Shane needed to manage himself better, because he was a much better person than he sometimes came over. And Shane bought in to it; he worked hard with Steve, and he'd come into meetings and say, 'Right, I've left the chimp outside in a box', and he'd be calm and give it a good go. And Steve worked hard with him too, although in the end none of us can totally get rid of that 'chimp' element.

If Sutton's character and mood swings were sometimes bewildering and draining, then Brailsford – aided by Peters and Boardman – was usually able to keep him in check, and whatever Sutton's foibles were they were widely tolerated because it was felt that his coaching skills made up for other shortcomings. If misgivings were raised about Sutton's language or behaviour by Board members, they were told not to worry, that it was all under control. Even if Sutton wasn't emailing training schedules and monitoring rider's training data, very little escaped his eye in training sessions on road or track.

By most estimations then, with more money, a new management team and a tweak of the 'feel' of the organisation, British Cycling 'really took off' under Brailsford's leadership and the medals tables in both world track championships and Athens Olympic Games are testimony to this. The sense in which British Cycling 'found its purpose', when the right mix of staff coalesce around a leader with a vision and the convincing sales pitch to sell it, had finally assembled in Manchester.

If 'the vision thing' was in place, the massive hike in funding from UK Sport while Brailsford was at the helm cannot be overlooked either. Thus, while British Cycling under Peter Keen had £5.4 million to juggle with in the run-up to Sydney and £8.6 million in the transitional Keen-Brailsford era between Sydney and Athens, UK Sport granted the Brailsford-led organisation £22.1 million to prepare for the Beijing Games – a near three-fold increase. Yet for all these riches, resources were still flowing towards the track rather than any other branch of cycle sport overseen by British Cycling. The profile and popularity of track racing was growing in the UK thanks to increased media coverage at the Olympics, but it was still nowhere near that of pro road racing. Was there talk of a road-based project in Manchester? Yes there was. Was there money for such a thing? No there was not.

Given Keen's original WCPP and British Cycling vision – obtaining Olympic track success as a means of generating credibility for the sport and pastime of cycling more widely – the events in the summer of 2004 justified Keen's long-held reservations about becoming too involved in the professional road scene. Keen's experiences as a trainer with Boardman during his career as a European pro in the 1990s had convinced him that professional road cycling was too mired in doping to risk WCPP investment. Becoming tangled up in the professional road scene would never be worth taking that chance. As the Athens Olympics approached events unfolded that appeared to vindicate Keen's hands-off position.

On 22 June 2004 Cofidis pro and high-profile British star David Millar – a former Tour de France yellow jersey and time trial world champion no less – had been arrested in Biarritz as part of a police inquiry into 'l'affaire Cofidis', in which several riders from the Cofidis team were implicated. Following a search of his French apartment, two vials of EPO were found and, after forty-eight hours of police questioning, Millar confessed to having used a variety of banned substances in his career, landing him with a two-year ban.

By coincidence, the recently appointed head of performance (and then acting British Cycling chief executive) Brailsford was in a restaurant dining with Millar when the French police arrived to arrest the Scot, since Brailsford was lining up Millar for the Athens Games. Millar was, after all, the reigning world time trial champion at the time of his questioning.

Millar's subsequent pronouncements on the problems of doping were among the more strident uttered by repentant professional ex-dopers and, whether he sought the role or not, he became the 'go-to' rider for journalists who wanted a frank comment on the latest doping scandal. Early in his professional career, the French had nicknamed the elegant and smooth-pedalling Scot 'Le Dandy', and that epithet stuck, until it was superseded by 'Anti-doping crusader', which clung to Millar like an olive oil stain on a white linen shirt for the rest of his career.

The road season, obviously, carried on without Millar though, in his enforced absence, the biggest British presence on the 2004 Tour de France that July was the media entourage. The race was won by Lance Armstrong at his most imperious, but there were no British stage wins, no British finishers in Paris, not even a single starter among the 189 men who rolled off the prologue ramp in Liege. Such was the profile and impact that British riders had in the professional peloton during this period. If British track riders were now top of a global league, their road racing brethren were still playing in division two.

As Keen had perfectly understood, professional road cycling was still a murky environment and, for all the UCI's efforts with its haematocrit limit, EPO test and introduction of out-of-competition testing in 2001, effective performance-enhancing doping was still rife in the peloton. Assuming Brailsford had any doubts about how polluted the professional peloton was in 2004, his experiences and conversations with Millar would surely have opened his eyes.

If the Tour de France was 'business as usual' – with or without British interest – the Athens Games track events later that summer turned out to be an even bigger cycling success for Team GB than Sydney. Given the budget that Brailsford and his new teams – management, coaching, equipment developers – had in the run-up to Athens, this shouldn't have been a surprise. This was the best-prepared and best-funded British cycling team that had ever gone to an Olympics, and results at World Cup track meetings and World Championships in the approach to Greece had been promising.

In Athens, Chris Hoy got the team off to a flyer with gold in the one kilometre time trial and the following day Bradley Wiggins maintained the momentum, with the 24-year-old winning gold in the individual pursuit. Wiggins crushed his erstwhile Australian tormentor, Brad McGee, in a one-sided final, then rode up to the barrier to embrace a tearful fiancée Cath, the first of many such scenes TV viewers would witness from GB track riders. In the team pursuit, with coach Simon Jones nervously and precisely pacing the line to indicate the quartet's progress, Wiggins collected silver with Steve Cummings, Paul Manning and Rob Hayles. Finally, to complete Wiggins' Athens set, there was a bronze, paired with Hayles, in the Madison. Wiggins' third medal came even after Hayles had crashed early in the race. 'Has it sunk in? Not yet. Perhaps after ten pints tonight!' laughed Wiggins, who was, of course, deadly serious.

There were no medals for the men on or off-road and no medals from the women either, but overall the performances were positive, signs of further progress. If the uplifting effect on morale in Manchester from the modest Sydney Games had been significant, then the improved Athens four-medal haul – two golds, a silver and a bronze – had a still greater impact. After Athens, endurance coach Simon Jones was named 'Coach of the Year' by Sports Coach UK, while British Cycling president Brian Cookson and Doug Dailey picked up OBEs in the New Year honours list. Cycling was inching closer to the mainstream, buoyed by increased coverage from the national broadcaster, keen to fly the flag.

The Athens Games also saw the first Olympic appearance of track bikes designed and built by Dimitris Katsanis, a British-based Greek, another happy outcome of the increased budget and the greater attention paid by British Cycling to using cutting-edge technologies. It was talked up at the time, but the comparison with other nations' spending on their track programmes was less commented on. When it came to investment in track racing, Great Britain was a global superpower, with a bigger budget than any rival nation and, as on the professional road scene, money talks loudly. With Brailsford happy to listen to new ideas and programmes, he was willing to spend money on anything that might help – whether coaches, sports science or equipment.

Bolstered by the UK Sport funding hike, Brailsford started spending money and hiring people from wherever he thought it might help. Brailsford's eclectic approach and search for talent from beyond Britain, outside cycling and outside sport saw him spending money from the Lottery coffers. 'There would be people who would be brought in, because Dave had an idea or was pursuing a new theory and then, when the idea didn't work, they'd be gone inside a year,' recalls Dailey, laughing quietly at the recollection. 'He spent fortunes.'

However, Katsanis' bikes had proved so successful that, on the back of his initial designs, the UK Institute of Sport was born. This was a joint venture between British Cycling and UK Sport, which funded, developed and 'commercialised' the road and track bikes – as well as handlebars, wheels, cranks, seat posts, saddles – used by British riders at Olympics and World Championships. The equipment is close to prototype, which sees British Cycling exploiting a fuzzy area in the rules, an approach common in professional sports, yet rarely used by 'amateur' cycling federations that didn't have the finances to exploit cutting-edge technologies. Well, with Lottery funding, British Cycling did have the financial wherewithal, and Brailsford and Boardman made sure it was used.

According to the UCI, the only equipment allowed at Olympic Games and World Championships should be 'readily commercially available' – meaning that if you went to a bike shop, you could buy the same equipment. As it stands, no shops stock UK Sports Institute equipment, and the orders for the hyper-expensive bike tech have never been revealed. Some feel that British Cycling is, quite simply, cheating, exploiting the interpretation of the term 'readily available'. In any case, it takes another nation to protest the legality of equipment and, surprise, surprise, Team GB isn't the only nation operating in this fashion, resulting in a stalemate of 'mutually assured disqualification' and an uneasy technological détente in track centres. Which is to say that if the German team lodged a protest about some Team GB technology, there's a very strong chance that Team GB would launch its own counter-complaint about German kit. When discussion turns to the 'marginal gains' employed by British Cycling or professional cycling teams, there's not much that is 'marginal' about a budget that dwarves those of your competitors, whether they are other national federations or World Tour teams.

Flushed by success in Athens, British Cycling employed more staff – influential coaches Darren Tudor, Dan Hunt, Jan Van Eijden and Matt Parker joined – and considered more ambitious programmes, funded, once again, by a significant raise in the UK Sport grant in preparation for Beijing 2008. The mood was giddy; it seemed the more money British Cycling spent, the more it came back in the shape of Olympic and World Championship medals. The general attitude of 'expecting to win' was becoming more firmly established in the strip-light labyrinth that curled around under the boards of Manchester Velodrome.

On the surface, the period after Athens was characterised by a succession of triumphs and good news stories. In July 2005 the International Olympic Committee announced that London's bid to host the 2012 Games had been successful, to scenes of wild jubilation in the capital. The news went a long way to refocusing many minds inside British Cycling, and it was clear that given the momentum inside British Cycling then the intensity – and likely increase of finances – were going to be ramped up higher still.

In purely sporting terms, between the Athens and Beijing Games the results from the 2006 Commonwealth Games in

Melbourne illustrated the depth of talent of the collective Home Nations. For all that the 'Commie Games' might be disparaged in other sports, with 'Great Britain's' constituent parts collectively taking on Australia, New Zealand and the improving Canadians on track and road, the competition in certain sports is genuinely world class, not a jumped-up colonial sports day. With twenty medals Team GB was clearly forging ahead – albeit almost exclusively on track – but Brailsford's version of British Cycling was delivering.

Inevitably, there were discontents behind the happier headlines and an organisation ready to rest on its laurels never stays at the top for long, so there wasn't much calm or stasis in Manchester. Between restless staff, ambitious managers, burnt-out coaches and riders, British Cycling's WCPP was in a state of flux.

Bradley Wiggins, flushed with a full set of three Greek-minted Olympic medals, had careered off the rails, going on a booze-fuelled bender and losing direction, at which point Brailsford called on Chris Boardman to try to mentor the wayward 'Wiggo' together with Wiggins' coach, Simon Jones. Wiggins had definitively revealed himself as a massive talent – who knew how far he could go – but he needed plenty of TLC and reassurance.

Boardman insists that his impact was minimal, and that the real work was done by Jones, though Boardman's description of Wiggins today would have served just as well a decade earlier. 'He's an enigma, I never really understood him. I don't think he knows what he wants to be.'

Inescapably, lurking in those Olympic bouquets are spores of decay and, unsurprisingly, the temptation to start believing your own press coverage grows too. Complacency was nestled in there too, that sense in which you think that you've 'made it' is very difficult to resist completely. After the Athens

Games and the 2007 world track championships in Palma – where British riders led by Chris Hoy, Victoria Pendleton and Wiggins scooped up seven gold medals out of a total seventeen on offer – the temptation to enjoy the success a little too long proved hard to resist for some. For others, a sense of restlessness emerged; having achieved long-strived for goals, the urge to move on is hard to ignore. Keen was not the only sports scientist and coach who felt the need for change, and head endurance coach Simon Jones left British Cycling after falling out with Brailsford.

The process of continual reinvention also saw changes to the coaching of the endurance track squad, some of whom were farmed out to European professional road teams. Now working at British Cycling as one its most successful coaches, Paul Manning was placed with the Belgian Landbouwkrediet team in 2006 and recalls that strategy with equanimity.

In hindsight, Manning now speaks of his three-season professional road career with Landbouwkrediet in a voice that is tinged with regret. 'In 2006 it was less about an opportunity to be a pro, more about working and an opportunity to be better in the next Olympic cycle. That was how I saw it. Maybe I could have made more of it,' muses Manning.

It's a measure of how the British cycling landscape has changed – in a pre-Team Sky era – that Manning would only be interested in an Olympic medal. Such was the focus on the track and such was the level of distrust in professional road cycling, that a rider with the ability of Manning barely considered a pro road career.

> I remember I won a road stage and a time trial at the Circuit des Mines, back in 1999, and Vincent Lavenu [manager of AG2R] approached me and asked if I might be interested in a pro road career. I said no, I was focusing on Sydney. It

was one of those conversations where there's a bit of the 'What if?' or the sliding doors scenario.

The pathway to a pro career was still ill-defined, and road cycling was still disfigured by a quagmire of doping. It was no wonder the velodrome and the stability of British Cycling held such appeal for Manning, Wiggins and others. Road racing, so long the bedrock and focus for British riders and teams, would have to wait a while yet before Brailsford turned his attention to it.

In light of later, multiple successes in the road races of Europe, the early 2000s had seen the few British professional road riders struggling to make headway. In world terms, British riders were on top on track, but lost on the road. A suspicious and sceptical Keen might have been content with this state of affairs, keeping road racing at arm's length, but Brailsford, with his love of the Tour and Classics, was not. Brailsford felt that British Cycling needed a road presence in Europe – but how to build it?

After David Millar's ban had removed the UK's highest-profile road rider, those still plying their trade in the top tier – Roger Hammond, Jeremy Hunt, Charly Wegelius – were, for whatever reason, unable to achieve big results, although Hammond flirted with cobbled Spring Classics glory. His third place in Paris–Roubaix while riding for Mr Bookmaker in 2004 was noteworthy, as was third in Gent–Wevelgem in 2007 with T-Mobile.

Wayward Olympic track superstar Wiggins had been riding for French professional teams since he signed for Française des Jeux in 2002, but had rarely shown anything other than glimpses of his slumbering talent in time trials and prologues. In four seasons with FDJ, Crédit Agricole and Cofidis, he had never started the Tour de France. In two starts at the

Giro d'Italia he had just one finish – 123rd and three-and-a-half hours behind winner Paolo Savoldelli, riding his national Tour as a warm-up before helping Lance Armstrong win the 2005 Tour de France.

The 26-year-old Wiggins finally made his Tour debut for Cofidis in 2006 and 'got round' the race famously won – then lost – by Floyd Landis as the Tour de France descended to farcical levels of doping intrigue. Landis had won, stood on the final Paris podium and, three days later, his positive test for testosterone was announced. When asked in a US press call if he had taken anything his reply, 'I'll say no', set the tragicomic tone. If there's an argument for citing one particular Tour as the nadir for modern doping, then 2006 might be it, though the competition in this arena is fierce. Keen's jaundiced view of professional road racing looked like it was still justified, and even though Brailsford nursed road-based ambitions, the time wasn't quite right; there was neither the talent nor the pathway – not yet.

In July 2007, showing the International Olympic Committee that it could handle a major event in its creaking infrastructure and sclerotic roads, London hosted the Grand Départ of the Tour de France, cheered on by massive crowds in central London, with a team presentation in Trafalgar Square and a prologue course that raced down The Mall.

Behind the scenes, in the London VIP tents pitched around the Grand Départ, Brailsford was engaged in serious networking. The Tour spectacle had attracted big players to town, the sort of people with access to marketing budgets who might be persuaded to back a major cycling team or a national federation. Or even both.

Among the people making introductions that day was Fran Millar, younger sister of professional David. Fran had been one of the founders of Face Partnership, which had impressed

Brailsford with its reinvention of track events at Manchester Velodrome, the Revolution series, in 2003, and she had been on Brailsford's radar ever since.

'In 2007 Face Partnership hosted a party for the Tour in London at the Royal Thames Yacht Club. I had invited the great and the good of British cycling as well as all the pros that I knew and a few other people. It was literally just a cocktail party,' recalls Millar. 'Well, Dave B and Shane had come along and Dave said to me then, "Shane and I have been chatting. We should set up a British team."'

The levels of success Brailsford had overseen at Athens in 2004 and the 2007 world track championships could turn anyone's head, fuelling ambitions and framing bigger, bolder goals. For a man who had made no secret of his love for road racing, for the head of a successful cycling nation lacking a real road presence, the Tour in London inspired Brailsford to try to rectify this sorry state of affairs.

Brailsford's fascination with the European professional scene had been clear for all to see. Famously, Brailsford could be at a World Cup track meeting and ignore the events on the boards to seek out a laptop to watch an obscure Belgian semi-Classic road race. It had always been obvious where Brailsford's true love was. One tale has British staff sitting in the stands at the Los Angeles round of the World Cup track series in January 2008, when Brailsford supposedly turned to Sutton and said, 'Fucking hell, we can't keep doing this, can we?' After dominating back-to-back World Championships and Olympic event track racing successively in Palma, Manchester and Beijing, there wasn't much left to prove or excite. When it came to cycling, as much as he loved winning track races, what Brailsford was passionate about was the Tour de France, the race that had sparked his love affair with cycling, fascinated by an event that was part soap opera, part heroic saga.

The popularity of the Tour in London and the enthusiasm of thousands of spectators who lined the English roads suggested that the UK, long indifferent to road racing, could be won over. That year there were only five UK riders in the 189-man peloton that sped through Kent, and not a single British team.

From Brailsford's perspective that needed to change and, while in London, he had met some people who agreed with him, over champagne and canapés at least. With a receptive hearing from key people in London in 2007, what price a strong showing from Team GB at the world track championships and Olympics the following year? There were clear signs of interest in the sport and potential for a new team. If British riders could keep medal-winning performances going, that would help seal the deal.

As it had turned out, that bright, optimistic 2007 Tour had ended ignominiously for Wiggins, when his Cofidis team withdrew from the race following a testosterone positive supplied by his teammate, Cristian Moreni. Any appeal that a full-time road career had for Wiggins had just taken a kicking. Still, if dreams of road-based glory had turned nightmarish, at least Wiggins had the comfort blanket of the GB track squad and the upcoming Manchester world track championships, as well as the looming Beijing Olympics.

Such is the gigantism of the Olympic Games and the media coverage it enjoys, the results of those 2008 world track championships are now little remembered. As a portent, the British performances were a taster of what would happen at the Laoshan Olympic velodrome, only five months later. In Manchester, the other powers of global cycling were treated to a morale-crushing dress rehearsal when nine out of a possible eighteen rainbow jerseys were won by Britain, three of them on Wiggins' back. What made the Manchester world's results 'worse' for the opposition was that so close to the Olympics, there wasn't much that other nations could do to halt the red-white-and-blue juggernaut that was heading to China.

After the hybrid Keen-Brailsford effort in Athens four years previously, the Beijing Olympic Games would be used to judge Brailsford's regime, his vision and energised approach. Brailsford had brought in a more disparate collection of back-room talent, empowered coaches, and lessened the reliance on number crunching while simultaneously investing in technology. There was no talk – yet – of those 'marginal gains' in any press conferences; instead there had been a shake-up of staff, increased spending and wasting lots of money, taking risks and pushing the rules to the limit. The World Class Performance Programme of British Cycling now bore Brailsford's stamp, with its bigger budget, staff-churn ruthlessness and relentless focus on excellence. Could the steamroller results obtained in Manchester really keep rolling all the way to the Chinese Games?

6

A CUCKOO IN THE MANCHESTER NEST

'C'mon Fran, it can't be that hard.'

'The Beijing Games? We were all walking on air and Dave B was walking on water,' chuckled Doug Dailey. Speaking nine years after the Chinese Olympiad, Dailey, the national coach turned British Cycling logistics chief still sounded thrilled by the Team GB results of 2008, as though struggling to grasp what had happened to his beloved sport. 'This was what we had been working and dreaming about for decades, and suddenly medals were falling from the sky. We were winning medals we didn't expect. It was incredible.'

Incredible is an accurate description of events. There were a total of eighteen cycling gold medals awarded and Great Britain won nine of them. In the words of Brailsford, British riders 'crushed' the opposition.

Chris Hoy's three golds – sprint, keirin and team sprint – were unimprovable, while the endurance riders also performed, with Wiggins' defending his individual pursuit and helping the team pursuit squad to its first ever Olympic gold. The British women also stepped up. Aside from Nicole Cooke's ferocious winning sprint in the road race and Emma Pooley's silver in the fourteen-mile time trial, Olympic rowing convert Rebecca Romero won gold in the individual pursuit, beating teammate Wendy Houvenaghel convincingly and still, somehow, having the lung power to roar 'Yes! Yes!' loud enough to be heard over the velodrome PA and applause. Romero's performance was emblematic of a cycling team that could seemingly do anything it turned its mind to, while Victoria Pendleton won sprint gold after setting the fastest time – and a new Olympic record – in qualifying.

It may be that the years between the Athens Olympics – the 2006 Melbourne Commonwealth Games, London's 2007 Tour de France Grand Départ, multiple triumphs at world track championships, Mark Cavendish's three Tour stage wins and European road race successes – culminating in the deluge of medals in Beijing, turn out to be a prelapsarian zenith for British Cycling. The bold vision of Keen's plan, the blend of staff and riders and promising earlier results all coalesced in Beijing. British track cycling was top of the world.

Subsequently, the financial temptations faced by many after Beijing complicated life at British Cycling, with growing egos excited by the prospect of London 2012 generating new problems. In hindsight, those were simpler times, with fewer of the complexities that would foment when Team Sky arrived in Manchester.

In the years before floods of titles and medals descended on British Cycling, the aims of many inside a low-profile sport were clear. 'It wasn't about fame or ego or money. All we wanted to do is be successful and win medals and that was it, that was all it was. It was a nice time and it'll never be back. It'll never be that innocent time when we were just doing this for the love of the sport,' reflects Chris Hoy. 'When you win medals, things change; people's attitudes change and the organisation becomes different.'

After Beijing there were those, according to one senior manager, 'who felt that they weren't being given enough attention or respect, and there was a bit of bitterness'.

The Beijing triumphs, mated with the anticipation of still more success in London, proved to be a fertile ground for sprouting egos inside British Cycling. 'Suddenly there were a lot of people who thought that they weren't given enough credit, getting distracted from their day jobs. Dave [Brailsford] was distracted by Sky, Shane was off somewhere, Steve Peters was doing lots of lectures, and it was all perfectly understandable, but it didn't help,' recalls one insider.

The knot of driven personnel that had worked so well in the years between Sydney, Athens and Beijing began to unravel. The management team responsible for cajoling riders and coaches prior to summer 2008 was not necessarily best suited to navigate the next great leap forward, with its myriad extracurricular distractions, speaking engagements and sporting celebrity. 'It was post-Beijing it started to get difficult, because of the success of those Games,' remarks Boardman. The most successful British sports team ever – never mind just British *cycling* team – having used cutting-edge technologies, training and sports psychology, found itself in the spotlight. People wanted to know about British Cycling and those 'marginal gains' that, so the world was told, had helped Team GB make history.

There are others, Board members, who are less diplomatic than Boardman in analysing the post-Beijing disintegration of Team GB, the beginning of the end of an age of innocence. As one former Board member of that time recalls:

Dave began to believe his own hype. After Beijing that was it. Dave made some poor decisions. He just wasn't as interested in British Cycling when Sky arrived and James Murdoch, his big mate Clive Woodward and the rest – Tony Blair, Alistair Campbell – were around him. When he was getting big fees for speaking to business leaders and saying stuff like, 'It's important to smile at your staff! Thanks very much, that'll be £10K.' Dave was losing interest in British Cycling.

In fact, it was in late July 2008 that the now infamous phrase 'aggregation of marginal gains' was actually seen in print for the first time, which casts doubt on the importance of the concept in the build-up to Beijing. If it was so significant, why had nobody been shouting about it more? The term, which would be increasingly bandied about when Team Sky arrived, had been retro-engineered at British Cycling as a neat explanation that would appeal to organisations looking for a Western tweak on the Japanese business theory of 'kaizen' – a strategy of continuously searching for small improvements. However, regardless of how consciously this 'method' was applied, as a catchy way of raising the profile of British Cycling, it was a huge marketing success, branding British Cycling as an innovatory enterprise rather than simply a well-run and well-funded cycling federation.

In fact, for many inside British Cycling – management and riders alike – the post-Beijing period was one of flux, relaxation, petty jealousies and contra-performances. To be charitable, most would accept that it was inevitable, that the 'post-Games blues' was a recognised sporting phenomenon and nobody was immune. Even the saintly and ultra-dedicated Sir Chris Hoy took some time off to sell Bran Flakes to the nation.

For squad members (track sprinters, the women's endurance riders) for whom a professional road team was an irrelevant distraction, it was obvious that Brailsford's work developing a Sky-sponsored road team was going to be problem. 'Well, I think the suggestion that Dave sort of lost interest in the track when Sky came along is a fair comment, though I'm not sure Dave would agree, or phrase it like that,' observes Hoy.

> But Dave is a motivated guy, he's always looking for new challenges, and I think it was a case of 'Why stick around doing the same thing? The next thing people said I couldn't do would be to have a team with a British Tour winner,' so you could see why he wanted to move on. But I think the trouble was he didn't want to let go of British Cycling because the London Olympics were coming. The London Games was enough to keep Dave wanting to be involved, but he wasn't around much. We'd see him once in a blue moon. Shane was the one that was running operations day-to-day.

The problem is that if the workforce feels management isn't that interested, if group focus and cohesion are lost then the potential for things to come unstuck is high. That Brailsford, such an important character and tone-setter, was absent was clearly a problem. Hoy, with his pathological love of planning, noticed the changes.

> People start to ask, 'Wait a minute, what's he doing? How come he's got that? Oh, she's doing this? Well I didn't get invited to that.' It's strange that, OK, you set out to win a gold medal, you did that and, well, nothing's really changed after all the success. We're back to the same old day-in, day-out painful training. That affected the coaching staff too, and I think it forced the team apart a bit. It took until around 2010 for alarm bells to ring. Dave had been away from the team then comes back and wonders

what the hell had been going on. Why weren't we dominating at World Championships? Why are the French and the Germans going so much faster? And we were like, well, where have you been?! Have you not being paying attention?

One of those expected to 'take care of British Cycling business' was Shane Sutton, except that with the Sky Procycling project on the go, Sutton was, like Brailsford, juggling too many plates, effectively working two demanding jobs. 'By 2010 people were really starting to get twitchy because the feeling wasn't the same,' says Hoy. 'Everything had been so slick and smooth before. Everyone had bought into the same philosophy. By 2010 it wasn't the same happy, coherent bunch of people that it had been preparing for Beijing – definitely not.'

Six years after London's Games, Sutton was still unwilling to paint himself as a hero, steering the good ship British Cycling through stormy weather. 'Well, when I look back to 2012 – and this isn't a criticism of Dave – but, yeah, I was basically in control of the day-to-day running. Dave was there for me and maybe he drifted a bit away, but we stuck to the vision, even if I was the man on the ground in Manchester.' When observers would subsequently scratch their heads and wonder how Sutton was ever given the head of performance job in 2014, his work in the messy lead-in to London 2012 should be borne in mind.

Dailey, who had been there, done it and got drawers full of old Olympic track suits, reflects on the period of Brailsford's semi-detachment.

Looking back I think, with Dave being a bit of a control freak, he hedged his bets and he didn't want to give up control of the track programme in the run-up to London, and that's why he got into a bit of a pickle and even got into trouble with Peter Keen, because Peter was now working for UK Sport, and they all tell me that they foresaw problems if British Cycling was working too close to a professional team.

The origins of many of British Cycling's future problems could be located at this juncture – the influential Brailsford drifting away and an ineffectual or distracted Board unwilling or unable to rein him in.

Yet who is to say that Brailsford's ultimate Tour de France goal was not both logical and commendable? Surveying British Cycling in summer 2007, witnessing the huge popular success of the Tour in England, basking in the 2007 world track championship results, noting the presence of a batch of young British riders, would there ever be a better time to launch a British-based World Tour team? Anticipating – correctly – even more success in 2008, Brailsford's determination to form a British road squad reached near obsessive levels.

Fran Millar, who was hired by Brailsford early in the Sky Procycling project, observed Brailsford's drive.

I think that when the Tour came to London, Dave felt, 'This is the real deal, we should be doing this. Look at it. Millions of people at the roadside, we're dominating on track, we've got these young lads coming through the programme, it's now or never', and he thought he had to grab the opportunity. Literally, from that point onwards, from August 2007 to around March 2008, he was like, 'Right. This is going to happen. I don't know how yet, but it *is* going to happen.'

Given the nature of the job – Brailsford was still head

of performance at British Cycling – it does seem strange, in retrospect, that more of a 'fuss' wasn't made about how he was going to assemble a World Tour team from scratch while simultaneously preparing a national squad for its home Olympic Games.

So why didn't the Board simply ask Brailsford to stand down as head of performance when he started planning a World Tour team? That thought may have been in some heads, but it was never formally considered. That reticence to insist – or even debate – that Brailsford should step down from his British Cycling post needs to be put in context. Clearly Brailsford had supporters on the Board; others, if they felt nervous about the development, were still reluctant to insist on removing the man recognised as the driving force behind British Cycling's medal-winning success in Athens and Beijing. Under the circumstances, who on the British Cycling Board was going to tell Dave Brailsford it would be better for all concerned if he was to vacate his office in Manchester? What if they 'removed' Brailsford and the London Games were a disaster?

It's also worth recalling that the initial discussion was to have a GB-branded road team, sponsored, as the track squad and under-23 road teams had been, by Sky. That idea, of a Pro-Conti team and national sponsor, didn't seem like a massive departure from what was already in place. As talks progressed, both inside British Cycling and with potential sponsors, that modest outline was shelved for something much more ambitious.

As many pointed out, the London Olympics were set to be the biggest sporting event in almost everyone's lifetime, and who at British Cycling *wouldn't* have wanted to be part of it? In the run-up to London, Sport UK would flood British Cycling with riches the likes of which had never been seen before. The British Cycling budget in the four years to 2012 – from UK Sport alone, without the additional money that the Sky sponsorship had brought in – was £26,032,000.

In fact, of the management team during the post-Beijing period, it was Boardman who identified the problems with uncanny clairvoyance. Fully eight years before British Cycling's internal troubles exploded in the media, Boardman had already spotted potential issues. Speaking in autumn 2008 he said,

> My only concern is the scale of the operation. The business has been run as a commando unit up to now and it's leapt in size. The Games has generated a load of new things to look at, such as the deal with Sky, and there are a load of things from before which were put off until after the Games. It has to change now, or it will fail.

Adding, 'But that's what makes it fascinating.' It was stimulating enough for Boardman to stay as part of British Cycling's senior management group, even if, in the end, it turned out to be fascinating in the same way as watching a slow-motion car crash.

Over the years, under successive regimes at British Cycling, there had been plenty of talk about forming a European road squad, so Brailsford's enthusiasm for the project – as well as that of other Board members – was neither secret nor surprising. In fact, even before he had got on the plane to Beijing, Brailsford had an envelope from Sky tucked in his luggage. The letter outlined the deal concerning Sky's sponsorship of the national squads and British Cycling, but also for a separate budget to run a World Tour team from 2010.

A decade after most of these events, observers of British Cycling are wont to forget what a profound shift in fortunes the 'long Beijing period' represented. With the remarkable results of the world track championships in 2007 and 2008, then the Beijing Games, the stock of British Cycling – organisation, riders and staff – was trading at an all-time high. Everyone loves success, and there were plenty of City and marketing high-flyers ready to take a meeting from the man at the top. The British cycling landscape was unrecognisable from the one poor 1984 national coach Jim Hendry had wandered, trying to secure a few hundred quid's worth of tyre sponsorship, or the 1988 national coach Dailey driving a second-hand car that had been bought for £1 from a UK professional team. Given the national squad's profile now, would there be a better time to launch a British team?

It transpires that among the pro team project meetings that consultant and Brailsford co-conspirator Fran Millar had attended in 2007, one contained members of the Sky marketing team and the conversation escalated quickly. Brailsford recalled, 'I think that was on a Wednesday, and we realised pretty quickly that we were talking a very similar language. On that Friday I was in Jeremy's office.' The 'Jeremy' in question was Jeremy Darroch, Sky's then chief executive and, though he couldn't tell a Pinarello from a Pokémon, he knew a great opportunity for his corporation when he saw it.

After searching for an Olympic sport to back, Darroch's marketing team told him, 'it's swimming or cycling'. Happily for British Cycling, swimming was trickier to brand (one can wonder about the sales value of Sky-branded Speedos), and with cycling's growing popularity allied to stellar elite success, the lure of cycling for Sky was well-nigh irresistible. With the best will in the world, you can't swim to work or school. To be fair to Brailsford, he would admit, 'If the truth be told, I think Sky found us just as much as we found Sky. They had done their homework.'

Such was Sky's enthusiasm for cycling that from a first serious meeting in March 2008 to the announcement of the sponsorship of British Cycling in Newport Velodrome took just four months. In fact, one of the appeals of British Cycling was that it had precisely no other sponsorship. Sky didn't want to share branding space on clothing with anyone, and with British Cycling, it wouldn't need to.

Fran Millar remembers how quickly things moved in 2008:

> By the time Dave actually met Sky we had already the concept, the brand, what the team would look like and how we were going to do it. The British Cycling sponsorship deal was done quite quickly, but Dave said, 'Oh I've got this Tour de France idea, would you be up for that?' So Dave literally texted me after the meeting saying, 'Right, you need to get down to London and meet this guy. I'm going to go to Beijing and you're going to get this off the ground.' All I could say was, 'Ah, OK.'

Sky Procycling was on.

Part of the sponsorship process and smoothing the deal involved UCI president Pat McQuaid. 'The first time I heard about the team was around Beijing, when I was talking to Dave [Brailsford] and we spoke about the philosophy of the team he was setting up,' said McQuaid.

> I was asked to go to a meeting with Sky in London. Sky contacted me independently of Dave, through the UCI, and I don't think that Dave was aware I was having this meeting. The marketing chief there said, 'You may have heard a rumour that we are considering sponsoring a team, so how do you see the doping issue?' And I said, 'Yes, there's been a history of doping, but we're doing more to combat it than any other governing body', so I gave them a lot of encouragement. From the UCI point

of view we'd be happy to welcome Sky as a sponsor as well as a new British team with a very strong anti-doping philosophy.

There, in very clear terms, is a blunt acknowledgement that the problem of doping in cycling, as recognised and feared by Keen in the 1990s, was still a pressing issue and one that a national federation with links to a World Tour team would have to face. The UCI president and a major multinational corporation knew there were risks and so, clearly, did Brailsford. Anecdotally but still credibly, by 2008 the sport was felt to be cleaning up its collective act, although it had been a slow process. Out-of-competition, unannounced testing had been introduced in 2001. By 2004 the UCI had introduced a test for homologous blood transfusions and signed up to the WADA code, while 2008 saw the arrival of the Athlete Biological Passport and mandatory whereabouts systems, as well as a test for human growth hormone. Those elements – allied to the increasing nervousness of sponsors and TV companies to support the sport – had helped calm the worst excesses of doping from the era that Keen and Boardman had raced through.

In spite of the ongoing doping problems, Brailsford had nurtured World Tour team ambitions because he had always been a huge fan of road racing and he had long toyed with the notion of setting up a road team linked to British Cycling. In fact, it's worth remembering that Brailsford had already set up a professional road team – recall the 2007 Halfords Bikehut outfit built specifically around Nicole Cooke, to prepare her and a women's squad for Beijing. More of which later.

As far as Brailsford was concerned, why *wouldn't* British Cycling have a road team? After all, there were departments and structures already inside British Cycling that each ran their own race 'teams'. Which is to say that there were men's and women's endurance and sprint squads, a paracycling group as well as BMX and mountain bike departments, each racing their own teams – so why not have a road racing department run along broadly the same lines? The infrastructure was already in place, from sports science to a human resources department. All that was missing, in Brailsford's eyes, was an organisation to run a road team. The initial conception, of a modest Professional-Continental squad, would have fitted into this format. In short order, however, those Team GB-on-the road plans were shelved, and a much more ambitious project began to emerge. The other British Cycling squads raced to win the biggest prizes – and so would the new road team.

It is inconceivable, however, that staff inside British Cycling could not have foreseen potential conflicts with a World Tour entity operating inside the same building, sharing staff and infrastructure. Whatever the practical or philosophical considerations in Manchester concerning the setting up of a professional road team – and those remained only as discussions early in 2008 – Sky signed up to support British Cycling international squads and domestic programmes for five years, announcing a deal worth around £24 million over the course of the sponsorship, on 24 July 2008.

The new Sky-sponsored Olympic-focused Team GB had broken cover and appeared in public in Newport Velodrome while, at another location in Newport, Fran Millar was hammering out business plans with executives from the media giant, detailing what a Sky Procycling World Tour team would actually look like, even though the official announcement of that part of the Sky deal was still seven months away.

Doug Dailey was as enthusiastic as any passionate lover of road racing would be, though it was clear to him that the arrival of Sky Procycling, a cuckoo in the nest at Manchester, was going to ruffle feathers.

We were joined at the hip with Sky. You couldn't tell where British Cycling ended and Sky began. We shared the same offices, the same staff, the same spaces at Manchester, and a lot of the staff, including myself, switched over to working for Sky and it was quite casual. I remember sitting in the office when the Sky thing was gathering momentum and it was so exciting. At one point I said, 'Christ Dave, I wish I was ten years younger, I'd love to get involved in this.' He just said, 'Come on then, join us, you take over the logistics,' and that was it. My job changed overnight, literally overnight. He just said, 'You handle the logistics, you've been doing it for years.'

Later, when Peter Keen would make accusations of Sky 'asset stripping' at British Cycling, it's easy to see incidents like this as evidence for the prosecution.

Rod Ellingworth was another early recruit to the Sky pro team project, poached from British Cycling, though if Sky Procycling hadn't come along, Ellingworth was ready to leave Manchester for HTC-Columbia anyway. Ellingworth, like many others in Keen's early intake at British Cycling, was devoted to the sport, a coach and man manager of considerable skill, someone whose life has been consumed by cycling. Ellingworth, a development coach at British Cycling, would go on to work with younger riders at Team Sky, regularly returning to British Cycling duties as a team manager with the Elite road squads at World Championships until 2017 when he stepped down, to be replaced by one of his first intake of riders, Matt Brammeier.

Although the project hadn't been officially announced, Sky Procycling was in serious development throughout 2008. Between them, Brailsford, Fran Millar, Ellingworth and Sutton had phones crammed with useful numbers and advice was sought on everything from potential team mechanics to ideal bus design. ('We've got an empty box on wheels, how do we optimise it?') Advice was sought and taken from David Millar, Mark Cavendish and other pros. 'Shane [Sutton] knew Scott Sunderland from some Aussie connection,' recalls Fran Millar,

> and Shane said that Scott was really well connected in the European scene, so Scott was involved early on and brought in Carsten Jeppesen as a general manager, because he had been doing the tech operations at Team CSC. We ended up with about twelve people working on the team, but Dave [Brailsford] and I flew all over, meeting and talking to people who had run teams.

Over ten years later not much has changed at the managerial heart of Sky, which features the same driven people at its core. Brailsford, Millar, Ellingworth, Kerrison and Jeppesen are all still deeply involved, while Sutton is still in touch with Brailsford too, although their relationship has cooled. Brailsford's notion that personalities and ambitions need to coalesce around a plan before it can really take off – which was true at British Cycling – turns out to have been equally critical in the development of Team Sky, but once that core has formed it becomes a formidable unit.

There were mutterings about how Sky should really have paid its dues and started with a modest Professional-Continental-level team, thus earning their place at the World Tour table. Others suggest that with major sponsors – particularly non-cycling sponsors – being so rare, any big name that showed an interest should be made as welcome as possible. Why make it awkward for new players with money to put into a sport struggling to attract sponsors?

Those considerations were put to the side when Team Sky

Procycling was finally officially announced to a small group of selected media representatives in the Lanesborough Hotel in London on 25 February 2009.

The surprise that greeted the news was minimal, given that it had hardly been kept secret from the moment of its inception in Brailsford's office, though the official news was none the less welcomed by a supportive media. When eyebrows were raised about the 'seriousness' of Brailsford's stated aim – to win the Tour with a clean British rider – his resolve merely stiffened. Brailsford was following the logic of the attitude he espoused and promoted at British Cycling, where the idea of a 'world class' programme was synonymous with 'Olympic gold'. If you were going to run a professional road squad, then the equivalent aim was, quite evidently, winning the Tour de France.

Speaking eight years later, Brailsford recalls the process. 'When we started to think about what we were aiming at, what was the ambition here? And then you start to think about the biggest races' – still with an evangelical tone in his voice – 'and then we reached that point where you go, "You know what? If we don't go with the goal of winning the biggest event then I'm not sure I can be bothered, so let's go for the big hit. Let's go for winning the Tour."'

The excited, cascading logic is still audible, as Brailsford continues:

And then we thought, 'You know what would *really* excite us? Winning the Tour with a British rider', and by now we were *super* excited, like, 'OK, now what?!' Right, then it was getting scary, because we had to decide whether or not to make that goal public. Hmm, shall we tell the world or just keep it behind closed doors, so only we know what we're going for? Shall we tell the world?

Buoyed up by the successes of previous world track championships and the Games in Beijing, emboldened by the fact that Keen's ten-year WCPP plan had worked so astonishingly well, the feeling of 'anything was possible' won out, and Brailsford went public with his clean British rider to win the Tour inside five years' pitch.

> After the multiple titles won in recent years, the GB attitude was no longer, 'Oh, I'm not sure we should be thinking like this,' or that our goal was to be gallant losers to the Aussies. By now it was more, 'Well, we've got 64 million people in this country, why the hell can't one of them win the Tour? Fuck it, we can do this. Let's go.'

In a sport still widely assumed to have a significant doping problem, the ethical intent of the team was laudable but, as it turned out, a weighty millstone. It was Brailsford's moment of hubris. 'We're going to find out what it's going to take to win the Tour de France with a clean British rider,' stated Brailsford in 2009, adding, 'We have thought very carefully about the criteria we are looking for, how we will screen the riders. We will have a very clear screening and selection strategy. There will be no riders who have failed drugs tests.' In the end, this was an ethical position – which also included sport directors, doctors and carers – that would come back to punch Brailsford and his team in the face, over and over. Had Brailsford and the team not opted for such a bold 'mission statement' it is highly unlikely that they would have been scrutinised and pilloried with such gusto later, although in early 2009, the media attitude to doping was less diligent.

Having said that, in some respects Brailsford wasn't really going too far out on an ethical limb, since former pro rider Jonathan Vaughters had run World Tour teams that proclaimed, loudly, that they were anti-doping and not using any injectable products. Vaughters' squad was, in fact, a 'no needles' team years before the UCI introduced that same protocol. By summer 2008 Vaughters' team had been transformed into Garmin-Slipstream, set up in tandem with Fran Millar's brother, David, racing again after serving his two-year ban and now reinvented as a loquacious anti-doping advocate.

In fact, Vaughters and Millar had an even bolder vision than Brailsford. After all, Brailsford just wanted to win the Tour de France clean. In David Millar's words,

> When we [Vaughters and Millar] came in, we wanted to change the whole *sport* and we wanted to prove that it could be done clean. We wanted to give confidence back to people and nobody believed it. When we came in in 2008, that was like the borderline of the Dark Ages in terms of doping and we were calling ourselves the clean team. We had our own anti-doping programme, saying we were doing this without needles, we want to prove that you can win the biggest races without drugs. In order to exist inside professional cycling, to say stuff like that in 2008 you had to be 'idiosyncratic' or nuts and dress in fucking argyle-patterned riding kit and be a bunch of misfits.

Measured against those terms – of wanting to change the perception of the entire sport – Brailsford's ambitions seem modest, particularly as Vaughters, Millar and their band of Argyle Irregulars had done much of the grunt work two years earlier. Crucially too, as Millar points out, 'Both Jonathan and I had "history" with doping, and we were very clear, it wasn't a "zero-tolerance" thing, it was an honesty thing.' That nuance between the two philosophies is important. Millar, a famous ex-doper who would happily speak out, gave credibility to a team racing under a clean banner in which talking about your doping past wouldn't get you fired.

Having said that, as much as Millar doubted that a competitive World Tour team could be assembled in which *every* rider and staff member would pass Sky's 'zero tolerance' criteria, Millar supported the aim to win without doping – insisting it was possible – and told Brailsford as much. Unwittingly – nobody could know it in 2008 and 2009 – issues of honesty, transparency and the limits of sports medicine would dominate cycling in a few short years, exposing Brailsford and his team's position to levels of scrutiny hitherto unknown in professional cycling, where 'don't ask, don't tell' was the tacit agreement that existed between the sport and the specialist media that covered it.

Unusually, British Cycling Board members Ian Drake and Brian Cookson were both initially on the board of Sky Procycling. To have, respectively, the chief executive and president of the parent federation on the board of a World Tour cycling team seemed to some to be a clear conflict of interest. What was overlooked by critics was the possibility that neither Drake nor Cookson (in particular) were committed Brailsford fans, and they might have wanted to 'keep an eye' on the new Sky Procycling boss. What, to detractors, was a conflict of interest could also be seen as a means of guaranteeing access and oversight. As later events revealed, if oversight was part of the Cookson-Drake plan, it really didn't work out that way.

Cookson was involved in the early Sky discussions and, even if he wasn't in the inner circle, he had more than a passing interest. 'The problem wasn't that the relationship between British Cycling and Sky was too close, it was that it wasn't close enough,' suggests Cookson now.

The original plan had always been to give the riders who British Cycling had developed a safe place to go and ride. We spent all that effort on riders and then basically threw them into pro life. They were open to doping, to not being paid, whatever, and so the original idea was to have a team where those issues would be addressed. That was the plan, to have a team with one-third GB riders at first, mix them with some experienced pros then add more GB riders to increase the percentage of British riders on the team over time. But that's pretty much the opposite of what happened. I think Dave just wanted to win and realised how hard it would be and how expensive it was with GB riders when you could just hire Belarus riders to sit at the front of the bunch and ride at 43 kph all day.

Cookson's recollection here is of plans for a 'Team GB pro squad' transformed into 'Sky Procycling', a state of affairs he was happy enough to go along with, swept along by Brailsford's energy and ambition. Such was the heady atmosphere that pervaded British Cycling at the time.

There were those who would complain that there was more than a simple conflict of interest in Cookson's relations with Sky Procycling and its ultimate owners, Tour Racing Limited. A decade on, the mild-mannered Cookson still bridles.

We didn't get paid and we had no shares. We were there as oversight, though any idea we were there to keep an eye on Dave is a bit wide of the mark. To tell you the truth I was pretty excited by the idea of the team. We went down to London once a month, then once a quarter and then less and less.

Quite clearly both Cookson and Drake weren't overly concerned by the way the Sky was developing, but again, given the post-Beijing honeymoon being enjoyed by the inhabitants of Manchester, that isn't a surprise.

Oversight apart, there can be no doubt that there were delicate issues to be dealt with. Brailsford was well aware of the doping issues facing him and his new squad, having been around the British pro cycling scene long enough to have heard the same stories as every other denizen of the sport. If Keen had been more comfortable with track racing, with its precise metrics and calculations, then road racing was a chaotic business, and there were so many variables in the what, why and how of the road it was dizzying. Certainly there were tactics and alliances in track racing, but nothing that came close to the complexity of road racing's epic national stage races, and understanding the people, tactics and 'rules' of professional road racing took time to assimilate. It needed experience, hours spent in communal manager's meetings and weeks driving team cars in race convoys.

All of which helps explain why one of the first staff to sign up to the Sky project had been 43-year-old Australian ex-pro Scott Sunderland. Brailsford knew he needed to hire managers with connections. Recruiting Sunderland and British cycling legend Sean Yates as chief sport directors was an important move because Brailsford was an unknown quantity, while Sunderland and Yates had over forty years of Euro-pro networking behind them.

Yates had gained his European credentials the hard way, the old way, packing his bags and heading to Paris to ride for the famous ACBB club as a 20-year-old. Yates won enough to secure a contract with Peugeot in 1982, going on to ride for Fagor, 7-Eleven and Motorola before retiring from racing at the end of 1996, having mentored the young Lance Armstrong in the Texan's rookie years.

Sunderland had done it in similar fashion, albeit that for him travelling to Europe required more of a commitment. Sunderland turned pro aged 24 for the TVM squad, hanging up his bike fourteen seasons later. No sooner had he retired than he was in Bjarne Riis' CSC team as a sport director, from whence he was plucked by Brailsford's lieutenant Shane Sutton in mid-2008 to help build Sky Procycling. Sunderland, who had lived in Belgium since 1991, was the first member of staff who signed a Sky contract and he, like Brailsford, had plenty to get on with.

Given Brailsford's history at British Cycling and the fact that Bradley Wiggins was the Brit most capable of mounting a credible bid for overall Tour victory, it was obvious that Sky needed Wiggins to lead them in Grand Tours. The problem was that when the Sky Procycling plan was announced to the press in February 2009, Wiggins was still contracted to Jonathan Vaughters' Garmin team. Wiggins' fourth overall in the 2009 Tour de France meant his stock had risen, but it also made him an even more attractive proposition for Brailsford. Wiggins, with his modish affectations and golden Olympic legacy, would be perfect. Except for the small matter that he was under contract till 2011.

It is almost unheard of in cycling that riders break contracts or leave teams mid-season, still less that a team will poach a high-profile rider from another team and invoke legal teams to help it do so. Plucking a young talent from a lower-division team isn't unusual, but for a new World Tour team to make an approach to a rider like Wiggins isn't really the done thing, while British rider Ben Swift's move from Katusha to Sky caused Russian eyebrows to be raised too.

But Sky being Sky and Brailsford being Brailsford meant that when it came to getting Wiggins into Sky Procycling kit, etiquette was going to take a back seat. One of the benefits of having a parent company like Sky meant that the team had access to some powerful lawyers who knew about employment legislation, even if they weren't so interested in the sporting 'rules' of professional cycling. In short, Sky got Wiggins.

In spite of the 'non-disclosure' clauses tied to the deal, elements of the story inevitably leaked out. The short version was that Wiggins – backed by Sky – was prepared to take Vaughters to court to test the EU employment legislation, arguing that Wiggins' contract amounted to some variant of restraint of trade. Vaughters, seeing no benefit in spending money the team didn't have on a court case it didn't want in order to hold on to a rider who didn't want to stay, agreed an out-of-court settlement to let Wiggins go. In Vaughters' understated phrase: 'It wasn't any fun, let's put it like that.'

'Legally, I can't say much about it,' says Vaughters,

> but Bradley has spoken a couple of times about how we were compensated, and that makes it sound like we got some kind of deal. The fact is that I never wanted to let Brad go. It wasn't like I had a figure in mind that would compensate the team. There was no figure 'X' in my head – I didn't want to lose him for any price. Ask yourself: how much was it worth to Sky to have the first ever British rider to win the Tour de France? To this day, I would rather have kept Brad.

According to Wiggins, he didn't take much convincing to leave Garmin. 'How big a decision was it to leave my old team? It took about five minutes over a coffee with Dave after one week of the Tour de France in 2009. Dave came round to see me in a little village near Limoges. We had a coffee in a supermarket and I said, "Yeah, I'm on board."'

While Wiggins had not yet been signed when the team's existence was first announced to a gathering of specialist press in February 2009, by the time the riders, bikes, livery and staff were rolled out in front of the mainstream media in London on 4 January 2010, Wiggins was being interviewed in Sky kit, his signing only having been completed a month previously. Filmed live by a Sky News television helicopter, team riders, fans and 300 invited members of the public rode through London before being introduced on The Mall.

Not even the chill January air could dampen the sense of occasion, and the talk was already of winning the Tour de France. Could the team do it inside five years, as Brailsford had proclaimed? 'Well, it's a lofty goal, there's no doubt about it,' explained Brailsford, adding, 'but there's no point in being involved in elite sport unless you are going to try to win. If you are going to go to the top, at the highest level, you've got to take the biggest events and try to win, and that's what we're going to try to do.'

In hindsight, for all the over-selling of the 'Sky is different' proposition, Sky had managed to do a good job of building a World Tour team from scratch and in such short order. Rather than make a few flashy rider acquisitions and run out of a dreary warehouse with some repainted second-hand trucks, Brailsford had paid attention to details, from bus drivers to sports science teams, and everyone required to run a World Tour team properly. On that front, Sky deserves considerable credit. Yes, they were splashing out money, but they were spending it in smart and not always obvious places.

In some less publicised ways, Team Sky was a unique proposition, even down to its relationship with its national federation (British Cycling) and its principal sponsors. At the formation of the team, Brailsford was still head of performance at British Cycling (albeit now on a reduced salary); he was also now team principal at one of the biggest World Tour cycling teams – a leader with one foot planted in both camps.

It was unprecedented in modern cycling and, by some credible estimations, saw Brailsford enjoying an income of around a million pounds during the period where he held two posts. That Aston Martin DB7 Brailsford turned up in at some races wasn't cheap to run.

Creating further close connections to British Cycling was the fact that from the outset there was a sharing of doctors, soigneurs and mechanics, although the arrangement was that Sky would pay British Cycling for use of its staff, if and when they were required. In light of future problems, the salaries offered by Team Sky to former British Cycling employees caused some resentment too, as Brailsford was able to cherry-pick the best elements from British Cycling, dipping into cash from the Sky war chest.

In spite of the logistical and practical complications of assembling a World Tour team from nothing, Brailsford and his dedicated team had moved with remarkable speed. In July 2007, Brailsford had been energised by the sight of the Tour in London, and from that point on, plans to form a team were being drawn up. By March 2008, talks with Sky were well underway; in July 2008 the deal was signed; Sky Procycling was announced in February 2009; and ten months later Brailsford and his squad were set for the opening road race of the 2010 season.

Early 'conspirator' Fran Millar gives an insight into Brailsford and the period in which Sky Procycling first came together:

> I think one of the brilliant things about Dave B is that he is a really optimistic visionary, and it can be immensely annoying because he'll say it referring to all sorts of stuff. I'll tell him that we don't have the time, the money, the resources, that I *can't* build a rocket ship and get you to the moon for next Monday, but he'll always think you can,

and his standard line is, 'Come on Fran, it can't be that hard!?' and there's something brilliant about that attitude, but also naivety too.

At the media launch just days before flying to Australia for the start of the 2010 road season, Brailsford explained,

It's not our ambition to change cycling, but we'll approach it in the same way as we've approached everything else that we do, which is to say we will pay attention to the details, we will look for marginal gains, we will use technology, we will look to other industries, we will benchmark off other teams, we will look for best practice in everything we do, so if we get that right then actually I'd like to think that we will find some new approaches. Now, what they will be, well, we don't know yet. But that's how we've worked so far and that's how we will continue to work, but it will be more about us as a team rather than trying to influence the wider sport.

Next stop, a municipal park in Adelaide, to put his philosophy to the test.

7

REALITY BITES

'We felt we were really getting somewhere.'

After nineteen months of scribbling on a whiteboard in a sunless Manchester office, Dave Brailsford's team would finally emerge in an Australian summer. Sky Procycling riders pinned numbers on their jerseys and lined up for the Cancer Council Classic in Rymill Park in Adelaide on 17 January 2010. After 51 hectic kilometres, the result was a win for Greg Henderson, the team's designated sprinter. It was the proverbial fairy tale start. The Sky Procycling stats read: raced one, won one. Although that modest victory wasn't quite 'as good as it would get', there wouldn't be too much champagne drunk on the Sky team buses in 2010.

In fact, there was one fine early result, when the Spaniard with a penchant for cobbles, Juan-Antonio Flecha, won the Het Nieuwsblad semi-Classic in February. Actually, Sky's first northern European campaign was more than respectable, with ex-Rabobank rider Flecha following up his Nieuwsblad win with third place in Paris–Roubaix.

However, if 2010 had started well, then the metaphorical wheels quickly came off the bus as the spring campaign fizzled out. Before Liège–Bastogne–Liège, Sunderland and Brailsford had exchanged 'heated' views in the team bus, with neither prepared to back down. Depending on which version you prefer, either Brailsford couldn't cope with Sunderland questioning his decisions, or Sunderland insisted his point of view as lead directeur sportif should carry more weight. However, since Brailsford was quite clearly the boss, there was only ever going to be one outcome.

'At the beginning of the year till I left at the end of April – I was just getting shut down all the time, even though I was senior sport director,' says Sunderland.

> In my opinion they wanted to do what they had done before, to run it too much like the track, and it just wasn't working. We were a new team, staff and riders, and instead of having that first season to settle down, Dave hyped it up and hyped it up. That put so much expectation on our shoulders, but if he had just come in quieter it would have been better. But no, Dave had to shout it loud from the rooftops – we're going to dominate this, we're going to do that.

Sean Yates, the lead sports director throughout Sky's first two seasons, saw some merit in Sunderland's analysis, although he also understood the clean slate approach:

> Another way of looking at it is to say that if you bring in staff who think they know it all and have been doing the job the same way for years, well, they don't learn and they're not so open to new ideas. But certainly it was tough, and there were gaps in the team's knowledge, because there

was hardly anyone who had experience of running a show on the road – as opposed to at a track meeting.

Of that first intake that made up Sky Procycling, Sunderland was the most experienced inside the professional peloton. When moving around races, shaking hands and exchanging news with riders, agents, managers and organisers, Sunderland was sometimes perceived to be running the team – after all, he had the reputation from decades in the sport; his was the familiar face everyone had been dealing with. Brailsford's profile, based essentially on British track successes, was much lower in European pro racing circles. However, as in any business, you can't disagree loudly with the boss for too long before someone will remind you who is paying your wages. Regardless of the validity of his criticisms and his experience, Sunderland left the team and – perhaps coincidentally – the team's results nosedived.

One senior figure who was – and remains – involved with Sky, was succinct in their appraisal of the 2010 season:

> We were shit. It was embarrassing. We had come in like *Star Wars*: we had done a big launch, we had spent all this money, we had bloody dry ice coming out the team bus when the doors opened; it was ridiculous. We had all this cool kit and an amazing bus and we literally couldn't ride our fucking way out of a paper bag.

Inevitably, with a new team, no matter how thorough the planning was, there were always going to be *some* problems. After Sunderland's departure in April, the following month the communications chief, Bryan Nygaard, informed Brailsford during the Giro d'Italia that he was quitting to set up the Leopard-Trek team. With packs of international media looking for some 'exclusive' time with your star riders, keeping everyone happy for three weeks – regardless of the actual racing outcomes – is a stressful business.

Casting around for a quick replacement for Nygaard, Brailsford turned to his erstwhile project manager, Fran Millar. 'Whaaat? Oh. My. God.' Millar laughs at the recollection. 'Nine years ago I went to the Tour as our press officer and there are people who still think that's my job. Anyway, we went to the 2010 Tour and we were appalling.'

As with every rider and every squad, a strong showing in the Tour de France could efface all of the season's other negative stories. If Sky had misfired through spring and early summer, there was always the Tour, the team's big goal. That July, Wiggins set off in the rain, delicately negotiated the slippery urban prologue around Rotterdam, and finished 77th, almost a minute down on winner Fabian Cancellara, a result that set the tone for the whole race. The team had checked the weather on a micro-station on the team bus and elected to send Wiggins out early, reckoning that it would rain on the favourites later. In fact, the opposite happened.

Rookie press officer Millar wasn't the only one who was having a hard time in an unaccustomed role in the 2010 Tour. Team leader Wiggins, the big money signing, was miles off the pace. He knew it, the team knew it, the whole peloton witnessed it and the Anglophone press was incessantly asking about it. After Brailsford's build-up at the team launch and years of Olympic triumph, the UK wasn't used to reading about reversals of fortune.

When the race hit the Alps, Wiggins cracked. For a rider prised at considerable expense to lead the new British superteam, Wiggins' performance was a disaster. Wiggins was so distraught that he wanted to skip the traditional rest day press conference, though to be fair he was never a fan of such events at the best of times.

'Bradley can be difficult; he can be hard work for a press officer, but I felt desperately sorry for him. It was just horrendous, the poor guy, it was so brutal. I remember walking past David [Millar] and Christian [Vande Velde],' says Millar,

and they were just laughing, like, 'Oh, you lot have fucked it haven't you?' Just laughing, 'Oh, you lot were going to take over the world and now you can't even get in the top ten of the Tour?! With the bike rider who you stole off us who now can't climb a railway bridge?' They were laughing and I was thinking, 'Oh this is just great.' It was so humiliating, all those dreams and plans were just ... pfft.

Wiggins had toiled, but after stage 14, at the summit of Ax 3 Domaines, he had had enough of dancing around when dealing with the media. Wiggins was now 16th overall with no sign or hope of improvement. The jig was up. As he was changing into dry riding kit, Wiggins was being prodded by journalists who were – supportively – inquiring about his travails. After offering a 'Dunno really' to the first journalist, when the next question was gently lobbed at him, Wiggins unburdened himself.

You want the truth? I'm fucked. I've got nothing. I just don't have the form, it's as simple as that, I ain't gonna lie to you. So I'm just trying my hardest, battling on, rather than give up, so, uh ... simple as that mate. I just feel consistently mediocre, not brilliant, not shit, just mediocre, on a plateau really. I just haven't got it right this year. I thought we had and I haven't got it right.

In the course of that impromptu 'conference' it was as if a weight had been lifted off Wiggins' shoulders and he could accept that his Tour was done.

In the awning of the Sky camper van, Wiggins started to carry out his own post-mortem on the sporting disaster he was at the heart of. 'It's a huge learning curve, this is the first year I've ever really tackled [the Tour] full-on and last year [2009] was a bit of a fluke.'

The team's inquest into Wiggins' poor performance in the Tour started before it had even finished. Sky coach Shane Sutton didn't mince his words. 'Before the Tour we were doubting that we were getting the right information. The numbers we were getting from Bradley in 2010 were, in layman's terms, bullshit,' he said, adding,

> Brad's come from earning a decent salary, he's a good bike rider [at Garmin] with a steady family life and everything else, to becoming a megastar at the end of 2009. You've got the likes of James Murdoch backing you and it's, 'Hey, I'm the Man' and I think he was quite blasé about it, but what he didn't look at was the hard work. In the end I said to Brad, 'What are you doing?' and I just went absolutely nuts. It just wasn't acceptable.

Regardless of any other more nuanced considerations, having Sutton going 'absolutely nuts' at you is probably going to force some kind of behavioural change ...

What had gone wrong? Why were the 2010 results so woeful? True, there were wins, but for Brailsford and his loudly stated Tour-focused ambitions, winning the Dutch Food Valley Classic or two stages in the Tour de Picardie were not what he had in mind when he launched the team. Even Wiggins' success in the Giro d'Italia prologue was small beer. Given the opening fanfare and build-up, Brailsford's new big-budget team had flopped.

Examined closely, there were significant elements hired by

Sky throughout 2009 whose experience rested, essentially, in British Cycling's track successes – the coaches and even sometime team manager Rod Ellingworth, psychiatrist Steve Peters, nutritionist Nigel Mitchell, coaches Dan Hunt and Matt Parker as well as the team doctor Roger Palfreeman. The wisdom of the characters who inhabit race convoys, the ones who know the roads, the climbs and the nuts and bolts of racing, the guys who are on first-name terms with both race organisers and commissaires, resided in Sunderland and Yates.

Ironically, Brailsford would be filmed wondering why the team seemed to be getting so many decisions on the road 'wrong' 'when there were only about ten minutes to decide and react' – precisely the job of a sport director like Sunderland. He, along with the equally experienced Yates, were two out of four sport directors hired by Sky for 2010, while the other two – Steven de Jongh and Marcus Ljungqvist – were recruited without a single season of experience as 'directeurs sportif' between them, given that they were both still racing in 2009. With Sunderland gone and the two other sport directors still learning their craft, it's little wonder Sky struggled throughout 2010.

Starting a World Tour team from scratch with a backroom staff inexperienced in the wiles of road racing – announcing that it would be 'clean' and its aim was to produce a British winner of the Tour de France before 2014 – as well as running British Cycling in the approach to its biggest and most-anticipated Olympiad ever, could accurately be described as a Herculean task. And it was on Brailsford's shoulders.

In terms of equipment, Sky was applying its budget from what it had learned from campaigns with British Cycling, but its arrival into the European peloton was not without issues, as Sky rider turned sport director Dario Cioni recalls:

I think it took time to adjust. We had the principals and all the commitment and when we got it right, it was great. Other times that commitment to doing it the 'Sky way' probably wasn't the best. Looking back, when you look at the way we came into the sport, with the presentation, we didn't creep in the back door. At the time plenty of people in the sport were thinking, 'Who the hell do you think you are?!'

So no sooner had 2010 racing ended than the core of the team sat down and wiped that Manchester whiteboard clean one more time. Prior to that season debrief, Brailsford decided a massive rethink was required. 'That off-season was full-on,' recalls Fran Millar, present at the brainstorming and riot-act reading moments at that year's end.

Having gathered a group of performance staff who had dominated world track cycling for the past three years to work at Sky, their plans for the road had hit the skids. 'I think they had probably forgotten the hard work it had taken to get to that position,' reflected Millar. 'They thought they could add on a few bits and it would be, well, not easy, never easy, but that they could do it. The reality, though, was that it had taken them almost a decade to get to their position on track; there was ten years of graft and cultural shift behind that.'

While the management pondered their mistakes, the critical and the curious media also had time to examine elements of the Sky Procycling manifesto and wonder how much substance there was in it. For all the professional presentation and carefully deployed buzzwords, what, concretely, was radically different about Sky Procycling in its first season? The team buses? Bringing a chef to the team's hotel at races? The omnipresent handlebar-mounted power meter head units on riders' bikes? The use of shared online training software to

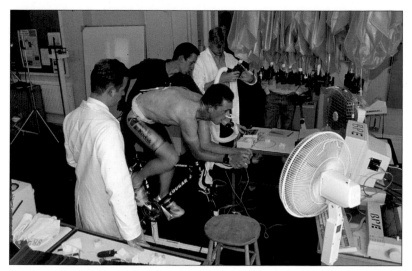

1. Bishop Otter college sports science lab, 1993. Boardman on a Kingcycle, watched by Peter Keen, Chris Shambrook (in red) and Andy Jones. Jones would go on to coach Paula Radcliffe and was involved in Eliud Kipchoge's 1-59 marathon time in 2019.

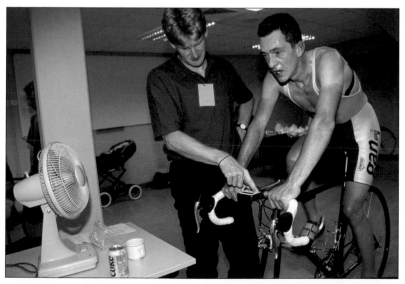

2. Underneath Manchester velodrome, still waiting for the great Lottery leap forward, Keen and Gan professional Boardman prepare for a 1996 Hour record attempt, while BCF exercise physiologist Louis Passfield lurks behind a pillar. The tech is still decidedly 'low.'

3. Happy with bronze in the 50km team time trial at the 1994 Commonwealth Games. (L-R) Team doctor Chris Jarvis, manager Doug Dailey, Maxine Johnson, coach Claire Blower, Julia Freeman and Maria Lawrence. Yvonne McGregor was the fourth rider.

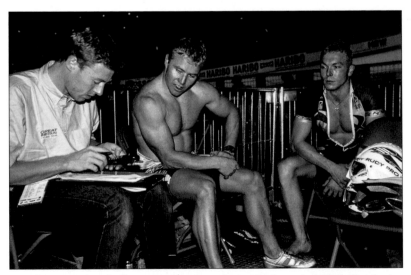

4. Simon Jones calculates a gear ratio as Craig MacLean and Chris Hoy look on at the 1999 World Track championships in Berlin. 'A breakthrough for us, we won a silver medal,' recalls Hoy. It was the only medal GB won.

5. Girls on top. Nicole Cooke and Emma Pooley show off gold and silver medals from the women's road race and time trial won at the Beijing Olympics in 2008.

6.Happy days. The Lottery money is flowing, the performances are improving, riders are winning. Victoria Pendleton, Laura Trott, Jess Varnish and Chris Hoy celebrate a Team GB UCI World Cup team win in London, months before the 2012 Games triumphs.

7. Dave Brailsford and Shane Sutton, the British Cycling head of performance and his coach and senior management member in a track centre, always planning, always pushing.

8. The 22-year-old Mark Cavendish is thrown into the Beijing Olympic Madison by Bradley Wiggins, watched by coach Sutton. The reigning world Madison champions would finish a disappointing eighth.

9. Dave Brailsford meets the media outside the Team Sky bus during the frenzy of the 2014 Tour de France.

10. Geraint Thomas casts an anxious glance back at his all-seeing boss Dave Brailsford on board the Team Sky 'Death Star' bus on stage seven of the 2011 Tour de France as crowds gather outside.

11. The body language doesn't lie. Relations between Wiggins and Froome during the 2012 Tour de France were strained, a consequence of events at the previous year's Tour of Spain.

12. After being dropped by British Cycling in March 2016, British track sprinter Jess Varnish took the Federation to an employment tribunal. She lost her case in January 2019, preventing her from suing BC and UK Sport. The Judge ruled that squad riders are not employees.

13. Even after leaving behind the stresses of leading Team Sky as its stage race leader, Wiggins was rarely comfortable in dealing with the media. After his retirement, accusations of cortisone abuse dogged him, further straining relations.

14. In spite of the accusations of sexism and bullying as well as the resignation of Head of Performance Shane Sutton, Team GB performed astonishingly well at the Rio 2016 Olympics, with women's team pursuit quartet (l-r) Katie Archibald, Laura Trott, Elinor Barker and Joanna Rowsell-Shand winning gold.

15. Beset by accusations of cortisone doping and Chris Froome's 2017 Vuelta Salbutamol case as well as Froome's 2019 leg-break and the loss of Sky sponsorship, Brailsford's team remained untouchable. Now sporting Ineos colours, in 2019 Egan Bernal became the first ever Colombian to win the Tour de France.

log and monitor riders' workload? The answer is: none of the above, since those were widespread practices in better-funded teams, though from the glow that surrounded Sky in the media early on, you might have thought Brailsford and his team had invented modern cycling.

Team buses had been part of the cycling scene for decades prior to Sky's descent from Tatooine with the model that David Millar famously christened 'the Death Star'. Sky's rolling Volvo palace was, however, the first team bus with dual axles and four – or five – feet longer than anybody else's in the parking lot, so there are bragging rights that Sky can legitimately claim. Was the Sky bus bigger and better appointed than anything previously seen? Yes. But extra special? Not really, though the early use of mood lighting was certainly bold.

Examined more closely, there was little that was hugely innovative about Sky's approach. When it came to trying to apply aerodynamic theory to road racing, there were plenty of recent precedents, including French manufacturer Gitane's development of an aerofoil tubeset for Bernard Hinault's time trial bike in 1979.

What, though, of Sky bringing along their own chef to races? Sky wasn't the first team to invest in this area either, with Bjarne Riis regularly bringing a chef along to bigger races for his CSC team, while the Rabobank team had also hired a chef years before the Sky chef assembled his first quinoa and pomegranate salad. And a decade before that, Sky's lead sport director would have experienced chef-cooked meals when he rode the 1992 Tour de France with the American Motorola team.

Overall most of those 'Sky will be different' ideas were not particularly innovatory; rather, they were more matters of budget, logistics and marketing. The concepts had been floating around the sport for several seasons; it was the budgets required to turn those ideas into actions that were the real novelty. Ambitious and intelligent teams required a budget to hire smart staff who could pay attention to details in every area that impacted on performance – from equipment, biomechanics, track hire and training to nutrition, travel and recovery.

Even the revelation that the team carried specific mattresses for riders around the Tour de France, so that the riders could be guaranteed the 'same bed' every night, was old hat. It was a strategy that had already been employed – by Rabobank – many seasons previously. The Dutch team had been inspired by their Tour de France-winning countryman Joop Zoetemelk's famous dictum, 'You win the Tour in bed.' Joop knew, in 1980.

Yates, the most experienced 'Euro dog' on the Sky bus, could see what Brailsford was trying to do:

> It was clear that he had a plan that had been based on British Cycling that the Sky money made possible, but it was more about trying to get the best people in and get them working on specific areas in projects that suited them; that was the key to the process. I was aware that there were a lot of staff. I mean, you need them, to do all the jobs that need doing in a team. No way do you get the best out of someone if they are doing five jobs. Nobody knows how to do five jobs properly, in the same depth, as one expert who has been studying altitude training for ten years.

As Brailsford surveyed the ruin of his plans after that traumatic first season, it was at this point, in the stressed-out autumn of 2010, that Australian Tim Kerrison first showed what he was capable of.

In keeping with Brailsford's tactic of lassoing expertise from parallel worlds, Kerrison had never coached cyclists before – his practical experience lay in swimming and rowing.

In fact, Kerrison wasn't even 'a cyclist', not even in the recreational or weekend warrior sense of the word. He had come to the attention of Brailsford when strength and conditioning coach – and future Mr Vicky Pendleton – Scott Gardner reckoned that his fellow Aussie would be a great fit for the new team.

Brailsford met Kerrison, who had been on the verge of signing a contract with the English Cricket Board, and lured him to Sky instead, installing him as head of performance. It was, beyond any doubt, one of Brailsford's key appointments. Surveying the small returns on their first season, Brailsford turned to his head of performance support and asked him to carry out a detailed examination of the cooling corpse of their inaugural season. In short order Kerrison put together a presentation for Brailsford, Ellingworth, Jeppesen, Helen Mortimer and Fran Millar. During his report, Kerrison explained that there were perhaps twenty-five areas that have an impact on performance and, quite improbably, Sky had tried to focus on all twenty-five of them. Brailsford recalls the impact of the analysis. 'I said to Tim, "OK, tell us what you've seen, what do you think", and he came out with this presentation and I just thought, "Holy shit, you really have been paying attention haven't you!"'

Rather than attempt to do everything and end up being mediocre, Kerrison suggested the team should focus on what he identified as four key areas – those having the biggest impact on performance. Kerrison, travelling around in his hired 'Black Betty' camper van, watching riders and collecting their race data throughout 2010, reasoned that training, nutrition – particularly as it related to body composition – altitude and heat were four areas in which improvement and focus would bring performance gains. Given their broad sweep, there wasn't much that was marginal in those observations.

Kerrison persuaded his audience that if those elements were in place then bike fit, clothing, aerodynamics and other 'details' could be added later.

First, however, the team needed riders who could perform in the environment where races were invariably won and lost, which meant they needed to be able to race in the summer heat of the high mountains. 'Tim said, basically, if you get that right, then the rest is gravy, frankly,' recalls Millar. For all the much-vaunted talk of the sophistication of the training, what Kerrison's analysis boiled down to was that you need to train for the same conditions you raced in. If you climb up and down mountains all day every day, guess what? You get better at climbing mountain passes. With hindsight, as Millar recalls, it seemed obvious. 'You're racing at altitude but you're not training and preparing at altitude? Why aren't you doing that?' Well, quite. In the light of the expertise that was assembled to create Sky Procycling, it seems almost embarrassing that some of this stuff needed saying at all.

Everyone had been so dazzled by the presentation and the clever little details (the riders get laptops and iPhones with Sky logos! The team has high-tech customised buses! The mechanics trucks were state of the art!) they were about to unleash on the European peloton that they had lost sight of the big picture. Talking to riders who raced in the first years, it seems the basics were overlooked. The phrase 'the aggregation of marginal gains' was already firmly attached to the team thanks to the link to British Cycling's successes, but after a brutal first year, it was clear that World Tour road racing was much more resistant to this strategy.

Everyone – from riders to media – had been sold the idea that a meticulously calibrated approach would be the main plank of the Sky Procycling method, yet, even where it had been implemented, it simply hadn't produced the hoped-for results.

In the development phase, Brailsford and his team had studied road racing and identified areas where they thought existing practices were sloppy and came up with an approach that had simple appeal: 'If we examine every aspect of road performance like we did on track, that'll give us a competitive edge and we can win big races with riders who don't dope.'

In fact, while the 2010 preseason intentions were good, in the whirlwind that descended on the team once the season started, with overlapping races and a hectic calendar, Brailsford's dreamy plans were never fully implemented. The ideas that had underpinned much of the success at British Cycling – such as being 'rider focused' – mostly remained as discussion points in Brailsford's office.

As it turned out, the 'rider focus' simply wasn't focusing on the most useful elements, and riders were often left to their own devices, as Jeremy Hunt recalls. Hunt had been a pro for fourteen seasons before he joined Sky Procycling, and he had ridden for some of the biggest (Banesto) and smallest (Oktos) teams in the sport. Arriving for the 2011 season, he found the best-organised squad of his career.

> That was the thing I noticed most. The organisation was at another level, and there were so many staff compared to other teams. As far as the training goes, I had been using a power meter for years (I had bought one in 2004), but after some initial discussion about training, when they could see what I was doing – thirty hours a week, every week, basically – they let me get on with it. In the run-up to a bigger race they'd get in touch to ask me how the training was going, but not really more than that.

Now, with the benefit of seven seasons between him and that traumatic first year, Brailsford has his own explanation.

Essentially, it was all too much. Which is to say that a combination of factors totally threw Brailsford and his staff, and he didn't take it well. 'I was just really, really, really disappointed,' he recalls:

Actually, more than that. It wasn't disappointment so much as I felt I had let everybody down. It was just, 'Oh God, Jesus, this is bad.' I think the thing was we had been really used to winning and enjoying success and all of a sudden it just hit us, the enormity of the challenge we had taken on. After a few seasons you do become a 'well-oiled machine' – like all the World Tour teams are – when it comes to the logistics. But the first time out, with new vehicles, new staff, new planning and processes, trying to get everyone to work in a certain way, trying to get everyone to buy in to a culture, sometimes faced with people saying, 'Who the hell are you? I've been doing this for twenty years! I know how to do my job. I don't need you to tell me, thanks very much' it was more difficult. It was like World War III at times. There were all those challenges going on, so I don't think it was just the performances in races. It was just getting everyone to really buy in to what we wanted to do and *then* trying to add the layer of performance on top of that. It wasn't just about the Tour, it was about the challenge of running the whole operation and of getting all the people aligned and purring along.

In Brailsford's phrase 'the enormity of the task' it's easy to see that as a reaction to Brailsford's inexperience and naivety of the World Tour professional road race environment. From 'playing tough and playing fair' against the track specialists of the world's cycling federations to taking on wily bands of professional road squads with – collectively – hundreds of years of experience in their ranks was, frankly, an impossible challenge. Confronted by the realities of World Tour road racing and surveying the landscape at the end of 2010, Brailsford accepted that things needed to change. The 'marginal gains' thing was not going to cut it in this arena.

As he had shown at British Cycling, Brailsford was not afraid of shaking things up and making drastic changes to staff or strategy, particularly when things were not going to plan. Brailsford and Kerrison got on well and Brailsford was fully behind his Australian coach's analysis. One of Kerrison's most important suggestions was that the team should use high-altitude camps as a crucial element of training and, over the seasons, this has become a key part of Sky's pre-race preparation. The notion of running a training camp in the middle of season, as opposed to well-established preseason gatherings, was something that Kerrison insisted could make a difference, though it was a far from novel approach. However, Sky could contemplate a more extensive use of these methods because it had the resources, both financial and human, to do so. But it also takes an understanding sponsor. If you are paying your star rider a big salary, when he's not even racing – generating zero media impact – you're not building the brand recognition you paid for. There's no return on investment when your big hitter is cloistered in a Spartan hotel clinging to a volcano with a Wi-Fi signal so feeble it makes uploading a group training photo to Instagram a trial.

When Kerrison's plans for two- and three-week training camps on Tenerife's Mount Teide were deemed ideal preparation for Grand Tour riders, the financial costs were considerable. Since Tenerife is anchored off the coast of Morocco in the Atlantic ocean, all bikes, tools, spares and materials would have to be freighted over. There would be no team cars either, so vehicles would have to be hired for the duration.

Support staff (one masseur per three riders, a doctor, maybe an osteopath) would have to be flown in and out, along with turbo trainers and massage tables – in short, all the paraphernalia that a team needs, along with the excess baggage costs entailed. What that adds up to is a significant investment and no publicity for the camp's duration. The mid-season camp was a high-risk investment, yet it was one that Sky was able to take.

From the outset, Sky was able to survey the terrain and spend money – on nutritionists, biomechanics, aerodynamicists, coaching, training camps, whatever. If Sky riders want to go to Tenerife, then there are rooms booked on a semi-permanent basis, the team has three nutritionists, not one part-timer, there's sports science support that is the best in cycling, aerodynamic expertise that can be called on and all of that can be applied to a group of well-paid and very talented riders who are ready to put their own ambitions on hold to ride for a designated leader.

'What they were doing didn't really contain any novel ideas,' reflects Slipstream owner and ex-pro Jonathan Vaughters,

> but that being said they were doing it for a big chunk of time, before others started to catch up. They were doing stuff better than anyone else, just because of raw finance. They could afford to spend money in areas where most other teams can't go. Overall I'd say they don't do a better job of innovating, but they're better at execution, because they have more resources at their disposal.

If Sky's approach to training was to undergo significant changes in 2011, then so were some coaches, with Kerrison becoming more of a hands-on trainer than an observer and data-analyst as he had been in his opening season. Additionally,

Ellingworth and Matt Parker, who had mainly been responsible for trying to coach Wiggins in 2010, were moved sideways to give Shane Sutton a crack at dealing with the struggling rider. Brailsford's choice to put Sutton on Wiggins' case was inspired, but Brailsford had seen Sutton at work close-hand before:

> The thing with Shane was that if he bought in to somebody, if he *really* bought in, he would make that rider feel fantastic and he'd move heaven and earth for them. He gave them belief and he'd go on a journey with the rider – Chris Hoy, Vicky Pendleton, Brad – every step of the way, every early morning, all the hard training sessions he'd be there, 'C'mon mate, let's go and do this today, we gotta get on with it', and he'd be coming up with little training and nutrition ideas. He was brilliant at it, just brilliant.

For a rider like Wiggins, whose confidence had taken a knock, Sutton was the perfect partner.

Sutton recalls the start of their road-to-the-Tour relationship not as one in which he simply wielded a big stick, but rather as one in which his considerate side was engaged too. 'Yeah, there was discipline,' says Sutton, 'but what you've also got to know is that I was sympathetic with it. People only see me as a hard bastard and for sure there were times I had to say, "C'mon Brad, that's a poor excuse, we've got to fucking crack on", but there was more to it than that.'

Sutton explains that,

> one of the reasons that we got together was because I said to him, 'Right Brad, we're going to play at baseball here and it's going to be three strikes and you're out.' I agreed to coach him but I said, 'Right, the first thing is that if you fail to communicate on three occasions, we're fucking

finished. If you don't pick up the phone to me, we're done.' Brad was notorious for that with Rod [Ellingworth] and the rest of them, just not keeping in touch. Then, I said, the second three strikes that you are up against is that if you don't comply with the work, then you're out. You need to communicate and you need comply but, I tell you, he walked across hot coals in that programme. At the same time we brought Tim [Kerrison] in, he was a fantastic numbers man and became a very good coach.

Sutton laughs at the recollection of the hours spent wrapped in well-padded anoraks, wrist on a twist grip maintaining a steady motor-pacing speed, one eye fixed on the bar-mounted SRM PC7 showing Wiggins' power output on Mount Teide, but sees the non-training elements of his relationship with Wiggins as being just as important.

I think the reason I got on with him was I knew him really well from the track side. I had raced with his dad too, but the fact of the matter was that I actually understood what Bradley was going through as well as the expectation on him, whereas most people didn't see what stress he was under when they created Team Sky. But I knew – I *knew* – that everything I could do for him outside the team, to make life as normal as we could within the programme we had for him, then we'd get a really good Brad Wiggins. And we did.

Kerrison's first months with the team had been decidedly low-key, involving him in watching discreetly and asking questions, but his impact on the direction and philosophy of the team from the autumn of 2010 would be pivotal. Some in the team had started to wonder what the hell his job was, other than to stalk them in his camper van. As it turned out, the information he gathered combined with his observations, allied to the working relationship he formed with Wiggins and Sutton, would help turn the team's fortunes around as early as March 2011.

Apart from providing that crucial overview and revision of training at the end of 2010, Kerrison would also go on to play a key role in coaching Wiggins and Chris Froome, as well as important support riders like Richie Porte. The Australian trainer's arrival at the team and the implementation of his ideas played a big part in generating the results that begin to show in 2011 and then, in such spectacular fashion, through 2012 and beyond.

Given that some on the team nicknamed him after US TV serial killer 'Dexter', you would be correct in assuming that Kerrison isn't the 'Fair dinkum mate' tinnie-guzzling Aussie of popular stereotype. Rather, Kerrison is cautious and quiet, and those character traits would become even more accentuated after accusations of doping began to saturate the media. Tim doesn't do small talk with the media, though given the relentless repetition of doping questions, it's hard to blame him. Kerrison didn't sign up to Sky to be an anti-doping spokesman fielding ill-informed questions from journalists who thought knowing a rider's precise VO_2 maximum figure would reveal profound physiological and sporting truths.

Brailsford and Kerrison, however, had hit it off and, Brailsford acknowledged, there was something of Peter Keen in Kerrison, or vice versa. 'Both are incredibly bright guys, the same sort of intellect, and, while it's true that they didn't get on with everybody, they command massive respect in the group.' A healthy relationship between coach and rider is crucial to the success of any programme, and it wasn't immediately obvious that the Kerrison–Wiggins pairing would work.

Kerrison recalls the start of his relationship with Wiggins thus:

> Well, I think if I had come in at the beginning of the first season in 2010 and tried to tell any of our riders what they should be doing in terms of training then I would have been laughed out of the room, but I think over the period of that year – when Brad didn't have a great year – I think he recognised that he needed to change something. Shane Sutton probably played a role in convincing Brad that we needed to try something different and that I was worth listening to. I think fairly quickly that at least some of the stuff made sense and it kind of snowballed from there really.

But even as plans to change the team's fortunes in 2011 were being sketched out, 2010 wasn't quite finished giving Brailsford's bigger dreams a reality check. Concerns over the close relationship between Sky and British Cycling had not been long in surfacing, and that unease led to an investigation into the dealings between the two intertwined entities. Ironically, support for the investigation had come from Peter Keen, by then the head of UK Sport.

Keen, the man who had been responsible for the original World Class Performance Programme, had been invited to the Sky Procycling launch at the Lanesborough Hotel in 2009, and it would be fair to say that Keen was not entirely convinced by the road project. 'It was on record that I had my doubts about doping in the professional peloton, but in another sense, you could say that what Dave [Brailsford] did was like asset stripping British Cycling and then floating it as an IP on the stock exchange.' It's a provocative analysis, though in light of subsequent events, perhaps it holds more water than is comfortable for many players. The assets of British Cycling – the riders, the infrastructure, knowledge and staff – were certainly initially used by Sky Procycling.

In any case, regardless of Keen's personal analysis, there was enough nervousness about the links between the government-funded British Cycling World Class Performance Plan and the private enterprise of Sky Procycling for UK Sport to push for a report to be carried out into the relationship. In March 2010, UK Sport and British Cycling jointly commissioned Deloitte to write a report called 'The Impact of Team Sky on British Cycling's World Class Performance Programme'. It would take a year to compile, and the decision to commission it would cause a rift between Brailsford and Keen.

As Christmas 2010 approached, news emerged that the year-long Deloitte investigation was close to completion. In private, Brailsford was furious about the report, which helped darken his mood at the end of that dismal first season. Coming under pressure from British Cycling, stinging from criticism over his big-budget team's lack of success and hearing grumbles of discontent from Team GB riders as the London Olympics approached, Brailsford faced challenges on many fronts.

In the end, the sixty-nine-page Deloitte report – released to the public in March 2011 – was relatively anodyne. It noted 'a lack of clarity' in the relationship between Sky and British Cycling, but the line that emerged from both British Cycling and UK Sport was, essentially, 'Nothing to see here, move along.' Liz Nicholl, chief executive of UK Sport said, 'The Deloitte review has done exactly what we hoped it would. It has provided us with very good insight at a crucial time and helped to give us assurance about our investment … The fact that the review identified no major risks to the World Class Performance Programme is good news for everyone involved.' Case closed, and one less thing for Brailsford to fret over.

With the Deloitte report out of the way, and Kerrison giving Sky a new direction, Brailsford still had to deal with issues concerning the Team GB track squads. In public at least, at Manchester Velodrome, the squad was still able to surf the crest of a media wave from Beijing, and with London 2012 hoveing into view, the mood was bordering on the hysterical – though not in a way that was funny. British cycling had been on an upward trajectory for years and British teams masterminded by Brailsford had dominated on track, so why would it change now? Behind the scenes, however, there was a real possibility of failure given that several key players had, to borrow a sporting cliché, 'taken their eye off the ball'.

How did Brailsford – literally and figuratively – keep the show on the road, starring him as mastermind orchestrating this monstrous two-ring circus? What is also widely recognised – even if not publicly acknowledged – is that in the approach to the London 2012 Games, Shane Sutton was essentially cracking the whip and running the show in Manchester, with significant input from Chris Boardman. Even after leaving British Cycling, Sutton still resists any invitation to play up his role.

> When I look back at the run-up to the 2012 Games, what you have got to remember – Dave was going to put good people around him, not just me. Dave maybe drifted away a bit, but we stuck to the vision – via Sky or GB. He was never really 'away' because he always knew what was happening, but obviously I was the man on the ground. He was at the Giro, then America, then the Tour, then Newport for a day. The track team hadn't seen him for three or four months, that is true. But in that four-month period there wasn't a day we weren't in touch, 24/7, in the middle of the night if need be. But in a way yeah, I did lead them into London.

The other important member of the pre-London team was Chris Boardman, who had stayed at a long arm's length from the Sky professional road squad, though he too was not as frequently in Manchester as he had been in the preparation phase for Beijing. 'I should have left British Cycling after the Beijing Games,' recalls Boardman. 'That was the plan, to leave the senior management team. But I went in to the velodrome to resign a year after Beijing and Dave persuaded me to stay on and do the research and development stuff, with my own team and budget and not really have to tell anyone anything, just work on all these little projects.' It also meant he could spend less time with Sutton and, since Brailsford was working on Sky Procycling, leadership clearly suffered.

While the fractious odd couple of Sutton and Boardman fought fires in Manchester, Brailsford busied himself trying to make his new pro road squad function, though he had more plates spinning than hands to keep them going. Doug Dailey, still 'embedded' in both camps, was caught in the middle:

> Dave was getting frustrated. I think some of the original Sky planning and costs were proving to be grossly under-estimated, and some of the riders who had been signed weren't quite working out. So Dave was going through a difficult patch and I was making heavy weather of the logistics, bringing riders in from Sweden and Norway trying to get them into a location, and they all required bespoke travel, day and night. It was endless.

Happily, even if there was still some turmoil in Manchester, Kerrison's new training approach started to pay off early in 2011, with Wiggins' third place overall in Paris–Nice, followed by a prestigious overall victory in the Critérium du Dauphiné, a normally reliable pre-Tour de France form guide. Wiggins, alas, crashed out on stage seven of the Tour de France, so whether or not he was in shape to win the 2011 Tour cannot be known.

Although the 2011 road season showed improvement, World Tour racing on the roads of Europe was proving to be a tougher nut to crack than it had been on the hardwood velodromes of the track circuit. From Sydney to Athens, from Stuttgart to Beijing, Brailsford and his staff had all savoured track-based glory at those various Games and World Championships. On the eve of the 2012 season, the Champs-Élysées – as well as the Poggio, Oude Kwaremont, Carrefour de l'Arbre and la Redoute – had managed to rebuff the Sky Procycling approach. If the mysteries of stage racing looked like they were starting to reveal their secrets, the Spring Classics were still blank spaces on the Sky map.

Thinking back to the upbeat talk in the Lanesborough Hotel in February 2009, recalling the media fanfare in January 2010, Sky's race-winning tally by the end of 2011 still didn't see Brailsford and his assembled talent with much to show for their efforts, or Sky's significant investment. The year 2011 had thrown up some very strong results, just not the ones that grabbed big media headlines or tallied with Brailsford's grand ambitions.

Sky's best result – certainly the best collective performances – had come at the end of the 2011 season in the most overlooked of the three Grand Tours, the Vuelta a España. Often seen as a consolation prize for the wounded or underperforming stars, a blooding-ground for Grand Tour virgins or a punishment race for riders who had upset their teams, the Tour of Spain is simultaneously brutal (the organisers love a mountain) and relaxed (because most rider contracts have been signed), with the end of season in view.

After breaking his collarbone in the Tour, an in-form Wiggins and coach Kerrison decided that racing the Vuelta would be a good idea, ensuring Wiggins had one Grand Tour – a three-week 'training' block – in his legs before the 2012 Tour de France. As it turned out, the 2011 Vuelta would be a revelatory event, with Wiggins and Chris Froome falling out, never to fall back in again: Wiggins threatened by Froome's ability, Froome feeling betrayed by Wiggins and senior management.

As far as the 2011 Vuelta went, the recovering Wiggins, Froome the revelation and Juan Cobo the eventual winner* swapped the race lead throughout, until the unfancied Cobo finally dropped Froome on the Angliru climb on the penultimate stage. Nevertheless, Sky Procycling put two of its riders on the podium of a Grand Tour – and only one of them was a surprise. Here, undeniably, were signs that Kerrison's approach and Wiggins' ability were up to the task of winning a Grand Tour. True, it wasn't the Tour de France, but the 2011 Vuelta was encouraging.

And all the while, as Brailsford and his expensive road squad showed signs of improvement, back at Manchester Velodrome, things were not going swimmingly well with British Cycling's track riders. In the apparent lack of 'equality' among the stars who had brought home the bacon from Beijing, there wasn't quite the same *esprit de corps* as before, and Brailsford's absences from Manchester hadn't helped unite the troops. Friction and niggles festered more than had previously been the case. 'I think it took till around 2010 before alarm bells really started to ring,' recalls Chris Hoy. 'Shane was, in his own words, "running around like a blue-arsed fly" trying to get all these different jobs done and helping different groups

---

* Following retrospective anti-doping tests Juan Cobo was stripped of his 2011 victory and the race win was awarded to Froome in 2019. This meant that Froome became the first British winner of a Grand Tour, a year ahead of Wiggins' 2012 Tour de France triumph.

of people and cliques. The shine had come off the Games by then. It started to come together in the end, but there was a bit of a wing and a prayer about it.'

In the early months of 2012, however, with the London Olympic Games looming, Brailsford was still working flat out with two demanding jobs. Filmed by Sky TV for a fly-on-the-wall-style documentary, *Road to Glory*, there were times when he cut a forlorn figure, perhaps revealing more than he intended as the cameras followed him.

Talking about Sky Procycling, Brailsford said,

> It's not like a hobby or a gang. It's not like [we] all necessarily get on, but professionally, we're obliged to get on and move this team forward. I just want to make sure that everybody is supported and at the end of the day we can say, 'We couldn't have done any better, we couldn't have done any more', and that's important. If we didn't care, well … I wouldn't be still here [in a deserted Manchester headquarters] at eight o'clock at night doing this, would I? I'd be at home!

He laughed a self-deprecating little laugh before adding, 'It's not much of a way to live your life, but there you go.'

Having surfed a wave of post-Beijing popularity, the Midas touch seemed to have deserted Brailsford, who, in the first two seasons of Sky Procycling, had been forced to confront the shortcomings in his team and his approach. However, with Brailsford having revamped his road team and belatedly re-engaged with the track squad in Manchester following some tough talking to riders and coaches, 2012 was set to be a big year.

8

WIGGY STARDUST

'Bliss it was in that dawn to be alive.'

Happily for Dave Brailsford – head of both Sky Procycling and British Cycling – 2012 started well and got better as the season unfolded. Bradley Wiggins won the time trial stage at the Volta ao Algarve on 19 February, while his Sky teammate Richie Porte won the overall classification. A little more than a month later, at the world track championships in Melbourne, Team GB put in a series of dominating, medal-winning performances in the Olympic disciplines. Everything and everyone was on track; the stars were aligning.

The modest successes in Portugal were just the beginning for Wiggins, as overall victories in Paris–Nice, the Tour de Romandie and the Critérium du Dauphiné followed before Wiggins arrived in Liège for the start of the Tour de France. It had been an unprecedented, dreamy run. Could Wiggins keep it up and claim cycling's biggest prize?

As much as any Grand Tour ever could, the 2012 Tour unfolded like a simple box-ticking 'How to win a Tour' exercise, and there were few tactical challenges for Team Sky. Thus, Wiggins didn't take the race leadership too early, enabling Wiggins and his team to keep a low profile in the opening stages before asphyxiating the opposition in the space of three days. Chris Froome won at the summit of La Planche des Belles Filles after a perfectly choreographed Team Sky lead-in to the final kilometres, enabling Froome to claim his first ever Tour stage, while Wiggins took the yellow jersey and followed that up by winning stage nine's 38 km time trial to increase his advantage. Psychologically, it was perfect for Sky and crippling for the opposition.

The time-trial heavy and mountain-lite route of the 2012 Tour – not forgetting rivals Alberto Contador's doping suspension and Andy Schleck's injury-enforced absence – meant it was always going to be Wiggins' best chance for Tour glory. The Tour being the Tour, there were pile-ups in the opening week, though unlike 2011 Wiggins avoided them, which was more than can be said for that year's Giro d'Italia winner, Ryder Hesjedal of Garmin, another threat forced out after stage six. In fact, the worst bit of luck Sky suffered was when Kanstantin Siutsou was skittled down and out on stage three. In the 2012 Tour, Team Sky's problems were mainly of their own making.

Wiggins' sport director throughout 2012, Sean Yates, revealed, 'I remember hearing Astana's Janez Brajkovič saying that everyone else was racing for second place and being pleased to hear it, because that was the mood in the whole peloton. Early on they basically lined up behind us and gave us a relatively easy time.' If the media was getting excited, if Brailsford was giddy and Wiggins was stressing, Yates was an immoveable rock anchored in the team car. The benefits of hiring a sport director like Yates who had 'been there, done that and got the celebratory T-shirt' were more obvious with every passing stage.

The 2012 season, inevitably, had started long before Wiggins' opening race on the Algarve, and he had got down to serious work late in 2011, as Yates says:

> Brad was doing forty-hour weeks in Mallorca in December. He was doing weight sessions before breakfast at seven in the morning before road rides. He was flying in by private charter to Mallorca and for Paris–Nice too. Nothing was left to chance that year. I think Brad knew it was shit or bust, with the way the Tour route was that year.

However, the Tour was not won in the tiny weights room in the Vanity Golf Hotel in Alcúdia either. The idea that Wiggins could win the Tour had been a much slower burner and, as then coach and confidant Shane Sutton noted, it had been fomenting for years.

> You're going to laugh but I was always a great believer that Brad could do something special on the road. I think that the track was a comfortable option for a long time though; it was like a bubble for him. He was already a legend on the track and I'm not sure he was willing to risk getting a kicking on the road. Obviously he could ride on the road to a certain level, but I don't think – and he'll hate me for saying this – he ever really applied himself properly in the early years.

But it was all very well for Sutton to hypothesise that Wiggins had the physiology to win the Tour, but when did Wiggins himself glimpse it? For Sutton it all changed in Italy.

> When he saw it in himself is the most important thing, and he vividly remembers when it actually clicked. I

remember Brad said to me that in 2009 at the Giro on one of the climbs Lance [Armstrong] started to go out the back and Brad's gone 'Fucking hell!' That was one of the key moments in Brad's career. When he said, 'Fuck me I've just dropped Lance Armstrong', that was a big thing.

Sutton had been close to Wiggins throughout his years of track focus, and had been a key character in Wiggins' training, but it was experienced sport director Yates, famously, who was driving the team car when Froome accelerated in the finale of stage 11 at the summit of La Toussuire. Yates' surprise, horror and blunt radio message to the rampant Froome – 'What the fuck are you doing?!' – was recorded for posterity for a TV documentary. It was no secret that there was friction between Froome and Wiggins, and not much of a secret either that Yates was more of a Wiggins fan, appreciative of Wiggins' immersion in the history of the sport. Wiggins, in so many ways, was 'old school'. Froome's school was more public school, St John's in Johannesburg to be precise.

Nevertheless, the undertow of tension between Wiggins and Froome wasn't defused by the explanations offered to the media – Froome's attack had been tactical, apparently – and the story wouldn't die. The strain between the pair born during the 2011 Vuelta had resurfaced and remained, indeed, for the rest of their time at Team Sky, where they rarely raced together again.

Undoubtedly Froome's aggressive riding was motivated by his desire to secure his second place overall because, unsurprisingly, there was a healthy bonus on offer for finishing runner-up in Paris. Inside Team Sky, relations between Wiggins and Froome deteriorated further, and Brailsford told Froome that Wiggins was ready to go home, which may or may not have been an exaggeration, but is still an insight into the mood. In the event, Brailsford moved quickly to pour oil on stormy waters, and Froome's contract negotiations were accelerated that same night after Froome's showing at La Toussuire, with an offer to match Wiggins' salary.

Froome and Wiggins managed their efforts and their rivals in the final mountain stages, holding station and sticking to the plan. It was only finally settled – for 2012 at least – when Wiggins put the peloton to the sword, winning the penultimate stage 19 time trial in Chartres and putting 1–16 into second-placed Froome in the process.

All that remained was for *maillot jaune* Wiggins to lead out Mark Cavendish, resplendent in his world road champion's rainbow jersey into the Place de la Concorde for the 'Manx Missile' to claim a magnificent stage win and wrapping Team Sky's 2012 Tour de France in a manner that couldn't have been topped. Six stage wins, first and second overall on general classification, fourteen days in yellow and, of course, the vindication of Dave Brailsford's stated aim. Team Sky had, in fact, won the Tour de France with a British rider less than five years after the formation of the squad. And Wiggins hadn't failed a dope test either.

On the Paris podium, Wiggins further delighted a generation of British club cyclists with his victory speech from the Champs-Élysées podium. Wiggins' 'OK, we're just going to draw the raffle numbers now. Some dreams come true and my old mother over there, her son's won the Tour de France. Thank you everyone, cheers. Safe journey home and don't get too drunk' was a pitch-perfect nod to his origins, to the sport's roots and his own club heritage, as well as a gentle piss-take of those expecting a profound statement or trite nonsense about 'following your dream'. Wiggins' speech was exactly the same one he could have given as guest of honour at any

British cycling club Christmas dinner. Those wry comments helped cement Wiggins' place in the hearts of club members, those few sentences a verbal 'wink' to the cycling culture he was formed in, the bedrock of the sport as it is practised by thousands of British riders. It was, in its own understated way, a profound moment for generations of British cycling stalwarts, from the mid-week club '10' time-trial 'pusher-offers' and time keepers, to the cake-bakers and tea-urn operatives, in the village halls that double as Sunday morning race headquarters and changing rooms.

In spite of the stories that started to seep out about Wiggins being difficult to deal with when things weren't going his way, Wiggins still 'connected' with British cycling fans; he somehow transmitted a sense in which he was still 'one of them'.

Wiggins' subsequent comment in the 2012 TV documentary *A Year in Yellow*, that 'kids from Kilburn don't win the Tour de France. You had to be from these exotic climes, Paris, Nice, Italy, Spain, all these places when you were reading about it as a kid' – became over-used, but it did sum up perceptions both of Wiggins himself and British fans who had followed cycling through many barren years. Prior to the advent of cheap foreign flights, torrents of information available on the internet, streamed live coverage of even the most obscure races and increased mainstream media coverage, cycling had been wrapped in a layer of mystique, remaining essentially – and romantically – unknowable. The names of riders and location of the races meant that, truly, blokes with names like Wiggins from London postcodes simply did not feature in cycling's ancient multilingual mythology.

Wiggins' 'kids from Kilburn' neatly expressed a dawning realisation that, in fact, you *didn't* need to be from continental Europe to win the Tour. Almost 100 years of history had accustomed British cyclists to internalising the 'fact' that being born on continental Europe was a prerequisite if you wanted to win the Tour, the Giro d'Italia or the Vuelta a España. In much the same way that Olympic and World triumphs of Boardman, Hoy and others had showed that British riders could successfully compete on track, Wiggins' performances throughout 2012 had the same impact on ambitious road racers.

Wiggins was the ideal character to 'front' this cultural shift, the embodiment of a rider who had received his cycling education in venerable clubs, who knew the history of his sport like the obsessive fan he was and then benefited from the late 1990s Lottery-funded transformation of British Cycling.

Wiggins' public face, his early television appearances and *A Year in Yellow* had positioned him as a cheeky chappie, and the British media loves a lad. Being a sporting legend is all well and good, but David Beckham will never be as loved by football fans as fallible idols George Best or Paul Gascoigne.

Clearly there will never be another year like 2012 in British cycling history, a season with so many firsts and dazzling highlights. After all, there can be only one 'first British winner' of the Tour de France, and the name in the record books is that of Bradley Wiggins. There had been ninety-nine editions of the Tour de France and no British rider had ever finished in the first three, far less won the overall prize. Now there were British riders on the top two steps of the podium.

As the squad celebrated among the team buses assembled in an impromptu 'trailer park' in the spectacular Place de la Concorde, all was momentarily well with the world. Of course, tensions would return and in any case, the Olympic Games meant that a portion of the team, both riders and staff, couldn't afford to let themselves go yet. Wiggins and Cavendish in particular had serious ambitions in London, British cycling superstars out to further cement their reputations at their home Olympiad. In winning the Tour, Wiggins had reached a new level of notoriety, and the Olympics offered an opportunity to climb higher still.

Thus, less than a week after the Tour triumph on the Champs-Élysées, the roads around Surrey were jammed with the same club cyclists 'Wiggo' had referenced as well as the newly curious spectators, all anxious to see Team GB position Cavendish into a gold-medal-winning position on The Mall. The men's Olympic Games road race, run on a glorious summer Saturday, felt like a celebration, a giant open-air party with even Surrey's notoriously bike-phobic denizens coming out to cheer.

In the event, the road races held on the opening weekend of the Games offered only meagre British fare because in spite of the best efforts of the four other riders (Wiggins, Froome, Ian Stannard, David Millar) in the British team to control the race and deliver Cavendish for a hoped-for sprint finish, Alexandre Vinokourov of Kazakhstan outfoxed Rigoberto Uran of Colombia after the pair had slipped clear from a leading group in the closing kilometres.

The following day, after a sodden ride around the same Surrey hills, Lizzie Armitstead boosted GB morale by finishing second in a two-up sprint behind Dutch superstar – and one of the greatest cyclists ever – Marianne Vos. Three days after that, Wiggins and Froome would once again share a podium, finishing first and third in the Olympic time trial. It was about as physically close as they would get to each other for the remainder of Wiggins' career.

For cycling followers, the multiple pleasures of the French summer and the London Games seemed like a dream in which the sun shone endlessly on British triumphs. After the Beijing Games, it was almost expected that British track riders would hoover up medals and, when they duly did, few bothered to ask how closely the team had come to failure or how fractious the preparations had been.

Mark Cavendish, a British Cycling trailblazer and bona-fide winner, could fulminate about how cruel the mainstream media had been in describing his performance in the road race won by Vinokourov as 'a failure', but it was a sign of things to come. The British non-cycling media only really likes you when you're winning. Or behaving badly. For a short period, the dream scenario for tabloid editors was 'Wiggo' doing both, simultaneously.

In truth, the run-up to the London Games for the rest of Team GB – the track squads – had been far from smooth, certainly not compared to Beijing. In the words of one insider at British Cycling,

> Dave [Brailsford] had buggered off to do Team Sky and it was left to Shane and Chris Boardman to hold things together behind the scenes. Chris was much, much more than just the guy who fronted the 'Secret Squirrel' club working on bikes and clothing. Dave would sound out Chris on so many things, especially relating to the track endurance riders.

The concerns over the track squad were real. Speaking just before the London Games, Brailsford confessed,

> I was under the impression that when we decided to go, the performance would come up. I was very confident. But in Apeldoorn, at the European Championships [in October 2011] I had a few moments when I thought, oh … It's like taking off in a plane, you pull the joystick back and the nose comes up. I was waiting for it to lift.

Happily, by March 2012 at the Melbourne World Championships, the squad achieved escape velocity and British cycling didn't come back down to earth for years.

Notwithstanding the bumpy run-in to the 2012 season – with underwhelming performances in pre-Games 2011 World Cups and defending women's Olympic pursuit champion Rebecca Romero leaving the squad – if the Team GB track squad had been a stand-alone nation, it would have finished eighth overall in the London Olympic medal table.

If most British cycling fans were blissfully happy throughout 2012 then there were others less besotted by Team Sky, and, given the manner in which the team raced the Tour, the epithet 'UK Postal' ricocheted around social media. The charge was that Team Sky was a smarter, newer version of Lance Armstrong's doped US Postal squad. How, fumed doubters, was it possible for a team to dominate the Tour unless they were doping? Given the leaks that were emerging throughout 2012 about the ongoing USADA report into the use of performance-enhancing drugs at US Postal, scepticism at exceptional cycling performances was a necessary prerequisite, but endless cynicism eventually corrodes the soul.

In the UK, there was no end of analysis, from erudite considerations of how the race was won to anonymised accusations of doping on social media. How had Wiggins done it? During seven seasons as a professional, with La Française des Jeux, Crédit Agricole and Cofidis he had showed little on the road in stage races – far less Grand Tours – so how had Wiggins claimed the biggest prize in cycle sport?

His Olympic and World Championship team pursuit and Madison partner Rob Hayles offered his take on Wiggins' transformation. Or, more accurately, Wiggins 'awakening' to his possibilities: 'You know, up until his fourth place in the 2009 Tour I wouldn't have said that Brad was a potential Tour winner. And, even if *he* thought it, he didn't shout about it either. What I knew though is that anything he has put his mind to on a bike, he's fulfilled it.'

Ironically, in light of the flood of doping accusations that Wiggins and the team were swamped by, Hayles reckoned the cultural shift and new anti-doping measures in the sport had helped Wiggins' cause. As Hayles explains (with more than a hint of frustration in his voice):

I think in some ways he's been lucky with the timing, since the playing field in Europe is a lot more level than it was a few years ago. If you look at the speed the Tour guys are riding up the forty- or fifty-minute climbs at these days, they are much slower than they rode them a few years ago, which is a good sign. Some people are saying that the watts-per-kilogram figures should be setting off alarm bells, but it's the longer climbs that are most revealing. You can explain that stuff to people till you are blue in the face, but the fact is that the Sky guys aren't putting out superhuman, ridiculous numbers.

Hayles – one of the small squad of endurance riders who had trained with Chris Boardman prior to the 1992 Olympics – had experience and memories of cycling that stretched back to the Dark Ages, the pre-Lottery era, and his defence of Wiggins also reveals how far ahead British Cycling had moved between 1998 and 2004.

People were asking about the secret of Sky, but it was just their attention to every detail that's important. I remember when Brad and I were racing together with Cofidis in Europe and with the World Class Plan for GB on the track – the difference between the two set-ups was amazing. The French were nowhere in comparison, and Sky is a lot more advanced than what we were in the World Class team back then. We were guinea pigs in some ways, and

Dave Brailsford has learned from whatever mistakes were made back then to turn Sky into the team it is.

Hayles is clear that the approaches pioneered by Keen and later amplified by Brailsford had given British riders a head start and new ways of looking at the sport. However, what both entities also shared were budgets that far outstripped those of their rivals, on track and road. It's not so much that the ideas were 'all new' but rather that any and all new technologies and techniques could be tried and employed. In 2018, the head of the Belgian Cycling Federation, Frederik Broché – who had previously worked at British Cycling for two years – noted that the Belgian budget was 'only between 10 and 20 per cent of British Cycling'. Considering that Belgium is one of the traditional bedrocks of the sport, that's a staggering gap.

The supporting explanation offered by agnostics was that Sky had assembled a well-prepared group of talented riders who were willing to sacrifice their own chances of stage wins or modest general classification placings to spill their guts for Wiggins. They did this in a year in which the race route also suited Wiggins' strengths, and in which three rivals – Contador, Schleck and Hesjedal – were KO'd. At Sky, Wiggins was a unique leader, backed by a group of riders who were much more talented, collectively, than the US Postal riders Armstrong had at his disposal between 1999 and 2001. Tactically and visually the similarity was superficially there – of one team riding on the front of the peloton all day – but the depth of talent at the respective teams bore no serious comparison.

The explanations and defences offered by Team Sky and its supporters, as well as the absence of drug test failures by its riders that year (or subsequently), did nothing to assuage the doubters. Even after the season ended, Sky staff were coming to terms with this post-Lance Armstrong landscape. 'I think in the past teams spent a lot of money on a couple of riders and didn't worry too much about anybody else. They paid for a few key riders to get them into the biggest races and that was it,' explains Team Sky coach Rod Ellingworth. 'We work with all twenty-seven of our riders, so you'd expect them all to move up a performance level.'

Questions of doping had always swirled around cycling, from its earliest competitions, but in the post-Armstrong era, the topic was far higher on the agenda than ever before. Suspicion would always be present, yet many insisted that things were changing for the better in this opaque domain.

David Millar, no stranger to the culture and practices of doping in cycling, was confident that the professional peloton in 2012 was a very different environment to the one he had entered as a young pro in 1997. Speaking after Wiggins had won the Tour, in which he himself had won a stage, Millar was unambiguous, confident of his position and strident in his defence of Wiggins.

> If you are doing 'the bad stuff' you have to be so incredibly secret about it, it really is like the dark arts. I mean, to get away with it you are talking about incredibly advanced doping, a lot of money and an amazing amount of logistics. It's not like you slip into it, not at the top end, and of course it does happen, but if we are talking about blood doping well ... it's such a different world now. I think that the anti-doping war is sort of being won. I think we've done a pretty good job there, and there's been such a shift in attitudes that we are kind of on top of it.

The announcement that Team Sky would be 'cleaner than clean' and win the Tour with a dope-free rider inside five years was laughed at, partly for having the chutzpah to say it, but also because assembling a credible World Tour squad which fitted the bill at that point in cycling's history was, as it turned out, impossible. Too many staff and riders had worked in the sport too long – including Millar's 'Dark Ages' of doping – for Sky's pristine ethos to be maintained.

In more candid moments, Brailsford hinted that the presentation of the team, allied with some of his early declarations, hit the wrong notes. Additionally, when he was first hoisting his 'Team Clean' banner, he couldn't know that cycling was less than three years away from Lance Armstrong's confessions and the revelations contained in the accompanying USADA report. Grim details contained in the 2013 Sorgdrager report into doping at the Dutch Rabobank team and by Denmark's ADD anti-doping authority in 2015 would also alter the media's reporting of doping – henceforth, the journalistic approach to doping would be more aggressively inquisitive.

If doping wasn't the only story in town, it was never far from the back pages or cycling websites. Now, the topic was approached with a directness and zeal that would have been looked on as inappropriate by cycling's press corps a decade previously. Brailsford and Sky would reap the whirlwind of this new media landscape, fanned in part by new social media platforms coming of age at the same time. Twitter, for example, would more than quadruple in size from 30 million global users in 2010, during the team's first year, to 151 million by the time Bradley Wiggins enjoyed his wonder year in 2012. And there were times when it must have felt that most users were accusing him of doping.

This history and context are important because Brailsford's 'clean team' aims played well to a gallery of new British fans intoxicated by British track successes, but in road cycling's broader culture, its media and fans took a more circumspect view of this rich upstart squad. After all, this was a sport where tradition – and the tradition of keeping your mouth shut – had held sway for almost a century. Brailsford's was a bold statement of intent, but it was twice doomed. It was doomed because in 2009 the connections between riders and staff who were 'clean' and those who were not were complex, and far deeper than almost anyone cared to admit. For those who advocated a scorched-earth 'Year Zero' approach, guilt by association was often assumed, and it was easy to join the doping dots because there was rarely much separation between the most flagrant dopers and riders racing clean. Riders who had raced for teams in which other riders had tested positive rode under suspicion, and pity help you if your training partner was under investigation by the Italian drug squad and mentioned your name in a tapped phone call. That was all it took for your name and career results to be considered suspicious and 'named' in an Italian judge's investigation.

Additionally, the lines in some doping cases were blurred to the extent that one rider's legitimate Therapeutic Use Exemption (TUE) medicine was another journalist's bang-to-rights proof of doping. The use and abuse of the TUE system in all sports would become a major issue; suffice it to say that during decades of blood and hormone doping, bending TUE rules – introduced in 2005 – had hitherto been considered small beer in the realm of performance enhancement. Essentially, a TUE certificate enabled riders to take otherwise banned or restricted medication while racing without fear of testing positive. The abuse of the TUE system occurred when riders and team doctors applied for TUE exemptions for substances that were not medically justified, or which represented a 'heavy duty' treatment for an ailment that could be treated with a less powerful medication – albeit with little or no performance-enhancing side effects.

It was against these wider, shifting attitudes that Sky's

'mission statement' and recruitment needs to be seen – as well as the reaction they generated. As Sky hired, those with longer histories and better connections in the sport shook their heads at the naivety of some appointments. Voices inside the team who advised against certain names were discounted as paranoiacs who saw doping behind every performance. What would turn out to be most troubling was that Brailsford – a student of road racing for decades – would claim ignorance of doping by team personnel whose careers had invisible asterisks attached to suspicious performances. Despite advice, Brailsford chose not to listen to those voices who counselled caution over certain hirings.

Thus, the recruitment of team doctor Geert Leinders was flagged up by team insiders as being incompatible with Brailsford's stated intention of running a team that excluded those who had been involved in doping. On believable accounts, Brailsford knew he was hiring staff and riders who at some level posed a risk to the reputation of the team, yet he somehow convinced himself it would never be an issue. Brailsford turned out to be gravely mistaken on that score, damaging the credibility of the team and exposing riders who had hitherto managed to avoid becoming embroiled in doping scandals, costing them their jobs. It left many with a bitter taste, while Brailsford's management was also called into question.

It was only after the racing was done, dusted and filed for posterity that the full extent of the stresses inside Team Sky during those weeks was revealed. At the time, given the media enthralled by a first British Tour de France winner and the subsequent Olympic medals, the cracks were easily papered over.

The whole of the 2012 season had felt like a jamboree for British cycling, at least from the point of view of road racing fans. The work that Wiggins had put in, buckling down as never before in the winter of 2011, training and dieting from

November, guided by Tim Kerrison with motivational coaching supplied by Shane Sutton paid off beyond the team's most optimistic expectations. Wiggins had won the Tour.

Yet even before the year was over, there was a hint of things to come when Wiggins revealed, 'I told them [Kerrison and Sutton] that I didn't know how long I would be able to go on training for the Tour and living the life it demands. It's too intense and makes too big a toll on your life and everyone else around you,' he wrote, with impressive perspicacity, in his autobiography, *My Time*. Between the exigencies of the lifestyle and the demands of the media, fans and a new personal management company, Wiggins wouldn't figure on the 'contenders' list for any other Grand Tours.

To be fair to Wiggins, he was already 32 when he won the 2012 Tour; he had been a full-time bike rider since the age of 17, and had won several World and Olympic titles. Additionally, the changing face of modern cycling, in which riders leaned on doping much less than in the previous decades, made different demands of its denizens, as David Millar, ex-Wiggins teammate at Garmin, explains:

> In the old days you'd prepare for about four months for a Grand Tour; you could turn up a bit fat then get on the gear. Now you have to work incredibly hard for months and months, surrounded by a massive team of people, doing training camps, altitude camps, and you get to that point where you are actually winning and people start bursting your balls. It's not surprising that they say 'Fuck you!' I think it requires some empathy, but then it also requires some empathy from the athlete, who needs to understand what people want to hear when it comes to disowning doping.

With a nod to Team Sky's budget and resources, Millar continued,

> I think you *can* compete without doping, and I think the thing with professional cycling now is that if you are a young rider and you want to achieve the best, you have to choose your team very carefully, and often that will mean not going for the money. In the old days all the teams were more or less the same: you turned pro when you reached a certain age and a certain level, you doped, you got to a higher level and everyone was more or less on the same playing field. The irony is that the playing field is so different now; everyone is clean, but the concept of a level playing field has totally shifted too. Now it comes down to the technical support you have, the money your team has to support you and afford to look for those little advantages.

Given Brailsford's long history with Wiggins, at three Olympic cycles with Team GB and as the Team Sky superstar who enjoyed that untouchable, unrepeatable 2012 season, Brailsford could see Wiggins wasn't likely to stay the demanding course. Over the years Brailsford – and Boardman, Sutton and Dr Steve Peters – had seen Wiggins wobble after hitting performance heights. Having achieved towering goals in 2012, it was hard to believe that, just as in times past, Wiggins wouldn't wander off the righteous path a little.

And all the time, while Wiggins kicked over the traces and as Team GB riders polished their medals, his nemesis was still pushing and planning. Chris Froome – with Kerrison – had been working out a programme for his run at the Vuelta; his 2012 season was far from finished. As Froome explains:

We decided to come here after the Tour. It was always a 'maybe', but after I got through the Tour I was still in good form and still motivated mentally, so Tim and the team said, 'Let's put you in it and go for it.' I actually had two days off after the Olympics, just as a bit of a mental break. Then I did a solid ten-day training block.

If Wiggins had decided that one Tour was enough, it was already clear that Froome had an appetite and desire that would see him outstrip his teammate.

With Wiggins' win in 2012, Team Sky had 'cracked it' in the sense it had delivered the first British winner ever, and proved it was capable of coping with the demands of the race. Winning the Tour had meant dealing with the pressures on and off the road (and inside the team bus), defending the yellow jersey all the way to Paris. But, as any team sports manager will say, the trick is in repeating the process. Winning one Tour is hard, but it's 'easy' compared to securing another, proving to the world and yourself that you didn't fluke it, that you only won because the field was weak, because the route suited your rider, because a rival was injured or took ill …

In celebratory mode, sure enough, after that 2012 Tour and the London Olympics, Wiggins cracked. Which is to say that having lived as a monk for the best part of two years, Wiggins decided he had had enough, and didn't so much take a breather as fly off the rails. Nobody begrudged him. Or rather nobody outside of Team Sky: he'd won Paris–Nice, the Tour de Romandie, the Critérium du Dauphiné; he was the first British winner of the Tour, he'd won Olympic gold, BBC TV sports personality of the year and had given the best winner's speech on the Champs-Élysées ever. What the hell, give him a break, pour him a vodka tonic in a glass the size of a goldfish bowl.

But Wiggins bailing out was doubly problematic. Not only

because no Tour contender could afford to enjoy too much time off, but also because his erstwhile understudy Froome was agitating to lead the team with a strong argument for doing so. If Wiggins was wavering, Froome was champing at the bit, insisting that a 'deal' had been made that guaranteed him team leadership in the Tour. In fact, the 'guarantee' was exactly what had not been promised in the contract Froome signed after his revelatory 2011 Vuelta.

Froome would reveal that the deal he had struck with Brailsford, with glorious ambiguity, said that Team Sky would 'support [Froome] in my ambitions at the Tour de France'. At the time the contract was signed, both parties probably thought they had what they wanted. The passing of leadership at Team Sky from 'Wiggo' to 'Froomey' – via the brief interlude when he was portrayed as the faithful 'Froomedog' eager to protect his team leader – was never going to be easy.

'Froomedog' had been supportively painted by fans on the Tarmac of Box Hill for the Olympic Games, but it was an epithet that Froome had already outgrown, even as his wheels rolled over it that July day. Wiggins was a bona-fide national hero, and Froome was never going to be taken to British hearts with the same enthusiasm, no matter how many races he won. None of which would matter much to Froome, who had struggled in ways that Wiggins hadn't when making his way to Europe and a career as a professional.

Froome's accent was polite colonial Home Counties English, with a slight South African inflection, but he was a child of a broken home, and for all that he went to a South African public school (paid for by his estranged father), he was happy in his black Johannesburg cycling club, ready to smuggle booze and cigarettes into his school to sell and fund his amateur race career. He was also capable of hijacking the Kenyan cycling federation president's email account in order to enter himself for the 2007 world road championships. Froome was the teenager who would get up at four in the morning to go (forbidden) training on his bike. He sounded posh, but the road he had travelled had been much harder than his accent suggested.

Curiously, the nickname 'Froomedog' had been Shane Sutton's invention. 'Ah, yeah, it came from "Froomedog Millionaire" actually,' Sutton laughs at the recollection.

> Froomey was always about money, like he always had his little businesses, selling ciggies down in his South African school! The Froomedog thing came about because him and G [Geraint Thomas] were sharing an apartment in Italy and something happened and G ended up owing some rent to Froomey and it was like €300 and they had a massive fallout over it – €300! – and Froomey was going nuts. He's so tight! So that was him – Froomedog Millionaire.

Yates, lead sports director on that 2012 Tour, found Wiggins much closer to his own heart and outlook. Yates, who went on to work with Tinkoff-Saxo after he left Sky, observes that Wiggins was well aware of the cultural significance of adding his name to the list of winners of Paris–Nice, joining such as Jacques Anquetil, Eddy Merckx, Stephen Roche, Miguel Indurain – Tour winners all. 'I think it's fair to say that Bradley took a real sense of pride and achievement in winning something like Paris–Nice,' says Yates. 'It was something that he had been dreaming about for a long time, having read about it in magazines from when he was little, and then, once he had won it, he had sort of ticked that particular box.'

Like Yates – like Brailsford – Wiggins was a student and lover of the sport and its traditions. Froome? Not so much. 'All Froomey cares about is money; that's what drives him,' was Yates' blunt assessment of what ultimately motivated the rider with the African heart and the British road racing licence. Given his personal background, perhaps that's understandable. When theories flew around the 2017 Vuelta wondering why Froome had snatched the points jersey on the final day by sprinting for 11th place, perhaps people need look no further than the €11,000 prize money on offer for the points jersey winner. Froome's Monaco training partners will all attest to his bottomlessly competitive outlook, where it seems like every climb is ridden hard and there are no shortcuts.

If Wiggins and Froome frictions had been evident from as far back as the 2011 Tour of Spain, they had ratcheted up a notch or two. In winter 2012–2013, Brailsford and the management team at Sky knew they had a problem with their two stars as their wives carried out a digital proxy war on Twitter and Froome (shades of the Froomedog Millionaire) went public on the fact that Wiggins still owed him a share of the Tour de France prize money.

If Brailsford's two stars were more or less equally physically blessed, then the balance would be tipped by different factors. Brailsford observed, 'I used to think, much earlier in my career, that talent times commitment equals success, but I'd say that's changed. Commitment is clearly still a massive part of success, but you could probably substitute that word with "hunger", "desire", "purpose" or "drive" – that's what you need to get the best out of your talent.' If it was a close-run thing in terms of raw physical talent, then when it came to a desire to win the 2013 Tour de France, Froome had Wiggins beaten.

Brailsford was pilloried by British fans for the perceived switch in allegiances to Froome, but there was never any other possible outcome, because more than anything else, Brailsford loves winning and, even more than that, he loves winning the Tour de France. Wiggins was displaying signs of wavering, but

Froome was eager. In a race between Froome and Wiggins, only one of them was under starter's orders, twitching in the blocks, ready to go.

Two potential Tour de France winners butting heads was something that, unpleasant as it might be, Brailsford could control. When it came to making tough decisions for the good of his teams, Brailsford had amply demonstrated at British Cycling that he was capable of making ugly choices. Dr Steve Peters had introduced the oft-repeated and useful phrase 'controlling the controllables' into Team GB and Sky early on, but there were many things that even Dave Brailsford couldn't control, try as he might. While he could exert significant influence on the behaviour and actions of his team and riders, the wider environment and culture of cycling was not Brailsford's to corral and mould.

So, in 2012, when the revelations about Lance Armstrong finally emerged, revealing ugly details of performance-enhancing strategies, the ground shifted again and media attitudes hardened still further. Of all the years to win a Tour, the post-Armstrong ones were those in which riders were subjected to the fiercest scrutiny, a state of affairs that hasn't let up. Of all the riders to be confronted by this inquisition, Bradley Wiggins wasn't the best suited, sitting at the heart of a team that had proclaimed itself proudly clean. Controlling training and racing was one thing, but keeping an emboldened media in line was another thing altogether. The doping 'thing' wasn't going to go away, not for Sky and not for any other rider or team.

Speaking at the end of that tumultuous 2012 season, team coach Rod Ellingworth – a former British pro roadman – was open and sanguine about the topic:

> Let's be clear, one of the key things to address doping is
> that we as a team have to accept it and expect it, because

the sport has been bad; we know now what was going on. So when a team is performing so well, with so many riders, then you have to accept and expect the questions. It's not going to be comfortable and it's not going to pass overnight. I know it's going to keep hitting us and keep hitting us, so I understand riders and staff frustrations at the questions, but we've got to accept it and – unfortunately – it's an area of our sport. I'll answer the questions, but we have to keep looking forward.

Ellingworth's insight was positively clairvoyant, because the questions about doping would not 'pass overnight', and 2012 was just a foretaste of what the team would be confronted with in the seasons ahead. The 2012 season had seen glorious successes on so many fronts, but those achievements brought with them another set of what Brailsford would describe as 'challenges'. The following year, 2013, would provide plenty; between the Froome–Wiggins power struggle and the ramped-up doping accusations, Brailsford-the-leader was about to be put to the test.

At the end of 2012, however, it appeared that all was still well with the cycling world and Team Sky. Brailsford would be named in the honours list, which saw him knighted for his part in leading Team GB to unthinkable successes at the London Olympic Games and masterminding the first British team and rider to ever win the Tour de France. The new friends, the media plaudits and puff-piece profiles and the well-paid speaking invitations that arrived in the wake of this unprecedented sporting glory would turn anyone's head. On a roll since the Beijing Games, the intervening four-year period had seen Brailsford's stock rise stratospherically high – there was even talk of a move into English football management – and he was flying close to the sun, seemingly unable to do anything wrong. Appearances can be deceptive, however, and hubris lay in wait.

9

THE CARNIVAL IS OVER

'We were starting to create the right ambience in the team then, overnight, it was Boom! "See ya".'

As it transpired, 2012 was the high-water mark for Dave Brailsford, Bradley Wiggins, Team Sky and British Cycling. It had been a season of historic firsts and spectacular Olympic successes, all buoyed by a supportive media, and it saw a steep rise in the membership of British Cycling, propelled by those triumphs. The 2012 season had seen Britain take Wiggins and Team GB to its heart in an infatuated summer romance; 2013 would see an ugly break-up, with accusations of broken promises and grubby behaviour.

Given the near meltdown in 2016, when British Cycling, Shane Sutton, Team Sky, Brailsford and Wiggins were all simultaneously on the media rack, the grim irony was that British Cycling had known there were problems in Manchester with Team GB during that spectacular 2012 season. While Britain was still celebrating its London Olympic and Tour de France superstars, British Cycling chief executive Ian Drake demanded an inquiry be carried out, in part after stories of improper behaviour inside Manchester reached him. Since it was an internal inquiry, no news of its progress leaked out – and not much would be revealed when it was concluded either. The impact of the King report, as it became known, would only really be felt four years later, by which point it was much too late.

From a media perspective, the thread that connected these tangled controversies and reports would be Dave Brailsford, the man who had been at the head of both British Cycling and Team Sky in the periods under the microscope. If Brailsford had enjoyed the plaudits that came with the successes of his organisations and riders, then he would, inevitably, pay a price for their claimed misdemeanours. From the moment the media latched on to the stories that swirled around Team Sky and British Cycling, Brailsford endured a sustained media flogging which he later described, with deadpan understatement, as being 'a tough two years'.

In reality, although British Cycling, Team Sky and Wiggins had basked in near-universal adulation throughout 2012, there had been signs of trouble even before the Olympic baubles were taken down in London. The 'dodgy' Dr Leinders story, as well as Brailsford's handling of it, would dent Team Sky's image, while the examination of the connections between British Cycling and Sky added to a growing sense of unease. While the earlier 2011 Deloitte report into relations between British Cycling and Team Sky had allayed some concerns, not everyone was convinced that the relationship was entirely benign or appropriate. To better understand future troubles – TUEs, Jiffy bags and even Chris Froome's 2017 Salbutamol case – the undercurrents that attached themselves to the sport and Team Sky in 2012 merit revisiting.

As Wiggins rode towards his – and Britain's – first Tour de France win, Brailsford's insistence that he had been running a scrupulously dope-free team had come under scrutiny by the Tour de France press corps and, for some, Team Sky had not lived up to its billing.

Specifically, given Brailsford's declarations about not employing anyone – rider or staff – with connections to doping, how could one of Team Sky's doctors, Belgian Geert Leinders, have been part of this avowedly 'clean' set up? In an interview with Dutch paper *De Volkskrant* in May 2012, former Rabobank sport director Theo De Rooy had implicated Leinders in organised doping at the team, setting off a chain of events that would shake Sky's credibility.

De Rooy claimed that the Rabobank management had turned a blind eye to blood and hormone doping, and trusted Dr Leinders to both administer and monitor riders' intake of banned substances. Thus, apart from normal medical duties, Leinders also helped riders avoid testing positive while minimising the risk of riders damaging their health.

Like most big teams of the era – roughly between 1989 and 2008 – many team doctors were simultaneously implicated in doping and trapped by their duty of care, though some clearly went further than merely keeping their charges healthy and ventured into more proactive doping activity. On one hand, doctors knew that riders were likely to dope, and that, if they went to a third party, the team would have no control over their drug intake. Given a number of unexpected rider deaths from heart attacks in the early 1990s – many attributed to the misuse of EPO – having a team doctor to 'look after' riders seemed like the least worst compromise.

Leinders had been hired by Sky Procycling in autumn 2010, after the tragic death from septicaemia of team carer Txema Gonzalez, and had been part of the medical team since. Questioned during the 2012 Tour about Leinders' appointment, Brailsford insisted, 'We needed some experience. That's why we decided to go and get him. Has he been a good doctor? Brilliant. The guy really understands. It's not about doping, it's about genuine medical practice.' All of which may have been true but did absolutely nothing to help square the dope-free, zero-tolerance circle that Sky was supposed to be operating inside. It didn't really matter that Leinders was a fine doctor who understood the ailments that afflicted pro cyclists; he had also been elbow-deep in systematic doping at another team. Given Sky's ethical stance, Leinders had no place on the team, no matter how good his bedside manner was.

When Brailsford was quizzed on doping he had tried to maintain a measured tone throughout the 2012 Tour, but the more volatile Wiggins opted for a different approach. In a Tour press conference after stage eight in Porrentruy, after only one day in the yellow jersey, Wiggins reacted furiously to a question about those who doubted his performances in the light of doping revelations:

> I say they're just fucking wankers. I cannot be doing with people like that. It justifies their own bone idleness because they can't imagine applying themselves to do anything in their lives. It's easy for them to sit under a pseudonym on Twitter and write that sort of shit, rather than get off their own arses in their own lives and apply themselves and work hard at something and achieve something. And that's ultimately what counts.

'Cunts,' concluded Wiggins, as he dropped the microphone and walked out. It was clearly heartfelt, but it was also not what anyone wanted to hear, being about as far from a willingness to engage in transparent debate about doping as it was possible to get. Wiggins' stress-fuelled outburst was almost universally condemned.

The Tour, trailing the largest media entourage of any race on the calendar, easily twice the size of the Tours of Italy or Spain, is an environment where any rider's media training would be sternly tested. Managing the media, coping with the same questions and dealing with doping accusations is a wearing business. There are few other sports where, minutes after finishing a gruelling five-hour effort, the legitimacy of your performance is being fiercely challenged. But if Sky was to deal with the Leinders issue and maintain both its image and its ethical stance, it needed the media onside, and it needed Wiggins to 'play the game' and engage.

'Let's face it, no rider wants to be in the press conference in the first place. They don't want to be there,' noted David Millar, no stranger to media demands at the Tour de France.

> It takes up a lot of your time: it eats into recovery, you're stressed, you're tired and mentally fried because you've spent the whole day trying to stay at the front, not making any mistakes and then people are asking you questions that you don't want to answer because it bores the shit out of you and, when it came to Brad 'answering' for doping, it just wasn't his responsibility. And there's an element of that that people forget about. I mean, clean guys aren't interested in saying they're racing clean. Why should the clean guys have to apologise for them, for guys like Valverde and Vino? They are the guys who should be saying that they're clean.

However, a foul-mouthed rant and an unwillingness to answer doping questions was not going to help Sky or Wiggins' position.

Throughout the 2012 Tour there had been little empathy coming from the internet. Mutterings of discontent and accusations of hypocrisy over the team's 'zero tolerance to dopers' stance and employment of Dr Leinders rumbled on throughout the Olympic Games. The dissemination of disgraced, disqualified 2006 Tour de France winner Floyd Landis' 2011 interview transcripts, the publication of Tyler Hamilton's tell-all book *The Secret Race* in September 2012 and then USADA's Reasoned Decision from its US Postal inquiry a month later meant the atmosphere was sulphurous. The net result was that the media was no longer willing to give any Tour winner the benefit of the doubt, and both Wiggins and Team Sky were in the firing line.

In the autumn of 2012, Brailsford would later privately admit that he thought about quitting, such was the barrage of criticism from the media. Instead, determined to take control of the story and re-emphasise the 'Team Sky is clean' stance, Brailsford, team psychiatrist Dr Steve Peters and Fran Millar decided to interview staff and riders, asking them to sign a declaration that they had never been involved in doping and were therefore unlikely to be tainted by future accusations.

After several uncomfortable weeks Team Sky asked its eighty riders and staff to sign a 'dope-free' document. Riders and staff shuffled, literally and metaphorically, some departing the team on account of an unwillingness or inability to sign and others because of normal staff churn – the blurring of the lines was convenient for some parties. So, amid rampant speculation, among those who left in the autumn of 2012 were lead sport director Sean Yates, Froome's coach and time trial coaching specialist Bobby Julich, sport director Steven de Jongh and rider Michael Barry. And, of course, Dr Leinders. Given the circumstances of these departures, what did it say of Sky's initial bold 'team clean' position?

In fact, Sky's Leinders problem was an inevitable consequence of the 'dope-free' stance that Brailsford had espoused.

If dopers are banned and doping is taboo inside a team, how can that help promote a culture of transparency – even internally? It seemed that 'zero tolerance' merely reinforced cycling's long-established rule of keeping your head down and your mouth shut.

Even then, the 'Great Sky Purge' left many of the sport's insiders unconvinced. 'All that policy did was separate the honest guys from the dishonest ones, and they got rid of the honest people and they still have the dishonest ones, because there were still people at Sky who lied and stayed,' insisted one well-placed insider, 'and sooner or later, it'll come out and be another mess. In 2010, Sky's zero-tolerance stance was ludicrous. Maybe in another ten years, yeah, it would be possible and maybe then teams *should* pursue that policy.'

Brailsford's public statements throughout the affair seemed at odds with other reports of warnings offered to him over hiring Leinders.

> Hindsight is a brilliant thing, and what we've all learnt is pretty horrific. Had we known then what we know now about Leinders, we wouldn't have touched the guy for sure. I'll take that [Leinders] squarely on the chin. It's something I'll always regret. I made an error of judgment, quite frankly. When someone looks you in the eye and lies to you ... I'm pretty angry about it.

Having worked with Brailsford from the genesis of the team, Fran Millar had seen Brailsford's style at first hand over many hours.

> I think one of the brilliant things about Dave is that he's like, 'Come on, let's go, of course we can do it', and there's something brilliant about that attitude, but there's also

naivety in it, and a lot of people didn't believe that naivety. But Dave often won't see the bad because he's so focused on where he is going. Back then, in the beginning of the team, if I said we should interrogate something further he'd be like, 'Don't worry about that. If they've told me they've not cheated, that's it, don't worry, crack on.'

The real 'error of judgement' that Brailsford referred to might actually concern his own mistake in deciding to ignore warnings offered to him by at least two people prior to Leinders' engagement. According to a well-placed Dutch source, the general manager of the Rabobank team had phoned Brailsford when he had heard that he was considering hiring Leinders to warn him off, saying the doctor's reputation was not in any way compatible with Sky's ethical position. The advice might have been heard, but it wasn't acted on – a remarkably similar course of inaction that would haunt British Cycling in later years too.

Another former Team Sky employee had issued the same warning. 'Leinders had double red flags from me, and Michael Barry did too. I said [to Brailsford] don't take Barry, it's going to come back and bite you. I pointed these guys out. But he went ahead I think because in his opinion he thought it was going to be OK.' In light of Brailsford's apparent, claimed naivety, these statements don't sit well, but they are consistent with Brailsford's swashbuckling management approach. 'Basically I think he thought he would get away with it, that it wouldn't be an issue and it would never come up.'

The hoped-for PR outcome of the Great Sky Purge of October 2012 might have been damage containment, a line drawn and a brutal restatement of Brailsford's 'Team Sky is clean' position, but the impact on the reputations of those who left was heavy. At a time when cycling was trying to make peace with itself, the Sky Purge and its 'no dopers' position hadn't put out the flames in the post-Armstrong landscape so much as kept the bonfire crackling.

Clearly those who left the team paid the biggest penalty, but morale inside the bus, among those who still had jobs, also took a hit. 'It was sad, the whole thing,' said one team member.

> We had struggled badly in 2010, we had improved a lot in 2011, people had worked hard and we felt we were really getting somewhere and then – 2012 – those guys had to leave, and it didn't seem right. I don't believe that any of them were 'bad'. None of them thought, 'OK, if these new ideas don't work, we'll just go back to Plan B, the medical model. Some of them were really, really good at their jobs, and we put them out the door. We were starting to create the right ambience in the team and then, overnight, it was like, Boom! 'See ya'.

In Sky's first two seasons, Brailsford had discovered that the world of pro road cycling was much more complex and cut-throat than track cycling, and that the level of media scrutiny focused on a team with aspirations to win the Tour de France was forensic. The tangled Leinders story, the manner in which it was handled and the shake-up of team staff also, inevitably, changed people's perception of the team. Could it really be trusted with its declarations? Was Team Sky, in the end, just like all the rest?

And all the while, as the Team Sky headlines tarnished reputations throughout 2012, that other, lower-key report was being compiled at British Cycling by Peter King. The truth is that CEO Ian Drake's motivation for launching the inquiry was two-fold. On one hand the chief executive wanted to ensure that the successes in Beijing and London were maintained, but he also wanted to get to the bottom of stories that some management behaviour, including that of Shane Sutton and Dave Brailsford, was 'out of order', and that staff and riders were unhappy. Drake asked former chief executive King to carry out interviews, compile a report into the allegations and write a 'state of the federation' overview. Were these problems a transient manifestation of the successes of British Cycling – people 'drunk' on accolades and hype – or were these accusations more deeply embedded in the culture?

With over a decade in post, former British Cycling chief executive King had stepped down at the end of 2008, but subsequently worked on the development of cycling facilities after the London Games. With his long experience as well as ongoing connections with British Cycling, King was well-placed to garner information. He was a still-familiar face, yet one who had some independence. King says that

> After I left as chief executive, I had been to attend Board meetings, but I had no real feeling for the 'vibe' at the velodrome, which is, I think, one of the reasons why Ian [Drake] asked me to carry out the report. There was a degree of unease that had set in by that point, despite the success of London. There seemed to be a lot of uncertainty about how things were going and how we had got to that point.

King spent autumn 2012 talking to concerned parties in order to produce a document that would become known – four years later – as the King report. King had spent enough time in the sport to realise that rivalries, cliques and accusations of favouritism would be part of what he would hear. But more than that, 'I'd say I was hearing things that I wouldn't have heard before, prior to 2012. It seemed there was unease where I didn't think there had been unease before.' A summary of anecdotes and comments about where the organisation was, as opposed to where it *could* have been – or should have been – the report turned out, in King's phrase, 'to be a forerunner of everything that has happened since then'. Having said that, King adds, 'I never got the feeling when I was there that there were lots of things wrong. People did say things to me in 2012, but then there are always going to be rumbles of discontent, and Team GB has always been held up as a "no compromise" institution which, perhaps, gives some people licence to "push the boundaries".'

King is reluctant to claim that things would have been different if only the Board had listened to and implemented all the report's recommendations. He chafes too at what he sees as an exaggeration of the problems by the media ('it's like there was a quiet news time in other sports'); yet still, as far as he is concerned, the chance to nip certain issues in the bud was clearly there, back in 2012.

King's report would be delivered to chief executive Drake in November, and King returned to his accountancy practice in Surrey. As far as King was concerned, the recommendations would be followed up and British Cycling could look forward to more success. Curiously, there was no significant discussion in the report concerning bullying or sexism, although, in one line, 'Several referred to a culture of fear, intimidation and bullying.' Clearly it was an issue, though not deemed to be serious enough to merit a specific recommendation in the conclusion.

According to a Board member involved, discussions of the report's findings mainly centred on moving Shane Sutton away from working directly with riders, and that Brailsford's position should be reviewed and the possibility of him being moved on should not be ruled out. Brailsford's absences and his focus on the Sky Procycling project were seen as a major problem, leaving a void where leadership at the top should have been – and had been – up to 2008.

> Some riders and staff just didn't like the way that Shane was talking to them and behaving. The report was condensed into about seven bullet points to help make sure that the success after London was carried on, that there was continuity. So Shane was to be taken away from coaching riders face-to-face to be more of a coach of the coaches, while Brailsford and Steve Peters were meant to stay on in Manchester till 2016.

None of this happened and, in particular, widespread concerns that Brailsford was no longer as committed to British Cycling now that Team Sky was taking up his attention were played down.

The then British Cycling president Brian Cookson agrees that this captures the thrust of what King's report contained.

> That was the outcome of the discussions at Board level and, as far as I knew, that was what was going to happen, because when the report was delivered I was distracted by my bid to become UCI president at the start of 2013. I would meet Dave [Brailsford] in the corridor in Manchester and ask him how things were, and he'd tell me everything was great, no worries.

When contemplating the inaction in Manchester following the King report, the wider context is worth considering. Recall, at the end of 2012, that British cycle sport was on the crest of the highest wave it had ever ridden. Apart from the Team GB performances at the London Olympics, there was also the Wiggins and Team Sky season that had seen triumphs in the

Tour de France, Paris–Nice, the Tour de Romandie and the Critérium du Dauphiné. Additionally, Sky had been voted team of
the year by the British public, while Dave Brailsford had been
named coach of the year, and Wiggins was a runaway winner
of the BBC's sports personality of the year. To have gone loudly
public with a report that pointed out that the edifice was built
on dysfunctional coaches housed in a building with a sexist,
bullying culture would have been seen as an act of bizarre self-
harming. Instead, it was condensed into a few action points
that, in the end, were simply not acted on.

Peter King's report never escaped British Cycling into the
wider world in 2012, because it was never intended to. While
the report's author and president both, quite credibly, say that
they were less involved in the day-to-day activities in Manchester in 2013, it needs to be pointed out that both were still on the
Board, and still attended Board meetings after King's report
and its troublesome findings were reviewed. Nobody at Board
level can recall either King or Cookson asking what action had
been taken subsequent to the report being given to chief executive Drake. If the report was shuffled to the bottom of the pile,
the Board has to shoulder responsibility.

Four years later, with the benefit of hindsight, British
Cycling's harshest critics would insist that the report was
actively 'covered up'. For others, the inaction following its
release smacks more of a combination of expediency and
embarrassment, all trussed up in weak management. Less
than a year after massive successes, with three years till the next
Games, who had the stomach for a messy blood-letting inside
British Cycling?

However, if King's inconvenient report was 'buried' in
2013, then Brailsford, the head of performance at British
Cycling, would still have his hands full as boss at Team Sky.
Inside his World Tour team a power struggle was brewing,

as popular superstar Wiggins and the increasingly ambitious Chris Froome fought a proxy war that would ultimately see Wiggins leave the team and Froome assume the leadership role. If Brailsford and the Board of British Cycling had managed to paper over the cracks appearing in Manchester, the public falling out of Wiggins and Froome in 2013 would be impossible for Brailsford to finesse.

The problem was unavoidable, because, at Sky, the strategy had always been clear – there is one leader, and the rest of the team rides for him. Would national superstar 'Wiggo' really ride for 'Froomey' as he had told journalist Brendan Gallagher in the 2012 Tour? Was Wiggins' comment, 'Chris will have his day for sure and I will be there to support him', more about peacemaking than future pace making? Had Froome really been 'promised' team leadership after he sacrificed his 2012 chances and helped pilot Wiggins to glory? There was a long and inglorious history between the pair, and the 2012 Tour had essentially been 'business as usual' between them.

Froome and Wiggins had managed to maintain public respect for each other through 2012, though this was a thin veneer, given their history. The friction between them dated back to the 2011 Vuelta, when Froome felt that the team had danced to Wiggins' tune rather than supporting him, and it still rankled. Recounting incidents in his autobiography, The Climb, written with journalist David Walsh, it was clear the rift opened between them back then was never going to heal.

It was during the 2011 Tour of Spain when Froome, riding for a contract with Sky – or indeed anyone – emerged as a credible Grand Tour contender, much to the surprise of the team. Just how profound the events of that year's Vuelta were went unremarked on at the time, but they shifted the team's balance of power, undermining the fragile Wiggins' confidence.

Remarkably, even as it had developed, the 2011 Vuelta

didn't have the impact on Team Sky most would have expected. For a team that had failed to make any impact in Grand Tours, you would assume that finishing with two riders on the final podium and leading the race would have been a positive event, a sign of real progress. In 2011, however, Froome's performance caused almost as much consternation as it did celebration.

'The atmosphere was terrible,' said one Sky staffer. 'People would leave the bus early to escape from Dave [Brailsford] because he was in a bad mood. You would have thought everyone would be upbeat and determined, the way the race was going, but it wasn't like that at all.' The strain of accommodating both Wiggins and Froome was already evident.

Entertainingly, in light of the accusations of doping that stuck to Froome following his transformation from climbing domestique to Grand Tour challenger, it seems Brailsford was just as bemused and suspicious of Froome's newfound talent as the doping conspiracy zealots. As one team member recalled:

I remember when Dave arrived he asked Tim [Kerrison] to show him Froome's data, to try to make sense of it. I'd say that Tim was pretty supportive of Chris and he pulled up Chris' numbers from the Tour of Denmark, where Chris had ridden really well on a tough stage; it was just that he had never been consistent. Tim seemed to get on quite well with Chris. They seemed more compatible than Tim and Brad when it came to training.

Sitting in Brailsford's seat, it was normal that he would at least be concerned about this 'new' Froome he was confronted with, given Froome's previous career at Barloworld offered little insurance that the Anglo-Kenyan's background was squeaky clean. When Froome had ridden his first Tour de France with Barloworld in 2008 his teammate Moises Duenas had tested positive for EPO and been arrested after police raided his hotel room and found 'a private pharmacy'. Brailsford needed to ask the hard questions. Add to that the fact that Brailsford had already told Froome earlier in the summer that he needed a new team for 2012 and suddenly, when Froome is looking for a job, he starts to perform like never before? The pressure Froome faced would tempt the most saintly of riders to stray into 'the dark side' to see what potions he could find to help ensure his future employment in the World Tour.

Nevertheless, Kerrison was able to produce data for Froome from the Tour of Switzerland earlier that year that showed he was indeed capable of performing in the high mountains. If Brailsford was suspicious, Kerrison soothed his fears and suggested that Froome really did have untapped potential.

In the end, Froome lost the Vuelta but won a new three-year, €2 million contract, a long way from the €80,000 he had started the year on, while the fraught internal politics at the Vuelta offered a preview of what the team would face in subsequent seasons. In terms of the psychological impact on Froome, his confidence in the team as well as his relationship with Wiggins, the 2011 Vuelta remains a significant event.

The story of how Froome saved his job at Sky with his Vuelta performance not only reveals the origins of complicated intra-team relations between Froome, Wiggins and Brailsford, but is a perfect illustration of how a big budget gives so much power to a team like Sky.

Towards the end of the 2011 Tour de France, Froome's then agent Alex Carrera was touting Froome around, since he no longer had a place at Sky. Essentially, most riders are hired between the Giro d'Italia and the Tour. Budgets are spent and rosters are filled during the summer – and Froome, who hadn't even made the Sky Tour team in 2011 – was facing unemployment. After two seasons at Sky, Froome's results were modest and his profile subterranean, which meant that Carrera didn't have much to sell on.

However, among those listening to Carrera's sales pitch at the 2011 Tour de France was Garmin team boss Jonathan Vaughters.

I remember talking to Alex and he said, 'Oh I've got this guy Chris Froome, would you be interested in taking him at Garmin? He doesn't have a job next year.' I said, 'OK, yeah, I think we might be able to do this.' Bjarne Riis [Tinkoff manager] and I were both in the mix for his contract, and I thought that there was something about this Froome guy, though I wasn't sure what, and we started to discuss a contract. We were then supposed to meet up on the first rest day at the Vuelta to negotiate and Chris, during that period, went from Dave [Brailsford] not being interested at all to offering him a £2 million contract. Well, when Dave let Chris go in July, part of his reasoning was, 'I've filled my team slots, I've spent all my budget and I can't afford anyone more', and suddenly he comes up with two million to pay for Froome?!

Froome, the rider rejected then re-signed, playing second fiddle to an inferior Wiggins in the 2011 Vuelta, playing a support role in 2012 and then 'promised' support in the 2013 Tour wouldn't be fooled again. Not by Wiggins or Brailsford.

During a January 2013 media day in Alcúdia it was revealed that the plan was for Wiggins to target the Giro before helping Froome during the Tour. Wiggins' word, combined with vague assurances from Brailsford, were, it seemed, good enough. However, the entente, as cordial as it appeared in public, came apart in May, and Froome's mental toughness was put to the test once again, though this time he wasn't backing down. For Brailsford, who wants to win the Tour de France more than he wants to be on anyone's Christmas card list, managing this issue would provide another stern test of his resolve and his comfort with others' discomfort. With the team's image and morale suffering in the wake of the Leinders scandal, an internecine war was far from ideal, because Froome wasn't as mild-mannered as he appeared to outsiders.

Froome seemed so polite in his public appearances, yet those closer to him knew there was a different side. As former Sky press officer Rob Jorgensen says,

> Chris is as mentally tough as they come ... I've worked with a lot of sportsmen over the years and he is right at the very top of everyone I have ever worked with – and I'm talking about hardened boxers, footballers, rugby players, all those people who are in the limelight, and I think in terms of mental toughness, Chris outweighs anyone else. But he doesn't come across like that.

Another member of Team Sky's management team was less circumspect in his assessment of Froome: 'He's a bastard. Cold and ruthless.' The description was delivered with a hint of admiration, an appreciation of someone who has managed to hide a diamond-hard strength of will behind a media persona that is a near caricature of the polite public schoolboy.

It's all very well having a freakish physiology, being coach-able, living like a monk and being a leader of men if, in the end, you can't cope with the psychological pressures that bear down on your fat-free shoulders. When push came to shove, given Froome and Wiggins were well-matched when it came to 'the numbers', if there was a competition to see who could cope better with the psychological demands of the Tour, then Froome was streets ahead of Wiggins – and the team knew it.

Such were the long-simmering psychological and financial

issues underpinning events of 2013. So when Wiggins let slip that he fancied having a go at the 'Giro-Tour' double, Froome demanded clarification, and the starter's pistol was fired on the great 'Who will lead Sky at the Tour?' story. The speculation lasted till Wiggins quit the Giro, complaining of a chest infection, then knee problems and, whatever the truth, the game was up. Wiggins, the defending Tour champion, the BBC sports personality of the year, the mod rogue and tabloid favourite, would not be in the Team Sky line-up in the 2013 Tour. Wiggins' days as the leader at Britain's World Tour team were over.

The furore over Wiggins' absence bubbled away until Froome looked like he was going to win the Tour, at which point Wiggins' non-selection became a non-story. Brailsford was pilloried on social media for 'daring' to sideline national treasure Wiggins in preference to Froome, but in making an unpopular decision Brailsford again revealed that he could make tough calls and accept the consequences. Social media could howl all it wanted, it wouldn't shake Brailsford – not now and not in the future either.

With Wiggins on the way out – of Grand Tour team leadership if not quite yet from Team Sky – Brailsford had found a readymade replacement for Wiggins in the slim frame of the depthlessly ambitious Froome. Happily too for Brailsford, Froome got on well with his fellow Monaco resident and key teammate Richie Porte and, better yet, was far closer in temperament and approach with his coach Tim Kerrison, Sky's increasingly influential head of performance.

Wiggins needed a lot more 'hand holding' than Froome, and the man doing the hand holding, so to speak, was Shane Sutton. The self-reliant Froome didn't need so much cosseting compared to Wiggins, having grown up, in cycling terms, with a Kenyan federation that was bereft of funds or organisation.

With that upbringing, Froome was accustomed to doing things for himself, developing a mental toughness that is masked by his spooky politeness.

It was just as well that Froome had inner fortitude, because, on his way to winning the 2013 Tour de France, he faced even more sustained accusations about doping than his soon-to-be ex-teammate did. Baited by Wiggins supporters, harangued by roadside fans and endlessly quizzed, in July 2013 there were times when Froome struggled to cope, recording a video diary that revealed an initially bewildered and then increasingly angry rider, tiring of the daily, repetitive doping questions fired at him.

Team press officer Jorgensen revealed that even Froome's calm came close to cracking:

> I remember at one point, he had been asked the same doping questions over and over and over, and he turned to me and said, 'Look, can't we just say we'll answer three doping questions and that's it?' and I told him he was better than that. You don't need to do that, you can handle this. We knew they were coming, and the best thing to do was to answer them.

With Froome in the ascendancy and the team falling in behind the 'new guy' who had demonstrated that he was well capable of winning Grand Tours, Wiggins announced his departure from Team Sky in 2014, confirming rumours that had been growing since his non-selection for the 2013 Tour. Instead, there was talk of a race programme designed to help Wiggins' possible selection for the 2016 Rio Olympic Games team pursuit squad. Wiggo was on his way out the door. It wasn't a massive shock. At a charity event in June 2013, Wiggins had more or less said that his days of being a GC leader were over. 'For me it was always about winning the Tour,' he said. 'I've done that. If I'm honest I don't think I'm prepared to make those sacrifices again that I made last year, with my family and so on,' he told the *Independent*.

Without coming straight out and saying it, Wiggins was now searching for new targets to further cement his position in the pantheon of all-time British cycling greats.

Sean Yates was, famously, the Team Sky sport director throughout that stunning 2012 season, and he still has a high regard for Wiggins, who has a similar affection for the 'old school' character of Yates. 'I think Brad was a supreme athlete and he achieved his various goals by being dedicated but,' he pauses, searching for the best phrase,

> it wasn't sustainable, in terms of the diet and the lifestyle and training camps. He did it, he won the Tour because he loved the sport and he wanted to achieve certain goals, but then he didn't think, 'OK, if I do it all again, I'll win another Tour, get another million in the bank.' I think he was motivated by ticking different boxes, not by enduring the same things year in, year out.

Yates, who had worked as directeur sportif with Lance Armstrong and Alberto Contador in his career, was in a good position to reflect on the demands of modern cycling.

> I think some people relish the challenge of training to make themselves better, year on year, to push themselves harder and harder at altitude camps, whereas Bradley was like, 'Fuck that, I'm not doing all that again', even if it meant him earning another five million. Froome, on the other hand, is a person who knew he was capable of winning the Tour, and after he had won it once, it was like

a means of making loads of money, doing something that he really liked and that he was well capable of.

After Froome won the 2013 Tour, it was clear to everyone that there was no longer a place, in any sense, for Wiggins in any future Sky Tour squad. There was never the slightest chance of Wiggins riding the Tour with Froome, so in 2014 Wiggins' greatest road racing triumph was the general classification of the Tour of California, prior to heading to Spain for the world time trial championship. On an undulating course in Ponferrada, Wiggins demonstrated that he was far from finished, with a stunning ride to win his first world time trial title. 'It was,' Wiggins would later reflect, 'one of my best executions of a time trial in my career.' Another world-class box was ticked, another line for an already impressive list of race wins. And a sign too that his final goal of a team pursuit gold in Rio – his fifth Olympic gold – was a real possibility.

With his Sky contract up, it was time to concoct a dignified exit strategy, both from the team and from his road racing career. Wiggins decided to quit the team, form 'Team Wiggins' and focus on new goals in the shape of Paris–Roubaix, the Hour Record and, to wrap it up, the Rio Olympic team pursuit. That would be enough to keep him busy as he headed for retirement.

Coincidentally, as Wiggins had been contemplating his return to his alma mater in Manchester Velodrome, Sir Dave Brailsford was plotting his own departure from the same building. The signs had been there when he hadn't travelled to the world track championships in Cali, Colombia in February 2014, and, after ten years in the job, he decided his time was up. With Team Sky soaking up his energy and plans to develop the team further, Brailsford finally had to accept that he couldn't go on leading both organisations. On 10 April 2014, Brailsford resigned, and left an organisation he had helped turn into Britain's most successful ever sports team. With little fanfare, Brailsford was gone. His resignation statement was anodyne, considering the impact he had had over the previous decade. 'That side of things [Sky] has got bigger, more global and certainly doesn't leave me a lot of time. The thing I am concerned about is to make sure the British cycling team is in the best possible shape it could be heading into Rio and that I feel that I'm contributing fully to make sure that happens.'

Simultaneously, lost in the small print and overshadowed by Brailsford's announcement, was news that much-lauded Team GB psychiatrist Dr Steve Peters was also leaving British Cycling, following Brailsford to Team Sky. The departure of these two characters – with their insights, experience and influence – would have a significant impact on Manchester's squads and atmosphere, even if backroom worker Peters' departure was not much remarked on at the time. That same month, Shane Sutton was promoted to the post of performance director, effectively taking over from his former boss.

With British Cycling now part of his past, Brailsford could work on the big issue facing him at Team Sky – how could he keep improving the team and its results? If British Cycling and its four-yearly Olympic cycles offered breathing room and time for reflection, the week-in, week-out helter-skelter of professional road racing was relentless, offering no time for respite.

The stressful handling of Froome – his retention, his battles with Wiggins, the need to ensure continuity – as well as win a Classic or another Grand Tour – meant Brailsford had plenty to work on.

In any case, British Cycling would still have the talent of Bradley Wiggins to wonder at. Wiggins might have decided that the lifestyle of general classification rider was no longer one he would submit to, but he had hatched ambitious plans for a rider who *really* wanted to make his mark as a cycling legend.

Wiggins decided on a final serious attempt at Paris–Roubaix, the throwback, more than any monumental Classic on the calendar, to another heroic era of cycling. Many Classic roads have changed, but a few of the cobbled sections of Paris–Roubaix were fundamentally the same as those bounced over by Fausto Coppi, Roger De Vlaeminck, Bernard Hinault and other bona-fide cycling legends. The filth and grit of Roubaix represented a direct link to cycling's motherlode, and Wiggins wanted to be part of that lineage. This was, after all, Bradley Wiggins, whose father had raced on the European Six-Day circuit; Wiggins, who had actually been born in Ghent, and who, according to his teammate Michael Barry, had carried a square of one of Tommy Simpson's woollen undervests in his back pocket throughout the 2010 Tour.

Wiggins, however, had more than an eye on Roubaix, because the line Wiggins traced through 'the Hell of the North' went further than the cobbles of Arenberg. Wiggins' route went all the way to the Rio Olympic velodrome, a *parcours* from Europe's roughest cobbles to the smoothest Siberian Pine boards in Brazil. In between, as a useful detour, he would also attempt the World Hour record at Lee Valley velodrome in London, a location that guaranteed raucous home support. Froome was welcome to the Tour de France and its demands and diets; Wiggins was charting another course, adding new lines to his palmares. The Tour? Wiggins had that T-shirt.

That winter Wiggins discussed his ideas with Brailsford and new British Cycling performance director Sutton, who knew what Wiggins was capable of and was keen to make him at home back in Manchester, no matter what. So the Australian contacted coach Heiko Salzwedel, who was working for the Swiss Cycling Federation at the time.

Quite frankly the reason I came to British Cycling was Shane Sutton. He persuaded me to come back. I mean, he gave me a blank piece of paper and said, 'Here Heiko, you can do whatever you want, as long as you provide me with that gold medal in Rio,' but his trump card was Bradley Wiggins. That was a very important thing for me when I made my decision to come back.

Salzwedel, the coach who had been consumed by cycling since attending cycling school in Cottbus as a 15-year-old, knew Wiggins was capable of winning in Rio. How would Salzwedel *not* be tempted by Sutton's offer?

It was clear that Bradley had potential; it was obvious to me in 2001. He went the extra mile; he did whatever it took. You talk about passion or obsession. Well, if these words fit anyone, they fit Bradley Wiggins. Actually, that line between craziness and greatness is very thin. When Bradley commits to a plan then he does it absolutely, with no regards to anything else. If he does something, he does it with every fibre, with everything he has.

Salzwedel, who had seen Wiggins develop at British Cycling from his early senior appearances and watched him perform at World Championships and Olympic Games, knew what he was looking at. 'He was the greatest athlete I ever worked with.'

Unknown to Wiggins, training in the same Manchester Velodrome, there was another rider not prepared to go quietly into that good night of retirement, though her departure from Team Great Britain would have far more serious repercussions than Wiggins quitting Team Sky. Track sprinter Jess Varnish was a name more familiar to fans of track sprinting, and she had no Olympic medals of any colour, but she was about to make big headlines. As Wiggins returned to an organisation whose underlying problems highlighted by the 2012 King report still festered, the departures of Brailsford and Dr Peters, combined with Sutton's promotion and Varnish's discontent, would prove to be a highly combustible mix.

10

EVERYTHING FALLS APART

'It comes down to one simple thing. How bad do you want it?'

Women's track sprinter Jess Varnish was not the most-decorated rider at British Cycling and neither did she have the highest media profile, yet throughout 2016, her name and accusations would dominate British sports headlines. The 25-year-old failed to qualify for the Rio Olympics with her performances at the March 2016 World track championships in London and, together with her team mate Katy Marchant, spoke her mind to a BBC reporter. Varnish's subsequent criticism of BC provoked a combination of soul-searching and witch-hunt that would have an impact beyond cycling to touch on other UK State-funded sports.

In the following two turbulent years, BC, British cyclists and fans were forced to confront the realities of what it took to win the biggest bike races – lots of money, natural talent, determination bordering on mania, psychological toughness and a willingness to walk a narrow ethical line.

Simultaneously the public would also be forced to examine,

as never before, the underside of women's elite cycling within Team GB. Magazine articles and 'tell-all' ghosted autobiographies had previously touched on sexism, but there was no way to avoid newspaper headlines or television and radio features.

Following Varnish's interviews, comments by other riders and Sutton's subsequent departure on 26 April 2016, BC launched an inquiry. Former head of performance Sutton faced nine accusations of bullying, discrimination and sexism which were investigated by an independent quintet commissioned jointly by UK Sport and BC. The group comprised rugby coach Stuart Lancaster, hockey Olympian Anne Panter and barrister John Mehrzad, chaired by Annamarie Phelps of British rowing. Theatre director Jude Kelly joined only for the final deliberation, and all had been selected under the aegis of UK Sport. Between May and November 2016, the panel heard evidence from Sutton and others. Early on, Phelps said, "I would encourage anyone still considering making a submission to do so, in complete confidence, to Sport Resolutions UK." With two women and two men on the UK Sport-assembled panel as well as anonymity to anyone who came forward, the group was seen as credible. Unlike the internal report carried out by Peter King four years previously, this process and its findings were played out in front of a curious and critical audience.

The Phelps team interviewed 44 witnesses, 108 written contributions were received and "11 files of other documentation were considered." A staggered, two-stage mailshot was sent to current and former employees using the BC database asking for evidence, and the story was big news in the run-up to the Rio Olympics. It's hard to imagine that anyone with evidence or something to say would have been unaware of the process.

When a summary of the report was leaked in December 2016, it revealed only one of the nine complaints had been upheld – that Sutton had used the word "bitches" – and that complaint hadn't actually come from Varnish, but rather another rider. The other eight allegations against Sutton were not proven and social media commentators and several journalists insisted there had been a whitewash.

After a process of Maxwellisation – whereby those involved are permitted to challenge and object to accusations made in a public inquiry before its publication – BC released the full 'Report of the Independent review panel into the climate and culture of the World Class programme in British Cycling' on 10 April 2017. The review had actually investigated a wide range of issues – from nepotism, theft, misuse of funds, governance, bullying – examining the 'culture' at British Cycling between 2012 and 2016. Its headline finding was that the "World Class Programme in British Cycling continued to be a resounding success." On the downside, point two of the Review's 'Key findings' was that "Good governance was lacking at British Cycling board level in relation to how it managed the culture and behaviours within the World class programme."

Overall, the 70-page report was far from the apocalyptic wrecking ball that many had expected, though Sutton was criticised by "numerous contributors" who said that "he did not possess the necessary skill-set to lead the World Class Performance Programme." There were criticisms concerning the 'culture of fear' which were made by "many staff members" while some athletes complained of "a lack of encouragement or support...beyond pure performance."

Reading between the lines it was clear the track cycling bias that had been inherent in Peter Keen's original 1998 blueprint was still generating discontent, with mountain bike, BMX and para-cyclists all registering their unhappiness at the regime. They were "second class citizens" and it had been ever thus, albeit that many of the more caustic quotes throughout the report had come from a relatively small number of people.

On the other hand, the report noted "despite repeated requests, there were no contributions from recent members of the endurance programme (both male and female) or the male road programme." In light of the atmosphere wrapped around the issues, this isn't a surprise. Perhaps the squad riders – like Ed Clancy, Stephen Burke, Owain Doull, Elinor Barker, Jo Rowsell – were whipped into towing the party line or possibly things weren't as bad as the newspaper headlines stated. The other explanation was that being focused in their preparations for the Rio Olympics, they simply ignored Phelps' requests. Whatever the reasons, their lack of contributions didn't help in convincing anyone of the credibility of the report.

After the Phelps Report was published, those still in post at British Cycling preferred to keep their heads down, refusing to get embroiled in a story if at all possible. Nevertheless, some more supportive Sutton stories emerged from BC insiders, a counter-balance to the monstrous image that had dominated the headlines. Thus, speaking of the Beijing Games, it transpired that Sutton had saved some high profile riders from a lot of embarrassment in China. "He helped one get a medal back that was left in a 'nightclub'– it was a brothel. A rider had come to Shane in tears, saying their relationship with their partner was finished if she found out where the medal was lost, so Shane went to the 'club' and recovered it. In some cases there were serious privacy matters that prevented Sutton or anyone else from going public, so none of that stuff came out," recalled one person present. Indeed, none of that 'came out' and Sutton's popular media image was fixed as an irredeemable and unreconstructed 'sexist bully,' while BC was hammered for its relationship with women riders.

If all accepted that Sutton had been a divisive and abrasive character, what was also almost unanimous was the sense that he had been harshly treated by riders who he had helped enormously. However, the court of public opinion and social media echo chambers hear few appeals and care little for nuance or detail.

While talented road rider and Olympic time trial medal winner Emma Pooley and former pursuiter Wendy Houvenaghel shared stories alleging bad behaviour on Sutton's part, the current crop of riders had less to say. In fact, what some of the women's Olympic squad had discussed – internally – was that they had been so angered by Varnish's comments that a boycott of the Olympics was mooted if Varnish was brought back in. This was another story line that never made it into the public debate while Sutton and BC were facing their fiercest criticism.

The complex and shifting nature of the relationships between rider and coach can surely never be better illustrated than by an examination of the one which existed between sprinter Victoria Pendleton and Sutton. British Cycling had enjoyed tremendous success through Pendleton, winner, amongst other things, of Olympic gold medals in Beijing and London as well as being six-time world sprint champion.

Pendleton was the happy recipient of the epithet of 'Queen Vic' but between 2005 and 2008 stories of Pendleton's 'difficulty' and 'fragility' sometimes emerged in media dispatches, though they were rarely too deeply delved into. Pendleton was a world class sprinter, but clearly needed delicate handling, which, in the light of her future allegations about Sutton, makes it remarkable that the pair worked so long and so closely together. It was acknowledged that Pendleton was subject to profound crises of confidence which Dr Steve Peters was instrumental in helping her deal with.

Sutton was also closely involved in helping Pendleton cope with the stresses and strains of sprinting and the two appeared to work well together – Pendleton invited Sutton to be her 'plus-one' guest in the Royal Box at the Wimbledon tennis tournament in July 2008, a few months before the Beijing Games. At the time Pendleton said she had invited Sutton "because he had done so much for me, on and off the track in the past three years." The line "all he had done for me" may well have been a reference to an episode that was not much reported at the time.

When Pendleton added her voice to criticism of Sutton, it was to the bemusement of many at BC. "I think he (Sutton) was pretty hurt by the way some athletes he had helped reacted," said one insider. "He was a man who gave up his weekends to decorate Victoria Pendleton's flat, doing papering and painting. Victoria had bought a flat with her boyfriend and they were doing it up, but they split up and the place was a mess and she was taking it badly. This was in the run-up to Beijing, so Shane went over and worked on the place for three weeks." Four years after her triumphant retirement at London 2012, following the Varnish accusations, Pendleton would join in the accusatory chorus demanding Sutton's head.

What was even less well understood was that Pendleton had also been tough with the young women sprinters coming up in her slipstream and pushed them very hard indeed, with Becky James bearing the brunt of Pendleton's attitude.

Given the highly pressurised environment in Manchester and, in particular, among the track sprinters where mind games and self-confidence are so important, it's not a surprise that tensions run high as riders of both genders try to establish a hierarchy that is as much psychological as physical. But when do mind games and legitimate psychological one-upmanship tip into group-think and bullying?

"When it came to bullying, I think a lot of them were unhappy because Jess had been the one doing the bullying and Rio double track sprint silver medallist Becky James had been on the receiving end," said one person closely involved.

"I saw Becky James leave a training session in tears because of the stuff that was going on between her and Jess," said one staff member speaking off the record. "I saw her going into Shane's office in tears. When the Jess story broke Becky was preparing for the Games and kept her head down and, afterwards, she wasn't sure if she was going to carry on till Tokyo or not so again she decided to stay out of it." Sure enough, Becky James announced her retirement from cycling in August 2017.

All of which, in the end, is simply background and context. That Pendleton bullied anyone or that Varnish was as good at dishing it out as much as she was a victim of bullying is, ultimately, beside the point. Rather, what these examples highlight is that bullying was 'allowed' to go on inside British Cycling *at all*. The real issue was that although bullying was recognised as taking place, nobody in senior management thought to tackle it. Or, if they did, they didn't deem it a major problem, seeing it as simply part and parcel of life and of elite sport.

What should be recognised is that if there's a grey area in sports medicine, then there's an equally opaque zone in 'motivation' and managing 'rider rivalry' too, where psychological manipulation crosses an ill-defined line and becomes personal abuse. The skill of a coach is not just in balancing physical training loads, but in rider's mental stresses too and there is no exact science to measuring either, no matter how much data you gather. The stakes in professional sports are high – livelihoods, reputations, medals, contracts, sponsorship, endorsements – so it shouldn't be a surprise when lines are crossed. What is more surprising is that there seems to have been so little concern about this behaviour, regardless of who it came from, whether rider or staff member.

The point here is not to deny or downplay the fact that a number of women riders had a hard time with the regime and characters inside British Cycling. Rather these anecdotes attempt to illustrate that their relationships with the parent body were invariably more complex than presented. At the time, British Cycling's reluctance to defend itself and its staff more stridently was widely perceived as a tacit admission of guilt. However, as any public relations expert would explain, when a powerful company seeks to beat down critical voices – especially female ones – the outcome is rarely beneficial to the organisation.

While much of the brickbats aimed at British Cycling were track-focused, the formation of the Team Bikehut-Halfords squad was mostly overlooked. It turns out that Halfords was keen to boost its bicycle departments, nestled among its car accessories. Halfords had approached British Cycling and Brailsford had persuaded it to put £250,000 into a women's squad which would feature a number of women who would go on to fine careers. They included Olympians Nicole Cooke, Jo Rowsell, Lizzie Armitstead, Wendy Houvenaghel and Sharon Laws. Additionally Emma Trott and Katie Colclough in the line up. Given this was back in January 2008 and women's cycling was even lower profile than it is now, Halfords management was initially reluctant and only agreed after two male riders – Rob Hayles and Tom Southam – were drafted on to the team to satisfy Halford's requirements for promotional materials featuring 'men on bikes' too. In the end, four of the women in the 2008 Halfords team would go on to win Olympic medals, while several others went on to pro teams. Colclough rode with HTC and Lulumon, Laws too enjoyed a long pro career while Trott ended her road career with the top ranked Boels-Dolmans team in 2014. Bikehut-Halfords may have looked like a token effort to some, but it had an impact on the careers of a number of women.

Sponsorship and resource issues aside, there should be no doubt that Sutton was a divisive presence and some riders

– mainly women – simply didn't appreciate Sutton's language or coaching style. Thus, anecdotes like this from a female Olympian: "There were times when if I heard an Australian accent coming towards me in a velodrome corridor, I'd would turn around and go the other way. And I know that I wasn't the only one who did that." Sutton might have meant well in that he wanted his riders to push themselves and perform, but his method of achieving that clearly did not suit all.

Paul Manning, the women's team pursuit coach had worked with Sutton for years and was well aware of his foibles. "Well, of course you had to deal with challenging stuff with Shane, but I think his default position was to try to help and improve, I don't think he was negative or dismissive, basically he was always seeing something to improve it was just...how it was communicated or how you were feeling when he said it. Inherently though there was a point in what he had said that you could take away and think about."

Such was the level of toxicity that attached to Sutton's name, few big squad riders were prepared to support him publicly. Over a year later, Chris Hoy offered his analysis of the Sutton character. "The number of times I've watched and listened to Shane and just thought, 'What are you doing? Are you crazy? I'd just be left there, shaking my head in disbelief but," Hoy pauses, "there was just something about him, an almost childlike enthusiasm, he's so willing to engage emotionally and those emotions are always raw, unfiltered. I think that's what really hurt him the most when the accusations about sexism came out. The thing with Shane was, he didn't care who you were, male or female, as long as you were working hard and doing your best to win medals for the team then he would back you."

In spite of his resignation in April 2016 Sutton's years of work – as well as the work of his coaches, the support staff he employed and the riders he had selected – would be on show at the Rio Games, whether the roguish Aussie who hadn't a politically correct molecule in his body, was physically track side or not.

In summer 2016, the Rio Olympics were almost as great a triumph as London had been, and, given there was no home advantage, the performances were even more impressive. The British medal tally held up with 12 medals and, for all the accusations of bullying and sexism, Sutton's alleged 'reign of terror' had still produced some remarkable rides. Chris Froome collected a bronze medal in the men's time trial and, even if the men's and women's road races saw Team GB come up short, the Rio velodrome was again the location of British domination. Britain won golds in the men's sprint, the team sprint, the men's and women's team pursuit – with two Olympic records to boot – and the women's omnium. Even Mark Cavendish stepped onto an Olympic podium for the first time in his career, with a silver in the men's omnium. The Rio tally was six golds, four silvers and two bronze medals and the British team's cycling medal total was twice as many as the next most successful nation, Holland.

If Sutton's coaching and the coaches under his aegis had coaxed yet another remarkable medal haul out of British riders in Rio, the negative stories swirling around cycling didn't stop after the Rio Games, with the Fancy Bears hack revealing TUEs used by Bradley Wiggins and Froome, as well as the endless speculation about the contents of a Jiffybag delivered to Team Sky at the 2011 Criterium du Dauphine. The cumulative result of the three inquiries – Phelps, UK Anti-doping and the Select Committee for Digital, Culture, Media and Sport into 'Doping in Sport' – as well as furious arguments and accusations online meant cycling was under intense scrutiny.

The questions raised by the various threads of inquiry spread far wider than the narrow question of whether or not

Jess Varnish had been bullied or unfairly dismissed from her sprinting job at British Cycling. Rather, the issues highlighted by the stories and three investigations forced the British public to consider the nature of elite sport, UK Lottery funding, the 'price' of Olympic medals, Tour yellow jerseys and the limits of sporting ethics. Sport is something enjoyed and participated in by millions of weekend warriors, yet the gulf in what constitutes 'amateur' and 'professional' was laid uncomfortably bare throughout 2016.

Broadly speaking, two troubling areas were opened up during that year. On one hand, what were the limits of permissible language and behaviour in elite or professional sport? And on the other, what were the ethical limits in British sport which, in keeping with global practice, had become more medicalised following the explosion of sports science and medicine in the 1980s. These were questions that casual sports fans had never been asked to contemplate. Britain's media and TV audiences revelled in the medals and flags, but when it was revealed precisely how those celebrated victories had been achieved, the national sense of unease was palpable.

"This isn't the civil service you know," said one insider three months before the Rio Games, "the atmosphere is terrible, everyone is really watching what they say. Not in the sense that there was anything really bad going on, but now there's a weird mood. But really, you can't run elite sports along the same lines as the civil service, no matter if we are publicly funded or not. I get that it's tricky because of the public money that comes in, but a coach has a relationship with their riders that varies depending on what it takes to get them to tick." The speaker was a bemused Olympic medallist – who also had had his run-ins with Sutton – but whose basic position was that there hadn't been too much wrong at Team GB and that Varnish simply hadn't been good enough to keep her place.

Although British Cycling could point to the Phelps and UK Anti-Doping reports and try to contain the damage done, after the Fancy Bears hacks into the WADA database, there was no way BC squad riders or Team Sky could avoid indelicate questions about their private medical histories.

Additionally, the fact that so many riders and staff had crossed back and forward from one organisation to the other, that Brailsford had headed both outfits and Shane Sutton had been a coach at BC and Team Sky, meant tangled narrative threads were impossible to keep apart. The shared sponsor, the shared headquarters and the Team Sky riders racing in Team GB kit at the 2012 and 2016 Olympic Games meant the two entities were almost interchangeable in the eyes of the public. One scandalous story inevitably infected the other body, regardless of demarcation lines and, in any case, the anti-doping regulations were the same for all elite cyclists.

If Wiggins and Froome had been caught up in a TUE and cortisone-based 'scandal' then what implications did that have for their performances at the Rio Summer Olympics? As far as WADA, the UCI and UK Anti-Doping regulations were concerned, Wiggins, Froome and Team Sky had followed the rules, but the Fancy Bears hack revealed how close the 'we race clean' position of Team Sky flirted with the black arts of cortisone doping that had been practiced from the moment those products had arrived on the market in the early 1960s.

When the Wiggins TUE news story broke, the undeniable performance-enhancing effects of Triamcinolone (also marketed as Kenalog or Kenacort) were introduced to a wider public. Cortisone has a well-documented therapeutic value in, for example, treating tendinitis, but the side-effects of fat-burning, anti-inflammation, reduced sensations of fatigue and a sense of euphoria – as well as the timings of Wiggins' doses – caused unease even among his supporters. In terms of sporting legality, Wiggins was in the clear, he and the team followed the rules, but ethically he was in a grey area that was so dark it might as well have been black.

There was a counter-argument that, in fact, there was no grey area. If Wiggins and his supporters had made up symptoms for a non-existent medical condition to enable a TUE for Triamcinolone to be granted, it was straight-up doping. If Wiggins *did* have a condition that permitted the use of Kenacort, it simply *wasn't* doping – those were the rules and you can only judge an athlete by the rules in force at the time. It was indeed black or white and grey didn't come into it. The argument was that you can't retrospectively judge riders and actions and that if a rider followed the rules in force at the time, nobody had the right to call their actions doping.

Wiggins finally appeared to defend himself on BBC television's Andrew Marr current affairs show on 25 September 2016 in a one-on-one interview with the host. In a nervous, stuttering performance Wiggins told the watching public that his TUE applications were "to cure a medical condition, and was... ... was about putting myself back on a level playing field in order to compete at the highest level." In other words, Wiggins and the team had examined the rules to see what was permitted.

The British public is proud of its tech boffins, its 'Secret Squirrels' cleverly dancing on a very thin line, but the same supporters are more squeamish about sports doctors doing the same thing where the rules pertaining to sports medicine are concerned. All 'cheating' is not judged the same. Reflecting on the TUE tale, one BBC sports journalist said, "I didn't get too many quiet chats with Dave B but I remember once he said that they were going to bump up to that line, the limit, of what was allowed, but that they wouldn't cross it. The problem was that ethically, there was a different line. But it's sport and in every professional sport that's the approach that the best teams have, they all push the limits, otherwise they're not going to win. Whether it's Formula 1 or cycling, it's the same approach."

Viewed from a perspective denuded of all ethical considerations, the use of such products behind the screen of a TUE certificate was perfectly in keeping with Sky's – and British Cycling's – modern approach to professional cycling. Which is to say that given that British Cycling's technical and research staff studied regulations and materials to see how close they could get to the limits without actually breaking UCI rules, nobody should have been too surprised that a similar approach also applied to sports medicine.

The driving principal is the same: 'What can we legally get away with in this area? How close can we get to the limit of the law without actually breaking it?' The attitude is identical. There are people who study the rules and see what is on the limit, but still within the regulations. A simple example? If the technical regulations pertaining to the aerodynamic arm rests on a pursuit track bike are not allowed to touch in the centre of the handlebars, you can put the left and right rests as close as they can get, present the bike to the UCI judge for the pre-race check with the foam elbow pads removed for inspection, then, when the bike passes the judge's scrutiny, put the padding back so that effectively your 'separate' left and right rests touch and make one unit. Is that cheating or rule bending?

The shift in perceptions around cortisone in cycling is a fine example of how flexible the lines between sports medicine and doping are. What's the difference between staying healthy and performance enhancement? Would a saline solution given intravenously to a dehydrated rider be doping? Is that same saline solution infused with paracetamol to dull the ache after a time trial effort doping? Were injections of ferrous sulphate and B12 that were said to avoid upsetting the gut a form of doping? What about a pain killing pill to deaden the road buzz jarring a still-repairing scaphoid bone?

Today it's common for riders to ingest performance-enhancing quantities of caffeine in commercially produced gels (and less commonly produced suppositories, which enable ingestion of a high dose without the risk of stomach upset) that would once have produced a positive dope test for, yes, caffeine. As recently as 1994 double world champion Gianni Bugno was initially banned for *two years* after testing positive for the stimulant. A career blemished by a doping positive and a two year ban, for what he disingenuously claimed was a freakishly strong *espresso doppio*. Today, all that's at risk from using caffeine is in an inability to get to sleep without recourse to pills...

As the UCI and WADA had developed more sophisticated anti-doping strategies in the 1990s and early 2000s, the use of the performance-enhancing doses of cortisone had made a come-back in the professional peloton. Its effects were nothing like as career-altering as EPO-boosted blood chemistry – Triamcinolone wouldn't add 50 Watts to a rider's steady-state power output – but it could help boost performance via weight loss and improve recovery during stage races.

The brutal, unavoidable truth is that – intended or not, desired on not – Wiggins use of Triamcinolone could have had performance-enhancing effects.

Another ex-pro who had a personal knowledge of its effects, as well as EPO, blood doping and human growth hormone offered this analysis. "If you had asked me in the 1990s, when we were racing, if Kenacort made a big difference to your performance, on top of those other products that were being used, I would have said no, not really. The thing is that if you are taking EPO and Human growth hormone, cortisone seems like, uh, the *frosting* on the cake. When those other products were being used, nobody would be taking a course of Kenacort and expecting a significant performance improvement. It would be more like it would keep you lean, you get a nice anti-inflammatory response for weeks, so you never get that puffy, bloated 'I'm not really recovered' feeling. And on top of that, it'll help you strip out a couple of kilos of weight too. Legally, yeah, no rules were broken, the letter of the law was followed, but ethically, it's indefensible. I don't doubt Wiggins had pollen allergies, but you don't need to treat them with Kenacort, that's like the nuclear option, just unheard of. You could treat a pollen allergy with an inhaler, something like Budesonide, but you'd have to inhale it for 14 hours a day to get the same performance benefit as injected Kenacort!"

So it was that a product used in 2011, 2012 and 2013 would come to light in 2016 with seismic repercussions for BC and Team Sky. If 2012 had been a dazzling high point for both British track riders and Team Sky, then events throughout 2016 would take the shine off that golden season.

The fall out over the Fancy Bears hack and TUE revelations pushed topics into the spotlight that, hitherto, everyone had been happier to leave in the shadows. On one level there were the ethical concerns with the way that certain TUE-approved medications were being abused. Almost nobody with experience of Triamcinolone use in cycling was willing to insist that its use was *entirely* and *uniquely* medically justified. How could they? It was clear there were other treatments available which came with negligent performance-enhancing side effects. So how did a team founded on a 'Do it clean' ethos come to a decision that using Triamcinolone fitted within its self-imposed standards?

Neither Wiggins, Brailsford nor Team Sky medical staff invented the abuse of cortisone, but the fact that a British team would operate in this manner sent a shudder through those fans who are happy to believe that cheating is something Johnny Foreigner does. The fact is that there were British doctors who had been working in cycling long enough to fully understand the theory and practice of blood transfusions, EPO and the other dark arts of doping. There was plenty British expertise when it came to walking the thin line between 'keeping a rider healthy and in optimum condition' and simply doping them. This is a body of knowledge that stretches back to the earliest days of Lottery-funded British cycling and Wiggins and his support team were playing by rules understood by British cycling long before the Team Sky bus arrived in the 'Village Depart.'

In this social media saturated age, where 'reputational damage' is a familiar phrase, wondering whether a course of action is ethical or not is fairly easy to ascertain. All it takes is a simple thought experiment. The question Team Sky management could have asked is whether or not they would be happy for Wiggins' use of Triamcinolone to be in the public domain. If the answer to that question was 'No' then, at the very least, Team Sky had a public relations problem.

And there's the rub. It was, at root, a public relations issue given that Team Sky had used Triamcinolone legally, within the WADA, UKAD and UCI regulations. That much was indisputable. However, it was still an fact that was not in the team's interest to have in the public domain. On one hand, it was a medical issue and subject to the rules of confidentiality enjoyed by every citizen, on the other, the use of this particular medication came with questions attached. If Wiggins needed Triamcinolone for his pollen allergies, why didn't he use it at his previous teams, at Cofidis, when he rode the Tour and the Giro? Had his allergies got worse? Or did he simply not care then because he wasn't riding for the general classification back then? On the other hand, was anyone outside of Wiggins' medical team, who didn't have full access to Wiggins' medical records, really qualified to comment?

Proponents of a 'scorched earth' approach – simply banning the use of cortico-steroids in cycling – were hamstrung by the fact that if the UCI introduced such a ban it would fall foul of the World Anti-Doping Agency (WADA) code, to which it had been a signatory since 2004. Conflicts of interest had always existed between the UCI and WADA and the difficulty in making every anti-doping regulation fit inside the WADA tent was complicated, given the competing interests of different sports. Cortico-steroids had long proved to be a prickly issue, as former UCI President Pat McQuaid revealed.

"I remember (UCI medical chief) Mario Zorzoli coming to me and saying 'Look, we have a problem with cortisone, there are riders who are preparing for the Classics – in particular – and they were taking a dose of cortico-steroids every Thursday before a race weekend so that they are really on song for Sunday.' So we introduced the rule about any rider who had an injection of cortisone had to have eight days off, which would take him over a week away from a race and maybe miss a Classic. That was pretty much all we could do," says McQuaid, mindful of the delicate relationship WADA would have with organisations like football's FIFA, where players can – and do – have recourse to large doses of cortisone to keep them 'fit' to play throughout the season. In world football, there's no eight-day ban from competition following an injection or infusion of cortisone. McQuaid continues, "I was on the WADA board at the time and brought up the problem that cortisone was being abused and I said that the UCI, needed WADA's support to frame some stronger regulation, but they were loath to do it."

McQuaid's experience reveals, quite clearly, the tensions that exist between the demands of fans, governing bodies and WADA, between the overwhelming desire of some to see an end to doping and, on the other, WADA's wish to keep organisations like the International Olympic Committee happy – and to continue funding WADA. The financial ramifications for global televised sport, the buying and selling of lucrative Olympic, athletic and football World Cup television rights as well as advertising and sponsorship revenues, require a credible, saleable product. Massive worldwide sports events, packages of entertainment, are precisely what WADA's anti-doping programme help provide credibility for. Global professional sport needs to be attractive to spectators and sponsors alike, and if WADA was to introduce swingeing new punishments – life bans for convicted cheats, a ban on the use of cortisone treatments, a more stringent TUE system – the implications for global football and athletics might negatively impact on the value of major sports franchises. Why would WADA clamp down on cortico-steroid abuse in a minor sport like cycling if the outcome was to jeopardise the most lucrative properties of the IOC, FIFA and the IAAF?

When Zorzoli and the UCI were blamed for enabling Wiggins and others' cortisone use, McQuaid felt sympathy with his former colleague. "He was in a hard position. I mean, no doctor will over rule another doctor in those circumstances. We knew the cortico-steroid abuse was a problem, WADA wasn't ready or willing to help and so we also brought in the 'no needle' rule for the same reason, to try to clamp down on guys injecting cortisone." For all the scorn heaped on Zorzoli, his reputation in the professional peloton was actually remarkably high, though after social media had passed judgement and him, he quit the sport. He was not the first actor to fall foul of the digital court of public opinion, so quick to judge on flimsy evidence, often unable to see a bigger picture. His 2015 departure did not noticeably improved the UCI's position on cortisone doping.

Given that the UCI had struggled to control decades of cortisone abuse, hindered by the conflicts of interest in other global sports, was it ever possible that BC and Team Sky were going to be able to navigate these waters without springing a leak at some point? It is unthinkable that any World Tour team has not had recourse to the medical use of cortisone at some point, the main and crucial difference being that the public has never been made aware of it.

Thus British fans were left scandalised by the cortisone revelations, wondering if it was all worth it, although given that the wider context was never fully explained, there was little chance of that. It was as if, like the Wizard of Oz, someone had pulled the curtains back on elite sport to reveal unpleasant realities that nobody had wanted exposed, not athletes, and not anti-doping authorities like WADA either.

After the years of media onslaught, how were both British Cycling and Team Sky going to rebuild their credibility? Was it even possible? Could British Cycling find a new management team capable of leading the organisation into a new phase while maintaining the success of the previous regime? Did Dave Brailsford have the stomach for another fight and, inevitably, more opprobrium? The latter turned out to be a far more pressing question for Brailsford than his former employers in Manchester. During the 2017 world road championships in Bergen, Brailsford was informed that Chris Froome had tested positive during the 2017 Vuelta a España This time it was Froome's career and credibility that was on the line, as well as his own. Out of the frying pan...

11

TAKE A DEEP BREATH AND RELAX

'If I had a few pints and met him in a hotel corridor I'd swing for him.'

Dave Brailsford could have been excused for thinking he was starring in a cycling version of the film *Groundhog Day*, in which he was forced to relive the same events over and over. The Team Sky boss awoke on 20 September 2017 to be greeted by word from Chris Froome, the first British winner of the Vuelta a España, that he had tested positive for Salbutamol during the Spanish national Tour. Another day, another doping story.

Froome had been warming up on a turbo trainer under the gaze of his coach when a UCI lawyer rang his mobile to inform him of his positive test. 'It was the phone call I never thought I would ever receive. Tim Kerrison was walking around and I told him, "I can't believe what I just heard." You do everything right, then this nightmare. I actually felt dizzy. I climbed off and immediately just started googling to learn what I could about Salbutamol, about thresholds,' said Froome.

Such cases were rare, but they were invariably dealt

with quietly, without fanfare, behind the scenes. The then UCI president, Brian Cookson, was also in town, and was informed of Froome's test on the eve of the presidential vote in Bergen (which he lost to David Lappartient) but, when it was announced Froome would ride the 2018 Giro d'Italia that November, Cookson assumed that Froome and Team Sky had managed to explain the adverse Vuelta test and no more would be heard of it.

However, a month later, the story – if not all the facts – would be leaked by an unknown source to the *Guardian* and *Le Monde* in France, and the newspapers simultaneously published the news on 13 December: Froome had returned an adverse analytical finding for Salbutamol following stage 18 of the Vuelta.

The common asthma medication Salbutamol fell into a class of drugs for which a positive test did not require the UCI to make the news public. WADA's position is that when Salbutamol is taken in normal therapeutic doses it does not have performance-enhancing properties – which is why riders haven't needed a TUE for Salbutamol since 2010. When it came to Salbutamol, concerns around false positives, debated performance-enhancing properties, as well as medical confidentiality, meant the UCI allowed riders privacy to explain themselves before judgement was passed.

Asthma sufferers use Salbutamol to dilate the air-carrying bronchioles in the lungs when suffering an attack and, inhaled via a puffer, Salbutamol alleviates acute symptoms. There is some research to suggest that used in larger, non-therapeutic doses, however – as a tablet or injection – that it has fat-metabolising and some anabolic properties, although the research is contested.

In any case, the 2017 UCI rules were clear, you can take Salbutamol so long as you don't exceed a certain limit – 1,600 microgrammes in a twenty-four-hour period – and Froome's sample indicated he had taken more than was permitted. The December headlines were just as unambiguous: 'Chris Froome fights to save career after failed drugs test result' in the *Guardian*, 'Abnormal dope control for Chris Froome' in *Le Monde* or 'Chris Froome tests positive and cycling history repeats itself' in the *New York Times*.

Following WADA and UCI regulations – when a positive for a 'specified' substance like Salbutamol rather than a 'prohibited' one is discovered, the athlete, the national anti-doping authority concerned and the rider's team are privately informed and the rider is given time to explain how the drug got into their system. Also, unlike with a positive for a prohibited substance like EPO, there is no mandatory provisional suspension for a specified substance, so the rider is permitted to compete while explaining their case. Thus, normally, the public would be none the wiser about a positive test for Salbutamol, unless the rider's explanation was rejected and punishment meted out.

In the four years between 2013 and 2017 there had been forty-one similar cases involving Salbutamol positives in world sport. In other words, it was rare, but not unheard of, and others had been acquitted.

Clearly a positive for a specified substance is treated differently from a strictly prohibited one. The distinction between a 'prohibited' and a 'specified' product is that one substance can be used subject to controls (a measured amount of asthma medication, for example, or cortisone authorised via a TUE), while the other, a banned substance, is simply that – there are no excuses for the presence of anabolic steroids in an athlete's sample under any circumstances. Specified substances are sub-classifications of banned products on the WADA prohibited list, their different classification basically allowing more flexibility in determining a rider's deliberate intention to cheat and the appropriate punishment. As the WADA Code notes, specified substances *'are simply substances which are more likely to have been consumed by an athlete for a purpose other than the enhancement of sport performance'*. Precisely like a bronchodilating asthma medication.

However, no matter what the details were, if Froome could not give a credible explanation for the amount of Salbutamol in his sample, he would be stripped of his Vuelta win and face a ban. More damaging still, Froome's previous race wins would be tainted by this failed test, which, in the eyes of doubters, added to the clouds of TUE suspicion that had clung to the team since the 2016 Fancy Bears hack.

As it transpired, the test and permitted limits for a Salbutamol positive were convoluted indeed. The amount of Salbutamol in any sample needed to be 'corrected' to take into account dehydration, as per a WADA rule introduced in November 2017, and the authorities also allowed for a 10 per cent testing error.

When it was boiled down, Froome needed to explain how his Vuelta urine sample contained 1,428 ng/ml of Salbutamol, when the permitted upper limit was 1,000 ng/ml – which is then raised to 1,200 ng/ml to allow for measuring errors. Additionally, the sample has also to be corrected for dehydration, from whence the official 1,428ng/ml figure. Froome was, from a legal and dope control point of view, 19 per cent over the decision limit, rather than the 100 per cent – double the amount – that was initially reported.

First reports in newspapers that broke the story had said simply that Froome's sample was twice the permitted amount – 2,000 ng/ml – a number which, when it escaped on to the internet damned Froome in the eyes of the public before the process had even begun. The 'fact' that Froome had 'twice the amount allowed', as per the *New York Times* story, or 'double the permitted levels of the asthma medication' in the *Guardian*'s exclusive, raced around the world before a breath could be drawn.

Following the leak, a number of his fellow riders said that Froome should voluntarily suspend himself while he compiled his defence. Froome refused, insisting he was innocent and that he had every right to race, reasoning that if due process had been followed and his adverse analytical finding hadn't been leaked, nobody would have been any the wiser and he – like others before him – would have been free to compete while his case was being assessed. Once the 2018 racing season started and he was obliged to face fans and media, Froome's mental toughness was put to its sternest test yet.

Team Sky boss Brailsford was also in for a rough ride, though he had had plenty of practice following his battles with UK Anti-Doping, his involvement with the Phelps inquiry into British Cycling, the Jiffy bag saga and his cross-examination by the Select Committee of Digital, Media, Culture and Sport. After navigating his way through those minefields, the mastermind of Beijing and London Olympic triumphs, the 2012 coach of the year, generously remunerated motivational speaker and Team Sky founding father was now confronted by his worst nightmare: his star rider had returned a positive dope test. As ever, Brailsford played bad news with a dead bat. There was no discernible outrage in his comments, merely a measured tone: 'There are complex medical and physiological issues which affect the metabolism and excretion of Salbutamol. We're committed to establishing the facts and understanding exactly what happened on this occasion.'

Brailsford was putting on a brave front, because this was potentially a much more damaging affair than any that he had faced before. If the Phelps report and Damian Collins' DCMS parliamentary reports were mainly British concerns and focused on Brailsford's past, this was a bang up to date and decidedly international doping scandal – a clear positive for a banned substance during a winning ride in the Vuelta and the news broken in the French media. Even Wiggins' Jiffy bag tale dated from 2011 and was in some sense old news when it first emerged in 2016. The Salbutamol story and its potential impact on Brailsford, Froome and the team, was much greater than any of the previous scandals, and far more difficult to control.

Yet again Brailsford's character and his team's philosophy would be forensically examined and, once more, the ethics of sport, the line drawn between doping/not doping would be front and centre, ultimately resulting in questions being asked about the reliability of WADA's test protocol. Brailsford was again beset on all sides by critical voices in the media, but he inevitably chose to tough it out, convinced, as he had been with Wiggins' use of Triamcinolone, that his rider and medical team had operated within the WADA rules and done nothing wrong.

One rider with experience of Brailsford over twenty years noted that his basic approach was unchanged, whether at British Cycling or Team Sky. 'He's a guy, when he's backed into a corner, he'll roll his sleeves up and say, "Right, let's fucking have it then." The harder it is and the more flak he gets, the tougher he is, though I'm sure the flak must be getting to him. But he's tough and he hates losing – he *hates* losing.' That phrase again: 'he hates losing'. Add that to 'he hates being laughed at' and it didn't take a psychiatrist to conclude that Brailsford wasn't going anywhere soon, no matter what the press wrote or how furiously the digital trolls hammered their keyboards.

If Brailsford had survived heavy hints that he should leave British Cycling in 2012 following the Peter King report, given he had weathered media barbs over Fancy Bears, UK Anti-Doping and Jiffy bags, and if a parliamentary select committee report had been repelled, then this Salbutamol business wasn't going to see him off either. For all that he and Froome had clashed in 2012, they shared the same stubborn attitude and approach. As one former Sky staffer put it, 'Despite the occasional moments of tension, Dave and Chris are both equally driven and focused, which is why they are so good together – they're far more alike in terms of resilience and will to win than most people realise.'

While Froome and his legal and medical teams gathered evidence for his defence, Bradley Wiggins finally broke cover in March 2018 after months of silence. Following the closure of the UK Anti-Doping investigation in November 2017 and the 5 March 2018 publication of Damian Collins' Digital, Culture, Media and Sport committee report, Wiggins came out swinging in a combative interview with BBC sports reporter Dan Roan, a tenacious journalist who, with Matt Lawton, had been a persistent interrogator from the moment Jess Varnish first accused Shane Sutton and the Fancy Bears hacking revelations emerged in 2016.

Wiggins was unrepentant and angry. Accused of crossing an ethical rather than simply a regulatory line, Wiggins was clear. 'Not at any time in my career did we cross the ethical line,' he insisted. 'As I've said before, I had a medical condition and I went to a doctor, back in 2003 when I was diagnosed with it, through the doctors at British Cycling at that time.'

Pushed harder on the ethical use of Triamcinolone, Wiggins deflected the question, but revealed the mindset of a world-class athlete preparing for the goal of his life.

> I am a rider riding for Team Sky, the biggest team in the world at that point. I am paid as the team leader and, as most riders in any sport, not just cycling – if you've got niggles, problems, a knee injury, common cold, you go

to the doctor in the team. We are hypochondriacs as athletes, especially coming to the height of the season, the
biggest race of the year, whether it is the Olympic Games
or the Tour de France.

Wiggins was clear, unabashed and unrepentant: medical care
is part of every serious team's preparation; it's just that nobody
shouts about it.

Wiggins' months of silence in the face of mounting allegations and theories had done nothing to help his cause or,
peripherally, the credibility of British Cycling's medical practices. The wide perception was that Wiggins had been hiding,
nursing a guilty conscience and trying to bolt together a credible story, while Brailsford was in the same position as Wiggins,
a mute witness in no hurry to implicate himself or his team.
Wiggins explained that he had helped UKAD and was legally
bound to say nothing until the reports and investigations were
completed.

Once that UKAD investigation got opened, I am gagged
for legal reasons, until I have acted as a witness. I was not
able to speak because there is a legal investigation with
UKAD, and I didn't want to jeopardise that. I'm fighting
a malicious allegation made by an anonymous source. I
was a witness to the UKAD investigation but this one [the
DCMS report], I haven't heard anything since this DCMS
thing started, and at the eleventh hour last week I was
asked if I would like to comment on it [the DCMS report].
I was asked five questions – [but] none of the questions
were the current allegations that have been made. One
and a half of the answers I gave were published in the
DCMS report.

Wiggins stated, without hesitation, that he had not been using Triamcinolone as a performance-enhancing doping agent. 'It wasn't performance enhancing in the sense that, for me, I had had asthma attacks that flared up through the pollen season, and this was an anti-inflammatory drug that was taken in order to prevent that happening, so I could compete on the same level I had competed all year with my rivals.'

Wiggins' fine point was that he had beaten his fellow Tour contenders throughout the 2012 season, from early March onwards, and that, really, he didn't need Triamcinolone to make him better, just to keep him from getting ill. As had been established by previous episodes, those who believed Wiggins was innocent felt vindicated, and those who were convinced Wiggins was a cheat didn't change their opinions either. It was impossible to believe that his Triamcinolone use hadn't had some beneficial effect, but it was harder still to believe he had won the 2012 Tour de France because he had taken an injection of a corticosteroid.

Would he have won the Tour if he had not taken that fateful dose of Triamcinolone? Wiggins paused. 'Well, had I had an asthma attack, no, probably not. No.'

Once again, the inescapable fact of the matter was that as far as UKAD, WADA and the UCI were concerned, Wiggins, Sky and team doctor Richard Freeman had played the game by the book, which had been written and signed off by WADA, the UCI medical commission and UK Anti-Doping. Everything else could never be more than speculation, particularly when it related to the infamous Jiffy bag and its mystery contents.

What *was* in the Jiffy bag, Brad?

God knows. Your guess was as good as mine. The first I knew that a package had been delivered was when [journalist] Matt Lawton phoned me up to ask what was in it.

I don't know what was in it. If it did have Triamcinolone in it, it didn't go in my backside. Which is what is being suggested, because it would have shown in my urine at the [dope test after the] National Road Race.

Wiggins' performance in the face of persistent questioning had been solid. His frustration and anger were evident, and it was clear that he didn't have all the facts or perfect recall, seven years after the first event. There had even been a hint of regret at his use of Triamcinolone: 'It's easy to think with everything that has happened now to sit here and go, "Yeah, I regret it ...".' It's happened. I can't turn the clock back,' he reflected, noting, however, that 'that was the treatment at the time'.

On 1 July, a week before the start of the 2018 Tour de France, the former Team Sky and Great Britain cycling doctor who had been implicated in both Wiggins' Triamcinolone and the Jiffy bag investigation also emerged. Like Wiggins, Dr Richard Freeman had kept a very low public profile after the allegations began to pile up and, as with Wiggins, this had been widely interpreted as the behaviour of a guilty man. In his television interview with Dan Roan, he too was unrepentant, and refuted accusations made in the DCMS report that Wiggins had repeatedly used Triamcinolone to reduce his body fat, given the product's catabolic properties. As Freeman evenly states,

Unfortunately he [Damian Collins, chair of the DCMS] didn't have medical information from me or from Bradley Wiggins. Bradley Wiggins' weight-management plan was a long-term plan, and when he was racing, well, take the Dauphiné example, he was at his race weight. So to say we want him to lose more weight ... I personally always battled to keep a rider at their race weight.

Freeman was also able to produce a document dating from 2014, two years before the Jiffy bag story broke, proving that he had indeed reported his laptop – containing riders' medical records – stolen in Greece. This explanation for the lack of Wiggins' medical records had been widely pilloried as a convenient excuse by critics of Wiggins and Team Sky, a fantastic tale totally lacking credibility and a sign of desperation in the Sky camp. If this was the sort of yarn Team Sky were reduced to, what else were they hiding?

The production of that single sheet of paper helped bolster Freeman's credibility – yet its existence had long been a matter of record to the UKAD investigators. 'It [the document] had been there all along, but people were so busy laughing at the "dog ate my homework" excuse they thought he had made it up. They didn't believe him [Freeman], but Nicole Sapstead of UK Anti-Doping had the document all along, as part of their investigation,' said one frustrated source inside British Cycling. There was a suggestion too that UKAD had been less than competent in its long dealings with British Cycling, and was therefore more than happy to see Team Sky take the brunt of the criticism and deflect curiosity from its own questionable record keeping and oversight.

For his part, Freeman explained that the infamous Jiffy bag sent to him at the 2011 Dauphiné had contained Fluimucil nebules – a formula then unavailable over the counter in France – thus the need for it to be sent from Manchester. For context, Freeman explained that between 2012 and 2014 over 275 medications were sent overseas to British squads and Team Sky. Additionally, like Wiggins, he stated repeatedly that he never 'crossed the line', and that the Triamcinolone he administered to Wiggins was to treat pollen allergies and allergic rhinitis.

Freeman's 2018 book *The Line: Where Medicine and Sport Collide* set out his side of the process by which Wiggins had first been granted a TUE in much greater depth, detailing the name of the specialist, the clinic, the time and date of his and Wiggins' visit to undergo tests that would form the basis of their request for those infamous Triamcinolone treatments. 'Would I use it as much in general practice? Probably not. Would I use it again in a performance-driven environment? Yes. Is it bad medicine? I don't think so, but that doesn't make it good medicine either. It was just the right medicine at the time,' stated Freeman.

Freeman also nailed another story that had been floated: that he had been bullied by Wiggins' then coach Shane Sutton into applying for Wiggins' Triamcinolone TUE, and that he had been 'bullied in a lot of different ways' by Sutton. Freeman's claimed bullying by Sutton dovetailed neatly with the wider perception of Sutton's character and stories that had emerged in the course of the Phelps and (earlier) King reports. Freeman, it seems, had been another victim of Sutton's abrasive man-management style. 'Initially, I was a bit ashamed to say, because nobody likes to say they're being bullied. Initially you try and appease a bully, but then ultimately you've got to stand up to the bully, and that's what I did,' explained Freeman, adding, 'but I was never bullied to give medication by Shane Sutton.'

By all accounts, Freeman had performed better in his interview than many had expected. True, he was still under investigation by the General Medical Council for his record keeping and practice, but for a man who had, by his own admission, suffered from depression, he was coherent and, at times, combative, clearly intent on defending his reputation, as well as that of Wiggins and Team Sky. 'I'm still receiving medical care, and I've got a great deal of thanks to give to my consultant doctor. I went down to the [DCMS] select committee the day before but that's when unfortunately I had what the layman would call a breakdown, and it was the final straw.'

Critics had previously been eager to point out that Freeman's last-minute no-show at the DCMS hearing together with his conveniently lost laptop containing medical records were evidence that he, Wiggins and Brailsford had plenty to hide. That Freeman then produced evidence that his laptop really had been stolen, allied with his revelation that he 'cooperated with UKAD in the form of two three-to-four-hour interviews with them, both recorded, as well as something in the region of 200 written answers to various questions they asked throughout the investigation', as well as producing additional written evidence, helped undermine the more outlandish theories of his critics.

The more extreme and troubling claims contained in the DCMS report – that Team Sky had used drugs, notably Triamcinolone, to enhance the performance of several riders, and that Wiggins had been injected nine times with Triamcinolone – rested as 'fact' in the published DCMS report. Despite coming from an anonymous source backed by no evidence from any other quarter, those serious but totally unsubstantiated claims made big headlines. The *Guardian* went with 'Remarkable drugs report shatters Team Sky's illusion of integrity'. Obviously, Wiggins and Freeman both rejected the allegation, which Wiggins called 'malicious' and accused Collins and his committee of using 'parliamentary privilege to make it legal, being able to say it without repercussions'.

The day after Freeman gave his interview – in part to promote his book – there was even better news for Brailsford, Sky and Chris Froome. The UCI and WADA had studied Froome's defence dossier and come to the conclusion that he had no case to answer. Specifically, 'WADA accepted that the analytical result of Mr Froome's sample from the Vuelta a España, which identified the prohibited substance Salbutamol at a concentration in excess of the decision limit of 1,200 ng/ml, did not constitute an Adverse Analytical Finding.' Effectively, the UCI had decided there had been no anti-doping violation, and WADA simultaneously announced it would not appeal the UCI decision. In other words, Froome was not guilty of any offence and was free to race at the Tour without punishment or reprimand.

Like both Wiggins and Dr Freeman, Froome had kept a low media profile while he was assembling his defence with his advisors. Although he had raced thirty-eight days – including a jaw-dropping first-ever overall victory by a British rider at the 2018 Giro d'Italia – he had stuck resolutely to his script to the point that the cycling media had more or less given up asking him what was happening. 'We are gathering evidence, the appeal process was underway, he had a right to race, he had done nothing wrong and fully expected to be exonerated.' And lo, on 2 July, it came to pass – Froome was exonerated by cycling's authorities.

Those supporters who had been prepared to give Froome the benefit of the doubt – or at least wait until more evidence was in the public domain – were vindicated. Those who felt ambiguous about a long-running saga were happy to move on, while the vociferous anti-Froome and Team Sky elements remained outraged, insisting that Froome had been whitewashed because of his name, his team and the money spent on his defence.

The latter was a strange angle of attack to take. If Team Sky had indeed spent money and time to demonstrate that the existing Salbutamol anti-doping test wasn't fit for purpose, shouldn't Sky be congratulated for exposing a flawed protocol? Shouldn't fans' ire be directed towards WADA or the UCI for continuing to use a test that could have – and possibly had – banned innocent riders? As Fran Millar of Sky put it, 'We've spent all this money have we? And that's wrong? Let me get this straight. You want us *not* to spend money and let a clean athlete serve a ban? Would that be your preference?'

Additionally, many critics felt his defence team had dragged their feet in assembling his dossier, which was initially reported to be 1,500 pages thick. Thus, the *Guardian*, which had broken the story seven months earlier, stated that 'Froome's defence appears to have rested on a 1,500-page report'. In truth, it was only around 160 pages, but, like his 'double the level over the permitted amount', the myth proved to be more resilient than the fact. As for Sky 'dragging its feet', when he finally spoke after the verdict Froome poured scorn on that notion. 'It's bizarre people would even think we would delay it. I wanted this over yesterday. To train and race with this over my head? Why would I want that for a minute longer than it had to be?'

In the end, short and none-too-detailed 'clarifications' from the UCI and WADA explained why Froome's case had been dismissed. As WADA noted, Salbutamol threw up 'complex' issues that varied enormously between individuals and sports and even between cycling races – one-day events or long stage races could very well generate different test results. It appears the fact that Froome had had so much dope-control test data from the Vuelta played to his advantage when compiling his defence.

Like Wiggins and Freeman, Froome had essentially kept his mouth shut and waited for the investigation to run its course and release its verdict before he spoke. As with Wiggins, his silence had enabled theories and 'facts' to proliferate. 'The most frustrating part was when I'd see stuff that was totally incorrect but supposedly leaked, because then everyone would assume it was a fact,' Froome said, adding,

The classic from the start was of my result being double the limit when it was less than 20 per cent over with the figure corrected [for specific gravity, taking into account dehydration] and with the decision limit of 1,200, not

1,000. That figure of 2,000 is half the calculation, but no one seemed to pick up on how it is established. They took the leaked information as fact. Then it was said that I would do some kind of plea bargain, which was never on the table. I would never have accepted anything other than a full exoneration from the word go. Knowing I had done nothing wrong, I was going to fight to clear my name, absolutely.

For his part, Froome's team boss, Brailsford, had somehow managed to keep his team together and maintain cohesion throughout the two turbulent years. After all, none of the scandalous headlines since 2016 had stopped his team either winning the biggest races (Liège–Bastogne–Liège, the Tour de France, Milan–San Remo, Sky's sixth Tour, as well as their first Vuelta and Giro), or recruiting and holding on to riders either.

When a story broke online in February 2017 claiming that riders were contemplating some kind of revolt unless he stepped down, Brailsford was outraged, though more at the suggestion that any serious media outlet would have given the story any credence. His texted reply to one experienced cycling journalist looking for a comment on this apparent coup d'état was succinct, 'Fuck off, you really should know better.'

For a time it felt that every Team Sky story revolved around the fact that Brailsford's position was untenable, that he was a liability and that his riders were restless. The stories ricocheted endlessly around social media. Thus, when negotiations on Froome's new contract were in early stages during summer 2017, there were reports that he was set to leave, such was his unhappiness with Brailsford and Sky's poisonous image. On 30 June 2017 Froome signed a new deal that tied him to the team for another three seasons. So much for Brailsford's toxic team and reputation. Froome's signing statement sought to undermine that angle: 'It's been a really successful partnership and I think one of the big reasons for that is the stability of the team.' In spite of the screams of protest and mountains of bad press, Froome highlighting 'the stability of the team' was a delicate 'fuck you' to critics.

The view from inside the team was that the press – led by noise on social media – was out to get Brailsford, and it was hard to avoid that interpretation with headlines like 'Team Sky: Sir Dave Brailsford must face the music – and then resign' in the *Guardian* or 'Brailsford must resign for Team Sky to survive' on cyclingnews.com. There was also 'Sir Dave Brailsford has to go' in *The Times*. And, with some irony, considering the newspaper's ownership, 'Why Brailsford has to quit Team Sky' in the *Sunday Times*, penned by journalist David Walsh, who had written a supportive book, *Inside Team Sky*, four years previously.

Was it true that some riders and staff were unhappy at the way the various bad news stories had been handled and had impacted on them personally? Absolutely. Were those rumbles of discontent a threat to the team? Hardly. The notion of a completely harmonious squad is a total fiction, of course – recall any number of spats inside British Cycling or any football team where a manager risks 'losing the dressing room' – but some element of Brailsford's management skill lies precisely in this arena. Some level of disquiet was always a feature of Brailsford's team, and he was perfectly sanguine about it. As far as Brailsford is concerned, harmonious teams do not necessarily deliver results, and his philosophy is that what is required inside a team is 'self' harmony rather than 'team' harmony.

What does that mean on the Team Sky bus? In practice nobody really gives a flying one about 'team harmony' so long as everyone is lined up and committed to the goal of winning the bike race. If every rider knows what they are doing and why they are being asked to do that job, the strong likelihood is that you'll get the desired result. If, on the other hand, management flaps about trying to ensure that everyone is happy, desperate to achieve a blissfully harmonious group, it's a waste of time and energy. Team Sky is not TV's hokey 'Waltons' family; it's a professional sports team intent on delivering results. Friction is something Brailsford can cope with, almost a default setting – and there had been a lot to deal with.

Reflecting on what was almost two years of constant fire-fighting and a barrage of criticism of Team Sky and Brailsford, director of operations at Sky Fran Millar observed, 'I'd say that you haven't been inside or even close to a high-performance sporting environment if you think that friction isn't normal, part and parcel of that sort of "ecosystem".' As a way of thinking about how Brailsford had dealt with the car-crash pile-up of stories focused on bullying at British Cycling, the Wiggins–Froome rivalry and rumblings of discontent inside the team, it's a useful perspective. Friction – internal and external – comes as standard in the elite sport package, and it was partly this sort of 'people-based' friction that had seen off Peter Keen from British Cycling in 2003.

Yet even here, in a particularly fractious run-up to the 2018 Tour de France, Brailsford's psychology could turn the 'hate' into a galvanising energy. For all that he and his staff would prefer not to be faced by booing French crowds and sniping Twitter trolls, that only really served to stiffen the team's resolve. After all the pre-race drama and debate, it would be Geraint Thomas who would win the Tour, with Froome occupying the third step of the podium behind Dutchman Tom Dumoulin. Thomas beat Froome everywhere – including to a famous stage win at Alpe d'Huez – and for all the potential for a 2012 Wiggins–Froome rerun, Thomas' form and nerve held.

Though nobody at Team Sky would admit it, Thomas' win was perfect, in public relations terms. Welshman Thomas was a more popular public figure than Froome, more relaxed in front of fans and cameras and a product of the British Cycling Academy initially set up by (then BC, later Sky) coach Rod Ellingworth in 2004. The fact that Thomas was, like Brailsford, Welsh, meant there was a stronger bond between the pair too. In his funny autobiography written three years before he won the Tour, *The World of Cycling According to G*, Thomas devoted a chapter to Brailsford, whom he described as being 'your best mate's dad ... a man who had seen you at your worst ... close, but not too close, stern without being a brute. All he cares about is cycling. You never see him relaxing, only hammering at his laptop ... he struggles to switch off from it all.'

As the 2018 season wound down it looked like Brailsford could at least try to relax, to take a step back. He wouldn't, of course; as Thomas noted, it simply wasn't part of his make-up. 'What I've finally got my head around is that you've got to keep going,' explained Brailsford. 'You've got to run, you've got to sprint, sprint as hard as you can, because everyone else – your competition – is running hard as well, so you sprint until the day you retire, because otherwise you are going to go backwards.' So on Dave goes, planning, recruiting, consolidating. Dreaming of being the manager of the first Colombian to win the Tour de France ...

Through all the reports, the leaks, accusations, the interrogations and relentless bad news, some of the uglier truths of elite cycle sport had been revealed to a naïve public. When you subjected modern professional sport to forensic levels of scrutiny, it turned out there was no place for sentiment and precious little romance. Racing the Tour de France in a World Tour team wasn't really like a three-week summer road trip with a bunch of cycling mates in a tricked-out charabanc; it was a brutal environment, and the line between medicine and doping was a lot thinner than most fans liked to imagine.

The horror with which many sports journalists reported on the medicalisation of the sport, the ethical dilemmas and less-than-full transparency that the Team Sky scandals revealed, rather suggested some had been asleep at the wheel or not delving too deeply in precisely how elite sporting performances had been achieved. If the same level of interrogation of football and rugby treatment rooms was carried out, if professional track and field athletes were asked about the precise details of their medical records and TUE applications, might the public become just as jaundiced? The DCMS report asked hard questions of athletics too, and Olympic champion Mo Farah had also been revealed to sail close to the medico-ethical edge.

The realisation that the imperative to look for 'marginal gains' was applied everywhere, from nutrition to sports medicine – not just in the air flows over skinsuits – seemed to come as an uncomfortable surprise. As far as Brailsford and his squad were concerned, they had played by the (professional cycling) rules and, as such, didn't deserve the hostility and opprobrium directed at them. The truth, of course, was that if Brailsford hadn't entered the scene in 2010 talking about 'doing things right and winning clean' then none of the grubbier linen being washed in public would have had anything like the same impact. Relative to the blood-and-hormone-doped nightmare decades, when Lance Armstrong battled similarly 'prepared' rivals, Brailsford and professional cycling in general was now squeaky clean. It's just that's not how the public saw it, because post-Armstrong, nobody believes anyone any more; the benefit of the doubt is no longer offered to any rider.

Of all the characters inside Team Sky, Brailsford, inevitably, was the one who faced the most flak. He was the man at the top, it was his team, he set the tone and, throughout two years of relentless criticism and sniping, he stayed the course. Brailsford had survived parliamentary committee sessions,

Fancy Bears, Jiffy bags and Salbutamol scandals, and in 2018 his team had won Tirreno–Adriatico, the Tour of California, the Giro d'Italia, the Critérium du Dauphiné, the Tour de France and the Tour of Poland. Every one of them was a World Tour stage race, and it was a winning record that no other team had got close to.

Professional cycling being the beast it is, if you win, someone else has to lose. Pro bike racing isn't a school sports day. Not everyone gets a prize, and sometimes more than feelings get hurt. Rivalry can spill over into enmity, and people get damaged along the roads in ways that Brailsford's famous 'compassionately ruthless' approach will fail to cover. In the course of researching this book, Brailsford was praised and damned in equal measure, often by the same people.

Which is to say that those who had worked with him for any length of time recognised his attributes, but weren't blind to his faults, in which a Herculean obstinacy blended with a ruthless streak that bordered on the sociopathic was often mentioned. 'I worked with him at British Cycling for years and did what I thought was a good job. I helped deliver medals at Beijing,' said one former manager.

> When we came back from Beijing I thought I was secure, but one day Shane Sutton came up to me and said, 'Sorry mate, Dave wants you out,' and that was it. Brailsford then made my life hell to the point that I left. I don't carry grudges, and I find it hard to blank people, but I can blank Dave, even in a hotel corridor if he passes me. I reckon if I had a few pints and met him in a hotel corridor I'd swing for him.

That might well have been a bit of an exaggeration, but the tone is clear, and the thrust of the story is far from unique.

And yet, for all his divisive character and public relations missteps, Brailsford has escaped almost untouched by vicious criticism coming from the many riders who have been through Team Sky. There are none ready or willing to 'dish the dirt' on Brailsford or Sky, even after nine seasons of activity and a considerable amount of staff churn. If there was a cunning doping regime operating inside Team Sky and ex-riders or staff pissed off enough by Brailsford's all-or-nothing management style, you would have expected a leak to have escaped the Team Sky Death Star by now. There's nothing like a disgruntled ex-employee to generate a crisis, whether that's Floyd Landis or Edward Snowden.

One insider, long acquainted with the machinations of professional cycling and Team Sky, had clearly been beaten down and bruised by the accusations, but insisted, passionately, that the 'popular' image of the team was inaccurate and distorted: 'Nobody understands the team. You have to be inside the team I think. We do do things the right way, and we work so hard to be the best. We wouldn't ever cheat. And we've made mistakes – oh, fuck me have we made mistakes – but none of them have been made from a position of malice.'

Perhaps the plain fact is that professional sports do a better job of hiding their dark undersides from the spectating public and supportive media than we care to admit. The list of ruthless managers in sport is not a short one, while the list of rules being bent and lines being pushed against is longer still, and much more opaque. While a private, professional enterprise like Team Sky has far more leeway in determining its culture and approach inside the arena in which it operates – what of a government-funded organisation like the one that Dave Brailsford had learned the ropes in: British Cycling?

During the two years that Brailsford and his team had been in a fierce spotlight, the new senior management team at

British Cycling had had time to bed itself in, take stock of the various reports the organisation had been implicated in, get to know its new sponsor, HSBC Bank, and plan for the Tokyo 2020 Summer Olympics. With new faces around the Manchester Board table and having digested critical reports, how was the form of the fresh regime? Well, as it turned out, perhaps not quite as good as many had hoped.

12

BE CAREFUL WHAT YOU WISH FOR

'These people don't have a clue what they are dealing with.'

After the deluge of Varnish and Sutton stories and the dissection of the Phelps, DCMS and UKAD reports, the news focus drifted away in 2017, and British Cycling was able to survey the damage. With former British Cycling boss Brailsford long gone, Team Sky having left the Manchester Velodrome and new British Cycling sponsor HSBC signed up, there was now a degree of separation from the ongoing travails of Team Sky. While Brailsford was still fielding critical flak, British Cycling was finally able to draw breath.

After eighteen months of traumas and the early retirement of CEO Ian Drake in March 2017, a new British Cycling senior management team assembled, read reports, met the media, paid their public penances and pressed on. In a briefing, someone muttered the anodyne benediction that 'Going forward, lessons will be learned' and the circus rolled into another velodrome in another town, with GB skinsuits now bearing an HSBC rather than a Sky logo.

Nobody really knew how heartfelt that 'lessons learned' cliché was, though, since inside British Cycling several senior people had felt that nothing had been drastically wrong in the first place. For many, the Jess Varnish affair that kick-started the process had been blown out of proportion by scandal-hungry journalists egged on by a fractious segment of social media, armed with their digital pitchforks and blazing torch emoticons.

There was even a credible source's version of events, in which Varnish had quietly admitted she never meant for things to get so out of hand and that, moreover, she had said so in front of a witness who had sent written evidence to the Phelps inquiry. In the parallel universe where that nugget of evidence had come to light, Sutton is still in his job, guilelessly suggesting that a rider should 'lose some timber'.

Few of those occupying positions of authority inside British Cycling had escaped unscathed from the bonfire of reputations, and although Sutton's was the highest-profile head to roll, others suffered too. Clearly, given the testimonies that emerged, there had to be investigation and accountability, even if some reputations suffered more than they deserved. In this regard, the name of long-serving staff member and CEO Ian Drake is at the top of the list.

A sympathetic but not uncritical British Cycling insider noted that when the troubled relationship between Brailsford, Sutton and the British Cycling Board was analysed, Drake – unfairly – came out the worst.

Ian had helped turn the sport around – we went from 11,000 to 135,000 members. He gave it his best shot, but you couldn't control Dave and Shane: they were loose cannons; they were part and parcel of this tremendous success; they were the shop window; nobody knew or saw that membership was growing week by week, you had to be in the backroom, in the know, to realise that. Joe Public could only see the Olympic results. It was all about Wiggins the national hero, and those of us who were getting on with the bloody job, our take was that whatever the management problems that Dave and Shane had, it must be a price worth paying, because the results were going through the roof. But Ian Drake helped build British Cycling's membership on the basis of international success, and it was Olympic and World medals that brought in Sky to British Cycling in the first place.

History will show that the unfortunate Drake went from being unsung meeting room hero to pilloried fall guy without enjoying the intervening period of public acclamation enjoyed by most of those around him. The manner of his departure and his rise and fall is illustrative of the core problem faced by British Cycling in that desperate two-year period. Drake was an old-school administrator caught up in twenty-first-century sports politics and media management scandals, scenarios he was ill-equipped to cope with.

Drake wasn't the front man that British Cycling needed in its moment of Varnish-inspired crisis, an amateur player all at sea in a ferocious new media landscape. Instead, Drake kept a low profile, as did most others, wary of being painted as apologists for sexism or bullying, regardless of how nuanced their positions might have been. British Cycling, its riders and the raison d'être of the WCPP were essentially hung out to dry, unattended, as the media laid into it. In the absence of a strong line of defence the accusations of Varnish and others became incontrovertible facts, damning British Cycling in the court of pubic opinion, fixing its popular image as a bullying, sexist institution.

As time passed, however, riders found their voices, offering alternative descriptions of the workings inside British Cycling's elite programme. In the run-up to the April 2017 world track championships in Hong Kong, different perspectives emerged. Sprinter Lewis Oliva appeared on BBC to say,

> Elite sport is brutal you know? Of course it is. And I've always maintained that with British Cycling it's a performance programme, it's not a day care centre. The other thing I would say is that, look, if athletes are really not happy with how the programme is and if you're really not convinced with how things are being run then take the opportunity to leave.

It wasn't only alpha-male sprinter types who were ready to speak out about the sometimes grim reality of elite-level sport. Around the same time, Jo Rowsell Shand also added her voice, as she called time on a ten-year international career that had seen her win two Olympic team pursuit gold medals, four team pursuit World Championships and an individual pursuit world title in 2014.

> Elite sport is really tough. It's not all fun and games. Everything we did on track was filmed and analysed, everything we did was scrutinised. And, if you're having a bad day, it is there for everyone to see. It's intense, but everyone is doing it because they want to win. They're not there to ride their bikes out in the sun. But elite sport is not for everybody. Cycling is as much about your head as it is your legs: how to cope with the pressure, how to cope with not being selected or losing is a big part of it. It's not easy.

Speaking about the supposedly fearful culture that existed inside the Manchester Velodrome, Rowsell Shand added,

> I didn't fear British Cycling. I accepted the commitment that was needed, accepted it and dedicated a decade of my life to it. British Cycling is not perfect, and people's complaints need to be addressed, but they have done a lot of good. I could have been a vulnerable target in the wrong environment because of my alopecia, but I wasn't treated differently for one second. No one said a word.
>
> I've come through the system and won two Olympic gold medals, and I wouldn't have been able to do that if I'd experienced sexism. I felt my medal was worth the same to British Cycling as the men's. It's hard to comment on other squads and their experiences – and I don't want to discount other people's claims – but my experience was that my medal was worth as much as, say, Ed Clancy's.

Paul Manning, working calmly in the background as the women's team pursuit coach, offered his own perspective. Manning was not seeking to defend Sutton or referring to issues raised by Varnish, but rather pointing out that elite sport is a fundamentally unsympathetic arena: 'It is like a jungle. There is a bit of that "survival of the fittest" that goes on. It's sport – that is sport.'

Olympic pursuit medallist Manning was one of the last of the old intake still at British Cycling, having risen through the ranks as a development rider in the pre-Lottery age to become the coach in Rio as his victorious pursuit quartet of Kate Archibald, Elinor Barker, Jo Rowsell Shand and Laura Trott set a world record in Brazil. Over his twenty years in the sport Manning had worked with the prickliest characters in British cycle sport – Peter Keen, Simon Jones and Shane Sutton – yet he learned and thrived. As the pragmatic Manning observes, with as succinct an explanation of the fine line between exhortation and going too far as anyone managed:

> When you're a rider, the best thing to do is concentrate on being the best you can be and ignoring, as much as possible, things going on around you. I say to my teams that I wasn't bothered with who was around me as teammates, I was bothered by what I was doing. I was focused on me and getting better. Coaches are there to challenge people. They maybe do make you feel uneasy, but I think that's a necessary evil. You need to challenge yourself; that shouldn't bother you. What should bother you is being made to look not good enough by the opposition. Getting beaten soundly, in public, by the opposition should feel worse. Anything else should be OK.

Louis Passfield, one of Keen's early sports scientist peers and coaches, is well-placed to offer this useful observation:

> There is something of a transactional relationship between an athlete and coach. Sometimes certain athletes will tacitly – or explicitly – need their coaches to be horrible to them in order for them to achieve what they do. That's part of the psychological make-up of some riders. Which is not to say that racism is right or sexism is acceptable – no medal should be won at the expense of humiliation of people.

That being the case, how does any human resources team manage those complex relationships?

By most accounts, those capable of performing at world level in cycling (or any other demanding athletic sport) are a strange cohort of souls, which is rather the point, really – they're not like you or me. They are not only physiological outliers but psychologically too; there's something different about individuals prepared to torture body and soul in the pursuit of sporting glory. The descriptors used in discussing elite athletes almost always include words like 'selfish', 'driven' or 'self-centred', none of which are considered desirable in the real world, yet the prevalence of those personality traits in elite cyclists points to the fact that managing them and their expectations takes special skills too.

The man at the centre of the Jiffy bag story and Wiggins TUE applications, former British Cycling and Team Sky doctor Richard Freeman, revealed just how 'strange' the world of elite cycle sport was in his 2018 book, observing that

> Sport, as I'm always saying, is not always healthy. Certainly I've had athletes competing on anti-depressants and I've had to withdraw riders from the intensity of their training programmes because of their mental health … I have been astounded that depression, eating disorders and self-harm don't stop success. Performance sport is a cauldron, no doubt, and you need to be able to stand the heat to play in the kitchen. Gold medals aren't given away.

In February 2017 Dave Brailsford, the character who put the capstone on the Manchester medal factory, also had his take on events published in *The Times*. Writing after a hostile grilling at a Team Sky media day the previous month, Brailsford reminded his critics what he saw as the role of elite performance at British Cycling. His words had uncanny echoes of Peter Keen's, from twenty years earlier:

I know this put some people's noses out of joint but my remit was to help make us the best in the world, not simply support the best in Britain. Elite sport is by definition not sport for all. It is edgy and it is difficult. Elite sport is tough. You play by the rules. You play clean. You play with the right values. You treat people with respect. But you must also never forget you are playing to win.

The common thread, unspoken but understood by many others, was clear – elite cycle sport is a brutal business, with little room for sentiment. For all the talk about expunging a bullying, sexist culture where winning at all costs was not the only thing but damn close. How would a new Board change that embedded culture, attitudes that had helped bring twenty years of unprecedented sporting success? British Cycling still needed international glory to sell itself to sponsors and attract new members, but could it maintain its run of medal-winning triumphs while paying more than lip service in atonement for previous sins?

This was the backdrop against which new Manchester staff were hired, tasked with recovering the reputation of British Cycling, convincing everyone – insiders and public alike – that the new regime would be different. No more sexist, bullying coaches, no more bad language, no more 'winning at all costs' but, hopefully, still winning, albeit with more 'sensitivity'.

So while riders continued to race and train, behind the scenes in Manchester a raft of significant appointments were made, signalling a change in outlook and cultural baggage. These moves were of little interest to a media more stimulated by shocks and gold medals than the fact that a couple of thousand new members had joined British Cycling. To be fair, Olympic medals *are* more exciting than boardroom reshuffles and office-based appointments were never going to send shock waves through social media.

Two days before Christmas 2016, after months of scandalous headlines, the press release announcing that a new performance director had been appointed at British Cycling went almost unnoticed. As it transpired, this was the first building block in the new British Cycling being built in Stuart Street's green and pleasant land.

The new man was Stephen 'Sparky' Park, whose previous job was as the Royal Yachting Association's Olympic manager. His job title at British Cycling – head of performance – was essentially the one previously held by Peter Keen, Brailsford and Sutton. Park clearly knew about high-performance sport, and he was a loquacious interview subject who could – behind closed doors – reveal flashes of the same ruthless desire for success as his predecessors.

Less than two months after Park's arrival, British Cycling appointed a new chairman in the shape of former Volkswagen USA chief executive officer Jonathan Browning, taking over from the long-serving Bob Howden. The 57-year-old Browning had been a non-executive member of the Board of British Cycling, so he had a good idea of the issues facing cycling from a boardroom perspective, not that that turned out to be much help to him ...

In light of the accusations of sexism, the appointment of ex-English Football Association operations director Julie Harrington as the new CEO in May 2017 looked like a clear statement. Her appointment, along with those of Browning and Park, were widely welcomed inside Manchester. The feeling at the time was that these were people capable of leading and manoeuvring big organisations, and the change in the manner in which business was done in Manchester meeting rooms was an improvement on the previous incumbents, well-meaning though they were.

As boardroom players, no one was in doubt of their

competencies, although whispered concerns emerged about their grasp of the nuances of 'cycling', the sport and its participants. Was this new trio part of 'the cycling family' raised in the custom and practice of the sport? No they were not. The temptation to draw parallels with traditionalists' suspicious reaction to Brailsford's new Sky team or Keen's WCPP revolution is strong. But both Brailsford and Keen had a firm grasp of cycling's mores, history and practitioners.

In spite of the Rio Games successes and the autumn 2016 announcement that HSBC UK would become sponsors of British Cycling from January 2017, morale in Manchester had been flat-lining and the new arrivals had, inevitably, caused some anxiety. After all, was there ever an organisation in which senior appointments didn't result in new rules and a few redundancies? When news broke of the £25 million award of Lottery funding to take the squads towards the 2020 Tokyo Games, it should have been a useful fillip. True, this sum was a £4 million drop in funding compared to Rio – which UK Sport explained was due to changes in the Olympic programme and the new increased HSBC sponsorship – but considering UK Sport chief executive Liz Nicholl had talked about funds being withheld unless reforms were put in place, this should still have felt like a win. Instead, the dark of a Manchester winter matched the mood of many inside British Cycling headquarters.

In fact, the first intake of the new regime didn't last, as Browning, with his cycling background, stepped down as CEO after only nine months in charge, having been obliged to reapply for his job – to be replaced by 'outsider' Frank Slevin, a chief executive from the troubled House of Fraser retail group. In short order Slevin promoted the idea that some new independent Board members – not those elected by the membership from the 'shop floor' of the annual National Council, but rather those recruited – should be paid between £30,000 and £40,000 a year.

Slevin and chief executive Harrington also oversaw the creation of a new post, an 'integrity and compliance director', a job filled by Rod Findlay, whose previous position was as director of business and legal services at England Golf. There were also newly created posts of 'strategy manager' and a 'cycling delivery director', who came fresh from her previous stint as chief executive of Modern Pentathlon GB. A few months previously, the occupant of the newly created equality and diversity post had also arrived. Jonathan Rigby, the commercial director appointed in 2018, had previously been head of marketing at Manchester United football club and the BBC charity Children in Need, a man used to spending large sums on behalf of massive global brands. By the end of 2018 nobody studying the composition of the Board and new executive leadership positions could be in any doubt that there had been a major shake-up.

New fiefdoms and layers of management were being created, but was there confidence that this new intake would improve British Cycling, either as the governing body of a grass-roots sport or as a medal-winning juggernaut? British Cycling had clearly been in need of changes at the top, but were these the right ones?

When a former Board member is moved to comment that 'There are people in British Cycling for whom this is a job – they're not actually that bothered about cycling' then you have to fear for the future direction of an organisation that had historically been staffed and driven by people with a ferocious passion for – precisely – cycling. The cycling education and background of the new British Cycling personnel had little in common with the old guard they replaced, who had been raised on chain-gangs, steel-framed bikes and outdoor velodromes.

It was as if, as one denizen of Manchester acidly put it, 'You don't need to know about cycling. Why on earth would that be important? Of course we all know what *sport* is, so why would they need to know what *cycling* is?'

One former Board member, still working at British Cycling in the post-Varnish world, said:

> I've been in a meeting where I heard someone from UK Sport say, in all seriousness, 'The fact that you've won all these medals over the years being as dysfunctional as you are, well, imagine how much more you would have won if you had got the culture right?' Seriously. These people don't have a clue what they are dealing with.

Which, as a statement, cuts to the heart of the matter. Is it possible for a relatively 'naïve' Board to manage elite cyclists and an organisation founded on competitive cycling? British Cycling might indeed now have a Board paying more attention to the issues raised by Varnish and others, but could it deliver the same medals as the old regime, with its intimidating culture?

The paradox at the heart of the issues raised was that UK Sport based funding on a federation's ability to win medals at Olympic Games. It seemed absurd then to criticise sports like cycling for fostering 'a win-at-all-costs mentality'. In Lottery-funded sport, if you don't win, you don't get funding.

Actually, it is rather more accurate to say that if you do not present UK Sport with a coherent, realistic strategy that *could* lead to athletes winning Olympic medals, then your funding would be in danger. If UK Sport considers that the performance plans of a sport are well-designed, then that counts almost as much as a medal tally, although medals clearly help a great deal. The fig leaf that less competent UK sports federations sometimes hide behind – 'we had our funding cut because we didn't win medals' – is not telling the whole story. If a federation was funded on the basis of plans presented and performance expectations, and those performances weren't forthcoming, perhaps the plan and coaching aren't worth giving money to? Funding is substantially allocated on the clarity, realism and credibility of your coaching structures and development pathways, not how big your medal cabinet is. That the two elements – effective pathways and big medal cabinets – often go together, should not be confused.

Ironically, the outraged cries from sports that have had their funding cut and the sympathetic public hearing such tales generally got reveals a contradiction in attitudes to elite sport. The public is distressed when competitors are pushed too hard, yet the same people are also angry when UK Sport determines that a sport isn't showing enough progress and subsequently cuts its funding. What is it that the public wants? Compassionate failure or ruthlessly attained medals?

Make no mistake, the connection between well-funded British cycling and medal-winning success is a direct one (while the same observation is also made of Team Sky's mega budget). One foreign-based coach, eyeing British Cycling's racing budget with envy, observed: 'British Cycling? It's like an F1 team competing against Willy Wonka's factory banger racing.'

In the end, the reality for a large publicly funded sports organisation like British Cycling's World Class Programme is that many, many jobs are on the line – coaching jobs, athlete payments, sports science, administrative, physio, strength and conditioning contracts – lots of salaries and mortgages. The pressure on British Cycling staff to hit targets, meet goals, to win and keep funding flowing and, therefore, to be able to stay in employment, is inescapable.

By 2018 Board and senior management of British Cycling had plenty to consider – and it didn't all revolve around the World Class Performance Plan. During the prolonged bout of soul-searching, there had been time to consider the bigger picture and broader 'problems' with cycling in Britain, most of which fell squarely within the remit of the national federation.

While media criticism had focused on the medal-winning WCPP group as being 'not fit for purpose' then, unspoken and ignored, were bigger questions that needed to be asked of the national governing body. The Olympians of the World Class Performance Programme had basked in the limelight, but they were only a small part of British Cycling's work. Given that the whole organisation was in self-analysis mode, wasn't a rebalancing required? Perhaps the grass roots needed attention? A former Board member noted:

> We've got something like 130,000 members at British Cycling, and there's a lot of emphasis on acquiring and retaining more members, but nobody is asking the members what they want British Cycling to be. And yet British Cycling spends millions on schemes and we're lobbying government for facilities. These are laudable, but it's got to the point that we're not really sure which way we should go.

When the HSBC UK sponsorship deal began in 2017 there were 'eye-watering' numbers being thrown about inside British Cycling, with 'special interest' groups and departments jockeying for budgets for the next Olympic cycle. The figures were huge, because there was now more money in British Cycling than there had ever been before, with HSBC putting in £8 million a year. Yet, astonishingly, there were budget cuts in some British Cycling departments. An organisation with around £32 million in financing, from sponsors, UK Sport, Sport England, HSBC and membership fees, was – somehow – making budget cuts of up to 20 per cent in some programmes. The new regime was certainly making changes, though the WCPP budgets were essentially left alone and, in the case of the equipment research and development, actually increased as Tokyo approached. The Board might have been new, but it understood that you didn't throttle the goose that was laying those golden eggs.

Strip away the moral panic and soul searching and British Cycling's World Class Performance Programme could clearly be held up as an exemplar when it came to elite sport – assuming the metric is medals and world titles won – with an approach that had left some damaged souls in its wake. If, on the other hand, British Cycling is also to be judged in terms of its success and strategy of growing a healthy grass-roots sport, then the verdict would be more equivocal.

After all, the heart and soul of the original BCF was amateur road racing; that, essentially, is what it was formed to manage when it emerged in 1959, while the membership, in paying for their racing licences, represented the only sustainable financing the sport had. Sponsors could come and go, but a membership was, in a manner of speaking, for ever. Their membership fees might 'only' account for around £5 million of British Cycling's annual budget, but those riders deserved consideration; their concerns about road safety and desire to race at weekends surely required support from Manchester?

Judging by the following observation, exasperation levels on the non-WCPP side of the British Cycling offices were at an all-time high:

I was looking at British Cycling-led rides, like Go Sky Rides, and I worked out that it was costing us £11 per participant to do one of those led rides. Effectively, that's us, at British Cycling, paying someone £11 to be taken out on a bike ride around a park. On the other hand, there are areas of British Cycling – like club racing – that don't get funded at all, things that are run by grass-roots volunteers. What the hell are we doing?!

British Cycling had been talent spotting in schools for years, though it was an increasingly tough market. BC's Go Ride coaches effectively have to sell themselves and cycling at £300 per visit, competing with other sports for a slice of shrinking school budgets. However, what was BC doing for riders who were the backbone of club cycling? Reports were worrying. 'I was part of the road commission at BC,' said one stalwart of the UK race scene, 'and there is awareness that there's a problem with participation in both road and track races. That's the ultimate irony, BC spent millions on tracks while training sessions and track leagues – in Newport, Halesowen, Newcastle and elsewhere – are frequently being cancelled because they aren't attracting the numbers.'

While some of this is down to a natural ebb and flow of interest – cycling cannot hold public interest indefinitely – how is British Cycling approaching these developments? News from Manchester was not encouraging. 'At a road commission meeting in 2019, BC listened to race promoters, so they know there are problems, but they don't have a plan. Literally. If you ask what the discipline-specific plan is for the future of road racing in the UK, it doesn't exist. They don't have an idea of what road racing would look like in four years' time, nor how they would support or develop it. There was no strategy for grass roots racing and it's the same in every discipline.' In an organisation built on four year plans and clear pathways, this is not reassuring. Given the managerial changes and staff churn that took place following the arrival of CEO Julie Harrington in early 2017, was there still a knowledge base inside BC to tackle these issues?

British Cycling is justifiably proud of its membership figures, but even here there's a tiny thorn in the carcass. 'They're (BC) always talking about the 130,000 members of British Cycling, but fewer than half of them are in clubs – where people learn how to race, about road etiquette, how to ride in a bunch – so when car drivers go mad at "cyclists all over the road" that might have something to do with it.' Clearly there are a lot more people riding bikes on Britain's roads, but what should British Cycling be doing to help them find their way?

So, away from international racing arenas, what, indeed, *was* British Cycling doing at promoting and growing a nation of cyclists? After all, Peter Keen's original plan had been to win medals, raise the sport's profile and thus drag cycling into the British mainstream – and not just in terms of support for elite competition. As British town planners started to contemplate the integration of cycling into city transport networks, the instances of friction between road users (amplified by GoPro video footage shared online) exploded. The case for cycling needed to be forcefully made, yet at British Cycling, the response was muted. 'In every membership survey carried out, insurance is the number one reason why people join British Cycling, and it's understandable, because they get well covered and it's pretty cheap,' said Chris Boardman, now policy adviser to British Cycling. 'And the number two reason is advocacy. And when those sort of results are examined, people inside British Cycling will say, "Oh yeah, it's really important", but there was only one person who had to deal with those issues: Martin Key, who was the campaigns manager.' There was, you could argue, a real and ongoing scandal at British Cycling. Why, in spite of the feedback from 130,000 members and in spite of the growth of cycling as a means of transport, were more resources not being put into an area its membership rated more important than sporting success? Where was the lead from the top of British Cycling? Where were the statements and policies fighting for its own membership on an issue riders considered important?

In some respects British Cycling had actually retreated from its 2016 activity levels. Boardman had a new job working for Greater Manchester, and he had poached Key and Kirsty McCaskill-Baxter to push a bold cycling infrastructure plan, although he and his team still consulted with British Cycling. However, the fact that three key people had moved away from British Cycling inevitably meant that advocacy inside British Cycling had lost experienced and effective staff. British Cycling was backing Boardman in his Manchester work, but nationally it had lost a high-profile, eloquent voice. As Boardman himself put it, 'British Cycling hasn't backed away from advocacy, but what they perhaps haven't been good at is letting people know about it.'

Although internal politicking between interest groups was obviously going on under the previous regime, the new management was grappling with the same interdepartmental struggles and, given that clarity of vision was never raised as a significant problem in any report, perhaps the 2018 management team led by CEO Harrington and chief executive Slevin cannot be judged too harshly. On the other hand, how has the new awareness generated by inquiries impacted on Britain's elite programme?

At the end of 2018 there were those inside British Cycling who were uneasy about the range of changes – or lack of them. Julian Winn, the GB woman's road team manager, was a passionate advocate of women's cycling, on or off-road, but, late in 2018, he decided to leave.

I had given a couple of presentations to the Board about

getting a proper women's road programme together for the Tokyo road race, a sort of 'Project Tokyo 2020', and asked for a budget to do a proper programme and I got nowhere. They are employing people now on big salaries, salaries that could pretty much pay for a programme for women, but there's no support for it.

The man who had helped manage Nicole Cooke to a gold medal at Beijing in 2008 saw little evidence of progress or a change in approach to women's road racing, and that, in the end, was enough to see him off.

For all the brave words about changes in attitude inside British Cycling after Varnish and others had spoken up, when it came to women racing, there was still a sense that they were a support class. As Winn says,

I've been at a couple of road world championships where the assumption is that I'll help out with whatever the men's teams want, which is fine, I'm happy to do that. But if I ask or expect anyone on the men's staff to help with the women? That's different. The women are still judged differently. At the World's in Doha, the men's team all went out after the race and there was a lot of partying pics on social media – which is fine. But the women's team rode a good race in Bergen in 2017, they executed a plan, it didn't quite come off, but they rode well. I told them to go out and have a night out, they deserved it, but I had a performance manager on at me saying it wasn't right. Well, it was OK for the guys, but not the women? How does that work?

At the European Championships at Glasgow in 2018, the staff numbers helping the women's road team were much smaller than the men's, which looked very much like business as usual. Off-road, the support – as well as the rider entry – for the women's and men's cross-country mountain bikers was smaller still, and borderline embarrassing. The racing focus was still, relentlessly, on those track medals. Almost two years on from the soul-searching and a 'year zero' potential for a rethink of priorities, what had really changed for Britain's mountain bikers, cyclo-cross champions or even the women's road squads?

If the accusations of sexism and bullying can be argued over – in terms of degree, how systemic they are and how much they sadly mimic the outside world – then the lowly status of mountain biking at British Cycling is still a source of frustration. Winn, a multiple cyclo-cross champion as well as 2002 British Elite road race champion, was also one of mountain biking's most vocal advocates inside British Cycling, and he found himself mystified at its position in the UK hierarchy.

If we put the same resources into mountain biking as we did into track racing, we'd have already had a world cross-country champion, I'm sure of it. There's no doubt we have the talent, but there's almost no consideration given to it, except in the year before the Olympics, when the management start to panic. But of course the talent is there – it's the same as cyclo-cross. If you go to a cyclo-cross race you'll see hundreds of kids racing, literally hundreds. But where do they go? I said to Shane [Sutton] that he should have a look at what cyclo-cross was doing because they were obviously doing something right to get those numbers participating. What has British Cycling got for them in terms of a pathway or resources or investment?

Even when talent is spotted and nurtured, the first reaction is still the same as it was twenty years ago. Winn again:

When [mountain biker] Evie Richards started to come through I had Iain Dyer come to me and say, 'Do you think we could get Evie Richards on track? She looks like she could be a good sprint prospect', and I said to him, 'What are you talking about? Leave her alone, she loves riding mountain bikes, she's good at it, let her do it.' Because that's still the British Cycling way of thinking: get the talent on track, riding in circles around a wooden bowl. And not everyone wants to do that. You think [2017 junior world cyclo-cross and world junior time trial champion] Tom Pidcock is interested in that? You think he wants to ride track? When it comes to grass-roots road racing and mountain biking, British Cycling needs to have a look at what it's doing – or not doing.

Which, as an indictment of the profundity of the rethink that had taken place at British Cycling, was rather damning. In many ways it looked like the same old discrimination, favour-itism and monomaniacal focus on track medals. Business as usual when there was a clear need for a new British Cycling, one that could capitalise on the sports success and the growing importance of cycling in daily (commuting) life.

Boardman's observation about British Cycling's advo-cacy work that 'letting people know about it' was problematic implying that, even if a credible voice in British Cycling had a coherent message or a defensible position, it would struggle to communicate it anyway. It was, in some sense, the very essence of British Cycling's problem. The damage control from the Varnish fallout had been inadequate and – if the experience of Winn and Boardman and others was representative – the post-Sutton era had shown little improvement.

In summer 2017, when a cyclist collided with a pedestrian who subsequently died, or absurd talk of making crash helmets compulsory and issuing licence plates for school children on bikes, where was the position statement from British Cycling? When it came to the broader 'mission' of British Cycling it shouldn't just have been the costs of Olympic medals, bullying, sexism and track medals that should have been hot topics.

'I've been very disappointed at the way things have gone,' said Chris Boardman.

> That the performances and the organisation, all of that success, has been dismissed. You start to wonder, in a Machiavellian kind of way, 'Why are so many people wanting to jump all over that history?' And I don't know, I really don't. But I have never been involved in any business that was as efficient and effective at improving cycling performances, for that period of time.

You might reasonably wonder why nobody in the upper echelons of British Cycling had stood up for the staff, for its riders, for the huge number of successes that British Cycling had enjoyed, while the organisation was being slaughtered by the media on an almost daily basis. Amid the gloom it was worth recording that Britain's cyclists were the most successful British sports team of all time, through three Olympic cycles. When furious outrage bounced around cyberspace, it was easy to forget that close to half the GB Olympic cycling medals won since 2000 had been won by women. For all the reports of a 'toxic culture that wasn't fit for purpose', riders are still fighting hard to get into the Manchester WCPP programme, and there has been no rush for the exit by disgruntled riders.

Maybe a credible defence could have been made by a more assured and confident senior management team? But nobody stood up to make that case as the brickbats rained down on

British Cycling and everyone attached to it. Certainly there were mistakes and terrible judgement calls, but there were many more people doing good work too. Who spoke up for them? Undeniably that too was a failure of leadership.

And yet, if there had been a post-Beijing management team capable of steering the organisation through this booby-trapped shifting cultural terrain, much of the trauma could have been avoided. It would have been realistic to maintain the original core values of unflinching excellence while incorporating improved oversight of behaviour and management. Given that the Peter King report had flagged up problems with personnel and attitudes in 2012, it would have been possible to create processes to deal with rider welfare, whistle-blowing and grievance issues. Clearly, given the public unravelling of British Cycling and revelations about the ways it managed its affairs, those processes and leadership were lacking.

In the approach to the Tokyo Olympics, the changes that had been made in senior management had yet to reveal their efficacy. In sporting terms, the goals had remained the same – track-focused – while those who had been made to feel marginal, those mountain bikers, cyclo-cross riders and women's road riders, were still on the outside looking in.

If British Cycling had stared into the abyss before turning its gaze inwards, by 2018 it didn't seem like it had come to any firm conclusions. Was it still, fundamentally, about 'winning at all costs' and ensuring the continuing flow of Lottery funding and HSBC sponsorship, or was it now paying more attention to making cycling more popular as a sport and pastime?

At a time when the nation and its cyclists needed to hear a clear re-statement of what British Cycling was about and what its future focus was, why did we hear so little? Presented with the perfect time to state, loud and clear, what British Cycling was 'about', there was barely a whisper.

At what distance will it be possible to write fully rounded histories of these people and events? At such close proximity, what exists so far are forty-six Olympic medals – sixteen won by women – over fifty world champions on track and road, three Tour de France winners, six Tours de France, two Vueltas, one Giro, a brace of one-day Classics, a world time trial championship, three world road titles (Cooke, Cavendish, Armitstead), four Hour Records and knighthoods for Sir Wiggo, Sir Chris Hoy and Sir Dave B. And that's not to mention the considerable number of junior and off-road international triumphs. At a more mundane but arguably more important level, Britain now has a cycling federation with 130,000 members, regular mainstream TV coverage of World Championships and Grand Tours that was non-existent in 1998, as well as an overarching public awareness of cycling that was unimaginable before the World Class Cycling Plan started generating medals and international success.

Prior to Jess Varnish's accusations, Fancy Bear hacks and 'Jiffy bag-gate', it might have been possible to write the history of the rise of British cycling as a glorious, heroic saga. Now its a mixture of uncomfortable truths and human fallibility, interspersed with moments of sublime performance and humour. Like life, in fact, like sport.

THANKS

A massive and heartfelt thanks to all those who were generous enough to talk with me. Some names are absent, by request. However, without them, no book.

Keith Bingham; Lionel Birnie; Chris Boardman; Ryan Bonser; Ian Boswell; Dave Brailsford; Simon Brotherton; Debra Brown; Johan Bruyneel; Simon Burney; Tom Cary; Dario Cioni; Jonny Clay; Gary Coltman; Brian Cookson; Paul Curran; Doug Dailey; Scott Dougal; Russ Downing; Rod Ellingworth; Stephen Farrand; William Fotheringham; Brendan Gallagher; Robert Garbutt; Sandy Gilchrist; Gilles Goetghebuer; Roger Hammond; Tim Harris; Rob Hayles; Jim Hendry; Graeme Herd; John Herety; Rob Holden; Chris Hoy; Jeremy Hunt; Alex Jaffney; Simon Jones; Rob Jorgensen; Peter Keen; Peter King; Simon Lillistone; Keith Lambert; Philippe Le Gars; Dave Loughran; Paul Manning; Neil Martin; Ken Matheson; Pat McQuaid; Fran Millar; Jonathan Mitchell; Jean Montois; Henri Montulet; Richard Moore; Graham McGarrity; Louis Passfield; Richard Plugge; Nicolas Portal; Jean-Francois Quenet; Keith Reynolds; Eric Richter; Jason Roberts; Alex Sans Vega; Heiko Salzwedel; Brian Smith; Dave Smith; Scott Sunderland; Shane Sutton; Colin Sturgess; Jonathan Vaughters; Darryl Webster; Charly

Wegelius; Phil West; Jeremy Whittle; Julian Winn; Pete Woodworth; Ben Wright; Sean Yates.

Thanks also to Penny Daniel, Jane Pickett and James Spackman at Pursuit books as well as David Luxton of David Luxton Associates for his guidance. Who knew writing a book was such a communal effort?

PICTURE CREDITS